Reviewers Praise **The Pink Swastika**

"The Pink Swastika: Homosexuality in the Nazi Party is a thoroughly researched, eminently readable, demolition of the "gay" myth, symbolized by the pink triangle, that the Nazis were anti-homosexual. The deep roots of homosexuality in the Nazi party are brilliantly exposed . . ."

Dr. Howard Hurwitz, Family Defense Council

"As a Jewish scholar who lost hundreds of her family in the Holocaust, I welcome The Pink Swastika as courageous and timely . . . Lively and Abrams reveal the reigning "gay history" as revisionist and expose the supermale German homosexuals for what they were - Nazi brutes, not Nazi victims."

Dr. Judith Reisman, Institute for Media Education

"The Pink Swastika is a tremendously valuable book, replete with impressive documentation presented in a compelling fashion." *William Grigg, The New American*

"...exposes numerous lies, and tears away many myths. Essential reading, it is a formidable boulder cast into the path of the onrushing homosexual express..."

Stan Goodenough, Middle East Intelligence Digest

"The Pink Swastika is a powerful exposure of pre-World War II Germany and its quest for reviving and imitating a Hellenistic-paganistic idea of homo-eroticism and militarism."

Dr. Mordechai Nisan, Hebrew University of Jerusalem

"Lively and Abrams call attention to what Hitlerism really stood for, abortion, euthanasia, hatred of Jews, and, very emphatically, homosexuality. This many of us knew in the 1930's; it was common knowledge, but now it is denied..."

R. J. Rushdoony, The Chalcedon Report

The Pink Swastika

Homosexuality in the Nazi Party

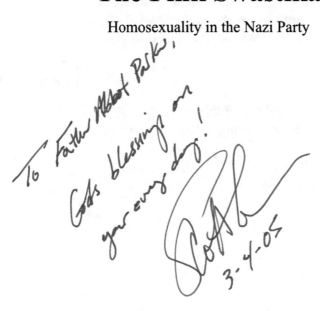

Scott Lively and Kevin Abrams

Published by Veritas Aeterna Press
PO Box 3691, Sacramento, California.
Ordering inquiries call 1-800-834-1508
or visit www.abidingtruth.com

First Edition Published July, 1995
Fourth Edition Published January, 2002

Cover design by Noah Lively

Fourth Edition 0123456789

ISBN 0-9647609-7-5

Table of Contents

PRELIMINARIES ... 3
- Preface to the Fourth Edition 3
- Foreword 9
- Introduction 17
- A Word to the Reader 26
- Acknowledgments 27

THE HOMOSEXUAL ROOTS OF THE NAZI PARTY ... 31
- The Divided Movement 38
- Karl Heinrich Ulrichs 44
- Magnus Hirschfeld and the SHC 48
- The New Hellenes 51
- The Clash of Cultures 57
- Adolf Brand and the "Community of the Elite" 60
- The Rift Widens 67
- Hans Blueher and the Wandervoegel 70
- From Boy Scouts to Brownshirts 75
- Gerhard Rossbach and the Freikorps Movement 82
- Ernst Roehm and the Development of the SA 87

HOMO-OCCULTISM ... 95
- Madame Blavatsky and the Theosophical Society 104
- Guido von List and the Armanen Order 108
- Jorg Lanz von Liebenfels and Ariosophy 111
- The Thule Society 119

THE HOMOSEXUAL ROOTS OF FASCISM ... 129
- Friedrich Nietzsche 133
- The Cultural Elites 135

**THE FOUNDING AND EARLY YEARS
OF THE NAZI PARTY ... 143**
- Hitler's Clique of Pederasts 145
- Was Adolf Hitler a Homosexual? 151
- Adolf, the Boy Prostitute 156
- The Bayreuth Connection 159
- The Nazi Rise to Power 162
- Power and Abuse 170

THE PERSECUTION OF HOMOSEXUALS ... 177
- The Path of the Paranoid 182
- The Sacking of the Sex Research Institute 185
- Anti-Homosexual Policies 189
- The Roehm Purge 195
- After the Purge 205

2

- Heinrich Himmler and the SS 210
- Was Himmler a Homosexual? 214
- Reinhard Heydrich: "The Blonde Beast" 219
- The Grynszpan Affair — Kristallnacht 222

HOMOSEXUALITY IN THE CONCENTRATION CAMPS ... 229
- The Guards and Kapos 233
- The Prisoners 242

THE NAZI HATRED OF JUDEO-CHRISTIAN MORALITY ... 249
- The Biblical Condemnation of Homosexuality 253
- Towards the Final Solution 255
- Homosexuality and Islamist Terrorism 269

HOMO-FASCISM AFTER HITLER ... 275
- The Fascist Roots of the American "Gay" Movement 275
- American Nazis 277
- "Gay" Nazi Skinheads 281
- Nazi Themes in "Gay" Culture 287
- Nazi Tactics in "Gay" Politics 290

THE HOMOSEXUALIZATION OF AMERICA ... 299
- Harry Hay and the Mattachine Society 301
- Alfred Kinsey and the Kinsey Institute 304
- The Sexual Revolution 307
- The Stonewall Riot and "Gay" Militancy 309
- Weimar in America 314
- Consequences 318
- Pederasty in the "Gay" Movement 320
- Scouts Under Siege 327
- Atrocities 332

CLOSING THOUGHTS ... 341
- The Danger of "Gay Rights" 341
- The Final Word 349
- Spiritual Truth 350
- Who were the Nazis? 352
- Left-Right Polarities 353
- Fifth Columns 355
- "Gay" Sedition 357
- Sons of Oedipus 359
- Akhtar's Metaphor -- A New Beginning 360

BIBLIOGRAPHY ... 363

INDEX ... 379

PRELIMINARIES

Preface to the Fourth Edition

When Kevin Abrams and I published the first edition of this book in 1995, we knew that it would cause controversy, contradicting as it does the common portrayal of homosexuals as exclusively victims of the Nazi regime. For this reason we were scrupulous in our documentation of homosexuals as the true inventors of Nazism and the guiding force behind many Nazi atrocities. We purposefully drew heavily upon homosexual writers and historians for our source material and used direct quotations from their writings whenever possible. The remainder of our sources are primarily mainstream historians of the Nazi era. We chose to place our citations in the text rather than in endnotes to emphasize the reliability of our sources.

Few contemporary historians, however, have weighed in, either pro or con, on the claims of this book. With some notable exceptions, the voices have instead come from ideologues on either side of the "gay rights" issue. Homosexuals and their allies (including some academics) denounce The Pink Swastika as baseless and hateful. Pro-family advocates praise it as authoritative and enlightened. We dare say that a majority of leaders on both sides of the "culture war" are familiar with this book. Yet we believe that the issues we have raised deserve broader public scrutiny and debate, especially in academia.

This fourth edition represents a renewed effort to put these issues up for debate before the American public. This edition is a dramatically expanded and strengthened volume. We have invested hundreds of additional hours in research and writing that is reflected in two new chapters and hundreds of additional citations that have been woven throughout the existing text. We have also added many helpful photographs and graphics. Our critics will note that we have considered their arguments and refined our own where appropriate.

What remains is the struggle to persuade academics and cultural leaders to address this subject, which begs the question of why have they not yet done so.

One reason, perhaps, is that <u>The Pink Swastika</u> addresses an aspect of Nazi history unfamiliar to most people, historians included. Indeed, no one could have written <u>The Pink Swastika</u> who was not a student of both history and of the so-called "gay" movement. The compilation of references to homosexuality from mainstream sources, while extensive, does not in and of itself provide a complete picture of the homosexuals' role in the rise and rule of Nazism. Only when that picture is overlaid with the work of "gay" scholars does the essential relationship between Nazism and the German "gay" movement become clear.

Ironically, a better explanation for why <u>The Pink Swastika</u> has been neglected is the dominance of "political correctness" in the academic realm; ironic because today's "PC" code suppresses intellectual dissent to a degree not seen since the Third Reich. Only today, the *verboten* subject-matter is anything that reflects negatively on the "gay" movement.

This trend is not new. In fact, one of the most remarkable facts we uncovered in our research is the near complete dearth of references to homosexuality in the Nazi Party in books published in the United States since the end of the 1960s. Nearly all of our mainstream U.S. sources (by

American writers) pre-date the 1970s, when the "gay" movement became a powerful political force in this country. However, other resources, mostly German works translated into English, have continued to enlarge our knowledge of the homosexual/Nazi connection. One important contributor is, of course, German academic Lothar Machtan, whose Hidden Hitler (2001), argues persuasively that Hitler's secret "gay" life defined his career.

In the 1960s, Nazi homosexuality was so widely acknowledged in America (at least among the "social elites") that the portrayal of Nazi thugs as homosexual was a frequent occurrence in Hollywood movies. One of the best examples is in *Exodus* (United Artists, 1960), the film adaptation of the Leon Uris novel about the creation of the State of Israel after World War II. In the film, actor Sal Mineo, playing a young man attempting to join the *Irgun* (the Jewish underground movement), fails to convince *Irgun* leaders that he is a genuine Nazi concentration camp survivor. Finally they are convinced — only when he breaks down and confesses that the Nazi guards "used me as a woman." To the *Irgun*, this was definitive proof that he had been a Nazi prisoner.

Allen Ginsberg, the homosexual "beat" poet was asked by a Justice of the Supreme Court in 1966 (during an obscenity trial related to the book Naked Lunch, by William Borroughs) whether at "some time in the future there will be a political party, for instance, made up of homosexuals." Ginsberg replied, saying "this has already happened in a sense -- or of sex perverts -- and we can point to Hitler, Germany under Hitler" (*The New York Times*, August 10, 1997).

These are but two examples which reveal the extent to which homosexuality was openly associated with Nazism in the past. There are many other examples in this book. Yet today, the record has been almost entirely purged regarding the homosexual/Nazi connection. This would be alarming enough if it were simply a trend in the popular culture and academia, but a similar whitewashing is also taking place in institutions responsible for keeping the record of the Holocaust.

Dr. Nathaniel Lehrman is a retired psychiatrist who read The Pink Swastika and was inspired to recommend it as a resource to the U.S. Holocaust Museum in Washington, D.C.. No political conservative, Dr. Lehrman has for many years contributed articles and editorials to liberal and humanist publications. After a great deal of effort, including an exchange of correspondence in which he challenged the museum to at least research the claims of this book, he was rebuffed. In a May 5th, 2000 editorial in the *Intermountain Jewish News*, Dr. Lehrman took issue with one of the frequent pro-homosexual events at the museum

> [F]or the conference to present a complete picture of gays in the Holocaust, it should also have included the key roles of Nazi homosexuals among its perpetrators. By failing to do so, the Museum fostered the myth of a "Gay Holocaust"....Why is the Holocaust Memorial Museum distorting the history of the Holocaust?

Another reader, Mr. Zan Overall, donated a copy of The Pink Swastika to the Museum of Tolerance in Los Angeles, the leading Holocaust museum on the West Coast. He was later told by a staff member that the book had not been placed in the regular collection but in a "special collection" available only upon request by a patron. He writes

> Wondering how a library patron might become aware of the existence of The Pink Swastika, ensconced in "the special collection," I asked if it were listed in the computer along with other books on the same general subject....She read off quite a number of titles listed there...and reported The Pink Swastika is not listed there (Overall: private letter).

UNITED STATES
HOLOCAUST MEMORIAL MUSEUM
100 RAOUL WALLENBERG PLACE, SW
WASHINGTON, DC 20024-2150

Help Us
Remember
the Forgotten
Victims
of the
Holocaust

Message on a Holocaust museum fund-raising letter (left) and a full section of books in the museum bookstore promote the "Gay Holocaust" myth, while the Nazi/homosexual connection documented in this book is entirely ignored.

Knowing how thoroughly these institutions have been infiltrated by "gay" political activists, we were not surprised that they have suppressed the evidence linking Nazism to homosexuality (see my article "How American 'Gays' are Stealing the Holocaust," in The Poisoned Stream, Founders Publishing Corporation, 1997). We are concerned that the same whitewash may be taking place at the Shoah Foundation as it collects the video histories of the last remaining Holocaust survivors. Its founder Steven Spielberg is the business partner of billionaire homosexual activist David Geffin. Unfortunately, the public perceives these institutions as the final authority on anything having to do with the Nazi era.

As we prepare to publish this fourth edition of The Pink Swastika, therefore, we are especially mindful that our small work represents perhaps the only significant attempt to counter a highly successful "gay"-sponsored revisionist campaign. We have thus endeavored to produce the most

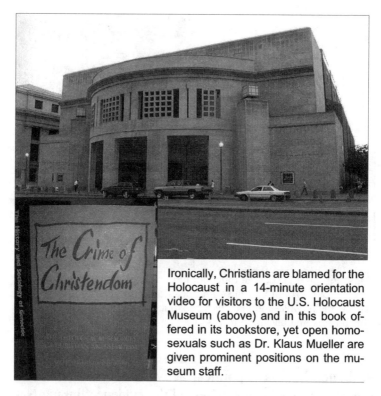

Ironically, Christians are blamed for the Holocaust in a 14-minute orientation video for visitors to the U.S. Holocaust Museum (above) and in this book offered in its bookstore, yet open homosexuals such as Dr. Klaus Mueller are given prominent positions on the museum staff.

thorough and accurate document of which we are capable.

This document is by no means the first, but is by far the most complete, resource ever prepared on the thesis that homosexuals invented and ran the Nazi Party. This is a thesis that has been frequently restated since the 1930s. It is a thesis with profound implications for our society, given the growing power of the "gay" movement. Yet most people in this country have probably never even heard it mentioned.

Our goal is not to replace one form of political correctness with another. We do not want our view to be imposed on anyone, nor the homosexualist view to be silenced. Our goal is to put these questions before the public and let the evidence speak for itself.

Scott Lively, December 14, 2001

Foreword

Kevin Abrams

I call heaven and earth to witness against you this day, that I have set before you life and death, the blessing and the curse; therefore choose life, that you may live, you and your children.
Deuteronomy\Devarim: 30:19

The Pink Swastika is not a work of fiction. Ironically, the authors have discovered that truth is often stranger than fiction. The Pink Swastika is a response to the "gay political agenda" and its strategy of portraying homosexuals as victims of societal and Nazi persecution. Although some homosexuals, and many of those who were framed with trumped-up charges of homosexuality suffered and died at the hands of the Nazis, for gay apologists to portray themselves as historical victims of Nazi persecution, on par with the Jewish people, is a gross distortion of history, perhaps equal to denying the Holocaust itself. The Pink Swastika will show that there was far more brutality, rape, torture and murder committed against innocent people *by* Nazi deviants and homosexuals than there ever was *against* homosexuals.

Today in the West, a new and aggressive homosexualism is making its bid for power. The media, psychiatry, science and academia have all been corrupted and pressed into the service of establishing homosexuality as a normal and acceptable variant of human sexuality. Those who are unwilling to bend to the new dispensation are bludgeoned into submission with slanderous accusations of intolerance and "homophobia." Our efforts will certainly fail to corroborate the politically correct propaganda offered by much of today's media, academia, psychiatry, various federal agencies, the courts and human rights organizations which are now driven by the new sexual ideology rather than by honest debate and inquiry. Coming in the wake of a successful public campaign conducted over decades, our book will also fly in the face of much of today's popular opinion. This having been said, we believe that The Pink Swastika will show clearly how the world the Nazis attempted to create is a world, not of the past, but of the possible future. It will show that, given its present course and left unchallenged, America could easily become the Nazi Germany of 50 years ago.

It is often said that the lessons of history leave us with a guide for the future. If this be so, then the lessons of the collapse of the democratic Weimar Republic and the social ideologies that preceded its defeat by the Nazis should provide us with insights into America's future. As a practicing member of the Jewish faith, I remain wholly unconvinced that by solely remembering the Holocaust we will prevent another. The ominous parallels between the Weimar Republic of pre-Nazi Germany and today's American republic are simply too pronounced to overlook.

This year, 1995, is the 50th anniversary of the end of World War II. It is also the 50th anniversary of Samuel Igra's book, Germany's National Vice, which we quote extensively. Largely purged from public view, Igra's book documents the homoerotic foundations of German militarism. Other books, like Dusty Sklar's 1977 The Nazis and the Occult, document the black occult roots of Nazi ideology. What The Pink Swastika does is to synthesize both the homoerotic and occult foundations of the Nazi regime.

It must be clarified — the Nazis were not Right-Wing Conservative Creationists; they were Left-Wing Darwinian Evolutionary Socialists. As a principle, an increase in pederasty and homosexualism parallels a militaristic Hellenic revival. History discloses that the most warlike nations are those whose male leaders were the most addicted to sexual relations with young boys.

The political agenda which has as its focus a plan to legalize and coerce a bewildered and unsuspecting public into accepting or regarding sodomy as normal or dignified, is based on falsehood, self-deception and skewed scientific research. In light of the medical record, history and the fact that sodomy represents a corruption of the natural and moral orders of creation, any positive affirmation of homosexuality is totally without merit. Human sexuality is never merely a physical concern, nor is it a purely private matter. It always has social implications. What goes on between partners influences society as a whole. In sexual matters, the issue is "what is advocated and what is practiced publicly" far more than what happens privately.

In a letter to the editor of the Toronto *Globe and Mail* newspaper, February 26, 1992, Dr. Joseph Berger, Assistant Professor of Psychiatry, University of Toronto, writes, "in my 20 years of psychiatry I have never come across anyone with innate homosexuality. That notion has been a long proclaimed gay-activist political position, intended to promote the acceptance of homosexuality as a healthy, fully equal alternative expression of human sexuality. It has zero scientific foundation, though its promoters latch on to even the flimsiest shreds of atrocious research in their attempts to justify the notion."

As they were during the Weimar period, 1918-1933, psychiatry and academia have been hijacked and pressed into the service of establishing homosexualism as the basis of a new *Kultur*. Professor Hans Blueher, a practicing physician whose specialty was psychiatry, was accepted by the Nazis as the apostle and higher authority of a new social order. Blueher's school held that male homosexual lovemaking is in itself a good thing and spiritually energizing. Blueher's teaching became popular in Nazi circles during the period between the two World Wars and promoted the idea that a well-regulated ritual of homosexualism was a unique force capable of creating the State and assuring its leadership. The resulting creed relegated women to a purely biological function and eliminated the family as a constituent cell in the community.

In 1973, the American Pyschiatric Association was also hijacked by American "gay" activists. Basing its decision largely on the skewed evidence of the 1948 Kinsey report Sexual Behavior in the Human Male, the APA removed homosexuality from its Diagnostic and Statistics Manual and declared it a normal variant of human sexuality. Homosexuals, sensing that the burden of change had been lifted from them and shifted onto society, were able to present themselves as innocent victims of what they referred to as society's bigoted and "homophobic" attitude towards them as persons.

Columnist Charles Krauthammer, in "Defining Deviancy Up," an essay published in the November 22, 1993 edition of *The New Republic* (pages 20ff), in describing the real effect of the APA decision, stated that a majority of society was made deviant while homosexuality was elevated to the status of normal. Krauthammer writes, "as part of the vast social project of moral leveling, it is not enough for the deviant to be normalized. The normal must be found to be deviant." In fact, the greatest single victory of the "gay" agenda over the past decade has been to shift the debate from behavior to identity, thus forcing opponents into a position where they are seen as attacking the civil rights of homosexual citizens rather than attacking specific antisocial behavior.

In an interesting and informative study, a critical analysis titled "Sexual Politics and Scientific Logic: the Issue of Homosexuality," by Dr. Charles Socarides (published in the Winter 1992 edition of *The Journal of Psychohistory,* Vol. 10, No. 3:317), Socarides quotes the warning of Abram Kardiner, psychoanalyst, former Professor of Psychiatry at Columbia University, 1966 recipient of the Humanities Prize of *The New York Times*:

> There is an epidemic form of homosexuality, which is more than the usual incidence, which generally occurs in social crises or in declining cultures when license and boundless permissiveness dulls the pain of ceaseless anxiety, universal hostility and divisiveness...Supporting the claims of homosexuals and regarding homosexuality as a normal variant of sexual activity is to deny the social significance of homosexuality...Above all it militates against the family and destroys the function of the latter as the last place in our society where affectivity can be cultivated...Homosexuality operates against the cohesive elements in society in the name of fictitious freedom. It drives the opposite sex in a similar direction. And no society can long endure when either the child is neglected or when the sexes war upon each other.

Victim-plunder ideology is at the core of "gay" political strategy. Homosexualists exploit the public status of homosexuals to impose their new definition of human sexuality upon society. "Victim ideology" and "reductionist" thinking is destroying America from within. Today's new victims see no reason to modify their own behavior. Victim psychology and philosophies undermine the legitimate workings of government and the justice, health and social systems. Like their Nazi predecessors, today's homosexualists lack any scruples. Homosexuality is primarily a predatory addiction striving to take the weak and unsuspecting down with it. The "gay" agenda is a colossal fraud; a gigantic robbery of the mind. Homosexuals of the type described in this book have no true idea of how to act in the best interests of their country and fellow man. Their intention is to serve none but themselves.

The Pink Swastika documents a hidden aspect of German history. The authors contend that homosexualism, elevated to a popular ideology and combined with black occult forces, not only gave birth to Nazi imperialism but also led to the Holocaust itself. The militarists in Germany were happy with Hitler. His teachings on "total war" and of a secret Jewish conspiracy against Germany provided a good screen for their own veiled preparations. From its very inception, it was the goal of the Nazi Party, working as a front for the German military industrial complex, to overthrow the Weimar Republic by whatever means necessary. The Pink Swastika documents how, from their beginning, the National Socialist revolution and the Nazi Party were animated and dominated by militaristic homosexuals, pederasts, pornographers and sado-masochists.

As Igra explains in Germany's National Vice, "the criminals who wreaked such astounding horrors on innocent civilian populations were not acting as soldiers drunk with the fury of battle, nor as patriotic fanatics, but as chosen instruments of a satanic religion to the service of which they had been dedicated by the systematic teaching and practice of unnatural vice" (Igra:94).

The Pink Swastika documents how the Society for Human Rights, founded by members of the Nazi Party, became the largest homosexual rights organization in Germany and, further, how this movement gave birth to the American homosexual rights movement. Its influence has grown. The President of the United States now receives official homosexual delegations at the White House who expect the President to repay them for helping him into office. They expected him to "normalize" homosexuality in the American military. As for the comparison made between homoeroticism and skin color, General Colin Powell, former Chairman of the Joint Chiefs of Staff, had this to say in a letter to Rep. Patricia Schroeder (D-Colorado), "Skin color is a benign, non-behavioral characteristic. Sexual orientation is perhaps the most profound of all human behavioral characteristics. Comparison of the two is a convenient but invalid argument" (*Salem, Ore.*) *Statesman Journal*, June 6, 1992).

American civilization rests on the basic principles of Christian morality, which have their origin in the Hebrew Scriptures. The reason why the Nazis first attacked the Jewish people and swore to exterminate them physically and spiritually is because the teachings of the Bible, both the Torah and the New Testament, represent the foundations on which the whole system of Christian ethics rests. Remove the Bible as the constellation that guides the American Ship of State and the whole edifice of American civilization collapses. For my Jewish brethren searching for a Biblical basis for the legitimization of homosexuality, I refer to the words of Rabbis Marc Angel, Hillel Goldberg and Pinchas Stopler and their joint article in the Winter, 1992-93 edition of *Jewish Action Magazine:*

> There is not a single source in all of the disciplines of Jewish sacred literature — halachah, aggadah, philosophy, muscar, mysticism — that tolerates homosexual acts or a homosexual 'orientation.' Jews who sanction homosexuality must do so wholly without reference to Jewish sacred literature, in which case their justification has no Jewish standing; or without reference to Jewish sources, in which case they act with ignorance or intellectual dishonesty. The idea, set forth by some of the non-Orthodox leadership, that the Torah prohibited only coercive and non-loving same-sex relationships, thus allowing for a contemporary, voluntary and loving same-sex relationship, is wholly without basis in a single piece of Jewish sacred literature written in the last 3,000 years.

Dennis Prager, a respected Jewish radio talk show host, commented, "There were two kinds of Jews in Auschwitz -- those who knew why they were there and those who thought it was just bad luck." Today Jews have assimilated ideas foreign to the Jewish perspective and many liberal,

16

secular American Jews, in adopting a tolerance for everything, stand for nothing. As the living, we owe a moral debt to that generation of Jews who were subjected to such inhumane and sadistic torture and extermination. The underlying causes of Nazi militarism are documented in The Pink Swastika. The Holocaust must be remembered for what it was, a war against the Jewish people and Western civilization.

MAY GOD BLESS AMERICA
Kevin E. Abrams, Jerusalem, Israel
June 5, 1995

Introduction

Scott Lively

I came to be interested in this compelling and sobering topic by a route familiar to many in our society today — that of the "victim." I did not seek this status, nor did I exploit or claim it, yet for many months I and others experienced what it was like to be on the receiving end of a full-scale, no-holds-barred "seek-and-destroy" campaign, orchestrated by "gay" political activists in the State of Oregon. The occasion of the uproar was a series of initiative campaigns aimed at preventing local and state-level legislation granting "minority status" based on homosexuality. The details of the initiatives and about the Oregon Citizens Alliance, the grassroots organization which sponsored them, would fill at least one book by themselves. But the long and the short of what led me to *this* book and its topic was the *astonishing tone of the rhetoric* which is routinely leveled by the defenders of "gay rights" at people who publicly oppose homosexuality. Amidst this rhetoric, the favorite names and metaphors were nearly all drawn from Hitler's Germany. Leaders and even petition-carriers on our campaign were characterized as every kind of Nazi, fascist, racist, hate-monger and Aryan supremacist. Bricks wrapped in swastika-emblazoned paper were hurled through the windows of businesses who had contributed to our campaign. Always, the Nazi rhetoric was loudest and most extreme among the homosexual activists and their closest political allies (Governor Barbara Roberts, a long-time homosexualist, characterized the ballot measure as "almost like Nazi Germany" (*The Oregonian*, August 26, 1992:A14)).

Some of the worst abuse came from homosexualists in the media. During the 1992 election cycle, I was contacted by an assistant producer for the CBS news-magazine show

"48 Hours," who wanted permission to feature OCA in a segment about "how mainstream Americans were responding to extremism in the gay-rights movement." Being familiar with media bias on the issue of homosexuality, I was very suspicious and insisted on personal assurance from the producer that this was indeed the focus of the program. Due to the tone of rhetoric in the local media I specifically demanded and received a promise that OCA would not be characterized as a hate group. Only after repeated assurances over a two or three week period of telephone negotiations did I seek and obtain permission for this project from OCA's chairman, Lon Mabon. I then devoted nearly two weeks of my time assisting the "48 Hours" film crew, facilitating dozens of hours of interviews and arranging camera locations for filming campaign activities.

The program aired on February 26, 1992. In the late afternoon I received a call from a friend in Massachusetts, where the program had just aired three hours ahead of our West Coast television programming schedule. "Watch out," she said, "they stabbed you in the back." Sure enough, the program was called "48 Hours on Hate Street" and featured a rogue's gallery of hate groups, including neo-Nazis and violent white supremacists. The segment on OCA was sandwiched between two such groups. In the local news program following "48 Hours," KOIN, the CBS affiliate in Portland, juxtaposed a report about OCA and a piece which included classic Nazi file footage and anti-Nazi polemics. Approximately two weeks later another television station in Eugene, KEZI-TV, included Nazi file footage in a news story about OCA (they later apologized). Newspapers across the state frequently editorialized against OCA, using the terms "Nazi," "KKK," "bigot," and "hate" liberally.

I had known for a long time that it is axiomatic that when name-calling (as opposed to reasonable debate) happens, the names one calls others usually reflect the things one dislikes about oneself. I think it occurred to me that there was something awfully overstated about the Nazi-labeling campaign, even before I received a set of carefully-documented notes on prominent homosexuals in the Nazi Party, sent by a person who had followed the firestorm of rhetoric brought on by our campaign.

In the years since I began augmenting and refining this first set of data, the nation has seen the trivialization of such extreme rhetoric. It is commonplace days to hear someone being called, directly or by inference, a "Nazi." Some people have attributed this to the impoverishment of our national discourse, the depletion of our language and powers of intellect, and I would agree. We are certainly losing our literacy, and much of our dignity along with it. Yet there remains the old and valid notion that those who repeatedly, loudly and unreasonably call others a name are often, consciously or not, describing themselves.

Though this book is limited to the examination of connections between the Nazi movement and the homosexual and occultist movements, I think that a larger and more chilling theme can be read in its pages. Can it be that the fascination with calling people Nazis is, for the modern "gay" movement and others in our society, an outgrowth of a deeper fascination with what the Nazis *got away with* in their own state? What are the attitudes that underlie the phenomena of the "nanny state," "political correctness," the cynical political promotion of racial and class strife, "dumbing down" the public, the attenuation of parental rights, sterilizing the public environment of Judeo-Christian religious references, and the increasing homogeneity of opinion and of news "slant" in the press? In a way, I think that American homosexual activists present an almost refreshingly *honest* view into the nature of these attitudes, compared to the sanctimonious presentations we hear daily from the press and certain special interest groups and political leaders.

Let us look for a moment at one of the more bald-faced revelations of the homosexualist's view of, and goals for, American society. In a point-by-point public relations strategy called "The Overhauling of Straight America," (*Guide Magazine*, November, 1987) homosexuals Marshall Kirk and Erastes Pill explain their modern makeover of Hitler's "Big Lie." This remarkable piece is a control freak's fantasy, a veritable binge of manipulative, coercive and deceptive words and tactics. It begins:

> The first order of business is *desensitization* of the American public concerning gays...To desensitize the public is to help it view homosexuality with indifference instead of with keen emotion. Ideally, we would have straights register differences in sexual preference the way they register different tastes for ice cream... (Kirk and Pill:7).

This behavior-modification mentality, combined with isolation of "straights" and others as groups or classes who assume the status of de-humanized targets of one sort or another, continues:

> the *masses* [emphasis ours] should not be shocked and repelled by premature exposure to homo*sexual* behavior itself...the imagery of sex should be downplayed...(ibid.:8).

> ...open up a gateway into the private world of straights, through which a Trojan horse might be passed (ibid.:8).

> ...gays must be cast as victims in need of protection so that straights will be inclined by reflex to assume the role of protector (ibid.:8).

> ...make use of symbols which reduce the mainstream's sense of threat, which lower its guard...(ibid.:8).

> ...replace the mainstream's self-righteous pride about its homophobia with shame and guilt (ibid.:10).

Not so many years ago, all of these statements would have been unbelievably offensive to most Americans, *even if they contained no reference to homosexuality*, precisely because they all advocate coercive tampering with people's most private domain, their thoughts, opinions and beliefs (Kirk and Pill call it "transforming the social values of straight America" — ibid.:14). Such attempts were thought to be the province of diabolical masterminds in sci-fi novels, or of Maoists or the dictators of banana republics. But we have arrived at a time in America in which Kirk and Pill simply add their voices (and the *tone* of their voices) to the many advocating the forcible or manipulative control of people's ideas (for example, "speech codes" on college campuses and in newspaper classified advertising policy).

The more of Nazi thinking I have researched, the more I have been reminded that our nation represents the first and greatest successful experiment in the opposite direction. At our founding we were the only nation, among many autocratically-governed states, which truly offered and guaranteed freedom of thought and expression. Our founding fathers attempted to write our inestimably precious freedoms in stone because they foresaw (indeed, it was going on even then) that there would be an incessant drift back to the power-in-the-hands-of-a-few school of thought. How far have we drifted today, and what does this mean for the behavioral fringe groups of our society (just as the Nazis were a behavioral fringe group of theirs), who feel compelled to re-shape American hearts and minds to resemble their own?

Let us return to Kirk and Pill to look at the mechanics of their strategy for "transforming" the society into what they feel would be a more acceptable form. Here are some of their suggestions:

Talk about gays and gayness as loudly and as often as possible...almost any behavior begins to look normal if you are exposed to enough of it...(Kirk and Pill:7).

Constant talk builds the impression that public opinion is at least divided on the subject (ibid.:8).

...the campaign should paint gays as *superior* pillars of society. Yes, yes, we know - this trick is so old it creaks (ibid.:9).

...it will be time to get tough with remaining opponents. To be blunt, they must be vilified (ibid.:10).

...we intend to make the anti-gays look so nasty that average Americans will want to dissociate themselves from such types (ibid.:10).

Each sign will tap patriotic sentiment, each message will drill a seemingly agreeable proposition into mainstream heads (ibid.:11).

The public should be shown images of ranting homophobes whose secondary traits and beliefs disgust middle America...the Ku Klux Klan demanding that gays be burned alive or castrated; bigoted southern [sic] ministers drooling with hysterical hatred to a degree that looks both comical and deranged; menacing punks, thugs and convicts...Nazi concentration camps...(ibid.:10).

These images should be combined with those of their gay victims by a method *propagandists* [emphasis ours] call the "bracket technique." For example, for a few seconds an unctuous beady-eyed Southern preacher is seen, pounding the pulpit in rage about "those sick, abominable creatures." While his tirade continues over the soundtrack, the picture switches to pathetic photos of badly beaten persons, or to photos of gays who look decent, harmless, and likable; and then we cut back to the poisonous face of the preacher, and so forth...The effect is devastating (ibid.:13-14).

A group called Parents and Friends of Lesbians and Gays (PFLAG) used this technique in an advertising campaign in the fall of 1995 against Pat Robertson, Jesse Helms and Jerry Falwell. As reported in the *San Francisco Examiner*, Sunday, November 12, 1995, "...a new television ad campaign [portrays scenes of] a teenage girl contemplating suicide with a handgun, [and] a young man being beaten by a gang as his attackers shout slurs...interspersed with actual clips of the Rev. Pat Robertson and other conservatives deploring homosexuality." Most stations turned down the ads, but they ran in Tulsa and Washington D.C. A print version of the ad (much less emotionally effective) was run in *USA Today*, November 21, 1995.

Interestingly, Pat Robertson's comments quoted in the ad were directly related to the subject of this book: "Homosexuality is an abomination. Many of those people involved with Adolf Hitler were Satanists, many of them were homosexuals. The two things seem to go together."

Without belaboring the point, these *soi-disant* propagandistic tactics, and even the verbiage in which they are couched, represent a twisted approach to the winning of American public opinion. Again, I was struck by the similarity (in deceptive tactics and puppeteer-like attitude) to the creators of the Nazi propaganda machine. Not only is there the classic Big Lie technique (say it "loudly and as often as possible"), but the homosexualists have elevated the old Nazi technique of vilification, used on the Jews by such adepts as pornographer Julius Streicher, to an art form. And the familiar Hitlerian emotional component of hatred is certainly there, as Kirk and Pill salivate over the imagined discomfiture of their "most fervid enemies" (apparently, pastors who have the misfortune to live in the South!):

The shoe fits, and we should make them try it on for size, with all of America watching (ibid.:10).

Two of the first and major commitments of the Nazis in their rise to power were the effective control of the information sources in Germany, and the careful building of a propaganda machine. This was the key to their power, and except for a strong military force, it is the most important enhancement to any autocratic power. Over the last two decades we have witnessed an appalling willingness among the American news and entertainment media to align themselves with one element of political thought, to allow themselves to be channels for the dissemination of one side of an issue over another. As new and contradictory voices (talk radio) have appeared on the media scene, they have actually been *opposed* by the existing media commentators. And in much of the entertainment media's program fare we find a not-so-subtle enactment of Kirk's and Pill's strategy (albeit on a number of issues, not just homosexuality). Indeed, Kirk and Pill assert that "gay Hollywood has provided our best covert weapon in the battle to desensitize the mainstream" (Kirk and Pill:8).

These are some of the issues to be broached in a study of the relationship of homosexuals and their political movements to the Nazi Party. The larger context of the study must be our own country, and the numerous groups who are now struggling to capture its soul and "transform" its society. How are we similar, and dissimilar, to the Germans of the 1920s and 30s? What lessons should we learn?

As a final note, the other inspiration of this book has been the recent claim of homosexualists that homosexuals were major victims of the Holocaust (this seems to be part of the "victim" strategy in Kirk's and Pill's design). The play *Bent* has been the springboard for a campaign, complete with homosexual add-ons to an Anne Frank exhibit which toured the U.S., to get the public to accept the idea that homosexuals were the most downtrodden and persecuted group in Nazi Germany. In this play, a homosexual prisoner "trades up" his pink badge for a yellow Jewish star to improve his status in the camp (S. Katz:145). This turn of events in the homosexualist propaganda campaign has been a sore affront to traditionalist Jews like my friend and co-author Kevin Abrams, who desires to protect the truth of history from the "Holocaust revisionists." It is to that truth, a signpost on the path of every free society, that we have dedicated this book.

A Word to the Reader

Two terms used frequently in this book, "homosexualist" and "pederast," will be unfamiliar to many readers. We use the term **homosexualist** to refer to any person, homosexual or not, who actively promotes homosexuality as morally and socially equivalent to heterosexuality as a basis for social policy. In our view Harry Hay, founder of the American "gay-rights" movement, and President Bill Clinton, who attempted to force the U.S. military to accept open homosexuals, are both homosexualists. Each has worked in his own way to legitimize homosexual behavior in America. Many heterosexual people are homosexualists. Many self-described homosexual people are *not* homosexualists. A homosexualist is defined by his actions in a sociopolitical context. This differs from Samuel Igra's use of the term in Germany's National Vice, which we have quoted extensively. Igra uses "homosexualist" to define sexual conduct only.

A **pederast** is defined as a physically mature man who engages in or desires to engage in sex with boys around the age of puberty, as opposed to a pedophile, who targets both male and female prepubescent children and/or pubertal girls. (Pederast derives from the Greek *paed*, meaning boy, and *erastis*, meaning lover). Self-defined "boy-lovers" who have formed "children's rights" organizations such as the North American Man/Boy Love Association (NAMBLA) in this country, and who formed the *Gemeinschaft der Eigenen* in Germany, generally seem to focus their sexual attention on boys *roughly* between the ages of 8 and 18 years, with an apparent preference for boys about 12 years old. Some sources quoted in this study use the terms "pederast" and "pedophile" interchangeably. We hope to reestablish the distinction between these terms (dubious as it may be) to facilitate a deeper understanding of homosexual ideology and the varieties of its expression.

English translation of German words using the *umlaut* (two dots above the vowel) result in different spellings of words like Fuehrer and Roehm (Fuhrer and Rohm). In this book we have chosen the form of spelling in which the vowel is followed by an "e." Spelling of German words varies among the authors we quote but we have taken the liberty of harmonizing the spelling in this book.

Acknowledgments

The process of creating a book involves, directly or indirectly, a great number of people who lend their inspiration. It is with deep respect that we express our gratitude to the many great historians, men like Konrad Heiden, who wrote <u>A History of National Socialism</u> and <u>Der Fuehrer</u>; William Shirer, whose book, <u>The Rise and Fall of the Third Reich</u>, became one of the most respected and classic texts on Nazi history; and, of course, Samuel Igra, whose obscure but important 1945 work, <u>Germany's National Vice,</u> reveals a hidden side of history seldom seen or acknowledged. To these who were there and who honestly reported what they saw and experienced, we are indebted. They are our guides to the future.

We would especially like to thank Dr. Charles Socarides, President of NARTH, The National Association for Research and Therapy of Homosexuality, for his support and encouragement. Dr. Socarides is a Clinical Professor of Psychiatry at Albert Einstein College of Medicine in New York. We would also like to express our gratitude to Dr. Joseph Nicolosi, Founder and Clinical Director of the Thomas Aquinas Psychological Clinic in California. Dr. Nicolosi has published insightful works on reparative therapy and homosexuality which offer hope and the option of positive change for the homosexual.

Other individuals with whom one or both of us have had the honor of working are Mr. Peter LaBarbera, editor and publisher of the *Lambda Report on Homosexuality*, a Washington, D.C.-based publication that monitors the homosexual agenda in American politics and culture; Steve Lequire and Terry O'Neil of *The British Columbia Report Magazine*; Rosebianca Starr, Vancouver, British Columbia; Lon Mabon, Chairman of Oregon Citizens Alliance (OCA) and Pat Smith of the OCA Research Department; Trevor Lautens, columnist for the *Vancouver Sun:* Paul Schratz, editor of *The Province Newspaper,* Vancouver, British Columbia; David, Avraham and Israel Feld, Maccabi Mossad, Israel; David Bedien, Director of Beit Agron Press Center, Jerusalem; Len Butcher, editor of the *Canadian B'nai B'rith Covenant*; Mrs. Irene Klass, Women's Editor of *The Jewish Press*, Brooklyn New York; Professor William Woodruff, Campbell University, North

28

Carolina; David Bar Illan, editor of the *Jerusalem Post*; Kevin Tebedo, Former Executive Director of Colorado for Family Values; Pastor Mary Rogers; Reverend Bernice Gerard of Sunday Line Radio and Television Ministries, Vancouver, British Columbia; Jan Willem van der Hoeven, Director for the International Christian Embassy, Jerusalem, and his wife Irene; Stan Goodenough, editor of the *Middle East Intelligence Report*; Rabbi Avraham Ravitz and Rabbi Schlomo Beneziri, Members of Knesset; Phil Chernovsky, Israel Centre; Rena Cohen, Sefat, Israel; Toby Klein Greenwald, columnist for *Washington Jewish Week*; Gershom Gale, editor of the *International Edition of the Jerusalem Post*; Aryeh Stav, editor of *Nativ Journal of Politics and the Arts*; Professor Mordechai Nisan; Ramon Bennet; Avi Asdauba, Yair Davidy, author of The Tribes; Shmuel Golding, publisher of *Biblical Polemics*; Aryeh Gallin, Director, Root and Branch Association; Christopher Barder, UK; John Hully, author of Comets, Jews and Christians; Rabbi Marvin Antelman, Chief Justice of the Supreme Rabinic Court of America; Gemma Blech; Dr. David Lewis; Dr. Mikha'el Snidecor; Maurits van Zuiden; Dr. Judith Reisman, author of Kinsey: Crimes and Consequences; Avi Lipkin; Gary Cooperberg; Paul deParrie and Andrew Burnett of *Life Advocate* magazine; Herman Bauer; Robert Orr; Libby Durea; Dr. Nathaniel Lehrman, Clinical Director, retired, Kingsboro Psychiatric Center; Gary Butterfield; Joseph D'Alelio; Josiah (Doc) Goldberg; Landon G. Mustell and Pastor Larry Dill, Sheridan Assembly of God Church.

Special thanks to Bill and Irene Bennett, Anne L., Kathy Bates and Charles Lowers for their editorial assistance, to D.E. and to Alan Abe for digging out countless familiar and obscure sources that document the truth of Nazi history, to Pat Gunnip for his generosity in underwriting research and other costs, and to Carol P. at OCA's research department who got us started on this endeavor by introducing us. Tim Duskin of the National Archives was especially helpful in directing us to important resources. There are several other people who helped in various ways but who wish to remain anonymous. We are grateful for each one.

I (Kevin) wish to acknowledge my teachers, Rabbis Mendle Altien, Lippa Dubrawsky, David Bassous, Mordecai Feuerstein, Avraham Feiglestock, Yitchak Wineberg — to you I owe the most.

Both of us extend a special thank you to our wives, Sharon Abrams and Anne Lively, who have struggled with us through this long and difficult process, offering their wholehearted support and many insightful suggestions. This book is for our children: Miriam, Aaron and Odette Abrams and Noah and Samuel Lively.

30

If it were possible to form a state or an army exclusively of homosexuals, these men would direct all their emulations toward honors, and going into battle with such a spirit would, even if their numbers were small, conquer the world.

Plato, from <u>Banquet</u> (In Konrad Heiden's <u>Der Fuehrer</u>, 1944:741)

It remains characteristic of the Germans, that they, outwardly the most brutally masculine of all European peoples, are the most homosexual nation on earth.

H.R. Knickerbocker, <u>Is Tomorrow Hitler's?</u>, 1941:34

Chapter One:

THE HOMOSEXUAL ROOTS
OF THE NAZI PARTY

It was a quiet night in Munich. The people moving along the streets in the heart of the city were grim. They walked heads down, hands deep in the pockets of their frayed coats. All around, the spirit of defeat hung like a pall in the evening air; it was etched on the faces of the out-of-work soldiers on every street corner and in every café. Germany had been defeated in the war, but it had been crushed by the terms of the Versailles Treaty. Everywhere the people were still mired in depression and despair, several years after the humiliating surrender of Kaiser Wilhelm.

In this atmosphere the purposeful stride of Captain Ernst Roehm seemed out of place. But Roehm was accustomed to being different. A homosexual with a taste for boys, Roehm was part of a growing subculture in Germany which fancied itself a superior form of German manhood. A large, heavy man, Roehm had been a professional soldier since 1906, and, after the war, had temporarily lent his talents to a socialist terror organization called the Iron Fist. On this night Roehm was on his way to meet some associates who had formed a much more powerful socialist organization.

At the door of the *Bratwurstgloeckl*, a tavern frequented by homosexual roughnecks and bully-boys, Roehm turned in and joined the handful of sexual deviants and occultists who were celebrating the success of a new campaign of terror. Their organization, once known as the German Worker's Party, was now called the *Nationalsozialistische Deutsche Arbeiterpartei*, The National Socialist German Worker's Party — the Nazis.

Yes, the Nazis met in a "gay" bar.

It was no coincidence that homosexuals were among those who founded the Nazi Party. In fact, the party grew out of a number of groups in Germany which were centers of homosexual activity and activism. Many of the characteristic rituals, symbols, activities and philosophies we associate with Nazism came from these organizations or from contemporary homosexuals. The extended-arm *"Sieg Heil"* salute, for example, was a ritual of the *Wandervoegel* ("Wandering Birds" or "Rovers"), a male youth society which became the German equivalent of the Boy Scouts. The *Wandervoegel* was started in the late 1800s by a group of homosexual teenagers. Its first adult leader, Karl Fischer, called himself *"der Fuehrer"* ("the Leader") (Koch:25f). Hans Blueher, a homosexual Nazi philosopher and important early member of the *Wandervoegel*, incited a sensation in 1912 with publication of <u>The German *Wandervoegel* Movement as an Erotic Phenomenon</u>, which told how the movement had become one in which young boys could be introduced into the homosexual lifestyle (Rector:39f). The *Wandervoegel* and other youth organizations were later merged into the Hitler Youth (which itself became known among the populace as the "Homo Youth" because of rampant homosexuality. - Rector:52).

Many of the Nazi emblems, such as the swastika, the double lightning bolt "SS" symbol, and even the inverted triangle symbol used to identify classes of prisoners in the concentration camps, originated among homosexual occultists in Germany (some, such as the swastika, are actually quite ancient symbols which were merely revived by these homosexual groups).

Ernst Roehm, Supreme Commander of the dreaded SA Brownshirts.
Yad Vashem

In 1907, Jorg Lanz Von Liebenfels, a former Cistercian monk whom the church excommunicated because of his homosexual activities (Sklar:19), flew the swastika flag above his castle in Austria (Goodrick-Clarke:109).

After his expulsion from the church Lanz founded the *Ordo Novi Templi* ("Order of the New Temple") which merged occultism with violent anti-Semitism. A 1958 study of Lanz, <u>*Der Mann der Hitler die Ideen gab*</u> ("The Man Who Gave Hitler His Ideas"), by Austrian psychologist Wilhelm Daim, called Lanz the true "father" of National Socialism.

List, a close associate of Lanz, formed the Guido von List Society in Vienna in 1904. The Guido von List Society was accused of practicing a form of Hindu Tantrism which featured sexual perversion in its rituals. This form of sexual perversion was popularized in occult circles by a man named Aleister Crowley who, according to Hitler biographer J. Sydney Jones, enjoyed "playing with black magic

Cover of Guido von List's book, The Secret of the Runes, 1908. The Nazis adopted many of these symbols.

and little boys" (J. S. Jones:123). List was "accused of being the Aleister Crowley of Vienna" (ibid.:123). Like Lanz, List was an occultist; he wrote several books on the magic principles of rune letters (from which he chose the "*SS*" symbol). In 1908, List "was unmasked as the leader of a blood brotherhood which went in for sexual perversion and substituted the swastika for the cross" (Sklar:23). The Nazis borrowed heavily from List's occult theories and research. List also formed an elitist occult priesthood called the Armanen Order, to which Hitler himself may have belonged (Waite, 1977:91).

The Nazi dream of an Aryan super-race was adopted from an occult group called the Thule Society, founded in 1917 by followers of Lanz and List. The occult doctrine of the Thule Society held that the survivors of an ancient and highly developed lost civilization could endow Thule initiates with esoteric powers and wisdom. The initiates would use these powers to create a new race of Aryan supermen who would eliminate all "inferior" races. Hitler dedicated his book, *Mein Kampf*, to Dietrich Eckart, one of the Thule Society inner circle and a former leading figure in the German Worker's Party. (Schwarzwaller:67). The various occult groups mentioned above were outgrowths of the Theosophical Society, whose founder, Helena Petrovna Blavatsky, is thought by some to have been a lesbian (Webb:94), and whose "bishop" was a notorious pederast named Charles Leadbeater.

The SA Brownshirts or *Stuermabteilung* ("Storm Troopers") were largely the creation of another homosexual, Gerhard Rossbach (Waite, 1969:209). Rossbach formed the *Rossbachbund* ("Rossbach Brotherhood"), a homosexual unit of the *Freikorps* ("Free Corps"). The *Freikorps* were independent inactive military reserve units which became home to the hundreds of thousands of unemployed World War I veterans in Germany. Rossbach also formed a youth organization under the *Rossbachbund*, calling it the *Schilljugend* ("Schill Youth") (ibid.:210). Rossbach's staff assistant, Lieutenant Edmund Heines, a pederast and murderer, was put in charge of the *Schilljugend*. The *Rossbachbund* later changed its name to Storm Troopers (in honor of Wotan, the ancient German god of storms. - Graber:33). Rossbach seduced Hitler's mentor, Ernst Roehm, into homosexuality. It was under Roehm's leadership that the Brownshirts became notorious for brutality.

Famous events in Nazi history are also linked to homosexuality; events such as the burning of the German Reichstag in 1932, the 1938 *pogrom* called *Kristallnacht,* and the 1944 attempt on Hitler's life. Even the enduring image of Nazi book-burning, familiar to us from newsreels of the 1930s, was directly related to the homosexuality of Nazi leaders. The first such incident occurred four days after Hitler's Brownshirts broke into Magnus Hirschfeld's Institute for Sexual Research in Berlin on May 6, 1933. On May 10 the Nazis burned thousands of books and files taken in that raid. The Institute had extensive records on the sexual perversions of numerous Nazi leaders, many of whom had been under treatment there prior to the beginning of the Nazi regime. Treatment at the Sex Research Institute was required by the German courts for persons convicted of sex crimes. Ludwig L. Lenz, who worked at the Institute at the time of the raid but managed to escape with his life, later wrote of the incident:

> Why was it then, since we were completely non-party, that our purely scientific Institute was the first victim which fell to the new regime? The answer to this is simple...We knew too much. It would be against medical principles to provide a list of the Nazi leaders and their perversions [but]...not ten percent of the men who, in 1933, took the fate of Germany into their hands, were sexually normal...Our knowledge of such intimate secrets regarding members of the Nazi Party and other documentary mate-

Among the burning literary works deemed unacceptable by the Nazis were hidden thousands of files documenting the perversions of Nazi leaders.

rial — we possessed about forty thousand confessions and biographical letters — was the cause of the complete and utter destruction of the Institute of Sexology. (Haberle:369).

The attack on the Sex Research Institute is often cited as an example of Nazi oppression of homosexuals. This is partly true, but as we shall see, the "oppression" fits into a larger context of internecine rivalry between two major homosexual groups. Magnus Hirschfeld, who headed the Institute, was a prominent Jewish homosexual. Hirschfeld also headed a "gay rights" organization called the Scientific-Humanitarian Committee (SHC), formed in 1897 to work for the repeal of Paragraph 175 of the German legal code, which criminalized homosexuality (Kennedy:230). The organization was also opposed to sado-masochism and pederasty, two of the favorite practices of the militaristic, Roehm-style homosexuals who figured so prominently in the early Nazi Party. Hirschfeld had formed the SHC to carry on the work of the pioneer "gay rights" activist, Karl Heinrich Ulrichs (1825-1895). Ulrichs had written against the concept of "Greek love" (pederasty) advocated by a number of other homosexuals in Germany.

One such advocate was Adolf Brand, who formed the *Gemeinschaft der Eigenen* ("Community of the Elite") in 1902. The *Gemeinschaft der Eigenen* inspired the formation in 1920 of the German Friendship League, which changed its name in 1923 to the Society for Human Rights. The leaders of this group were instrumental in the formation and the rise of the Nazi Party. Adolf Brand published the world's first homosexual periodical, *Der Eigene* ("The Elite" - Oosterhuis and Kennedy:cover). Brand was a pederast, child pornographer and anti-Semite, and, along with many homosexuals who shared his philosophies, developed a burning hatred of Magnus Hirschfeld and the SHC. When Hirschfeld's Sex Research Institute was destroyed, the SA troops were under the general command of Ernst Roehm, a member of Brand's spinoff group, the Society for Human Rights.

The Divided Movement

This was not the last time homosexual leadership of the Nazis would attack other ideologically dissimilar homosexuals. Later in this discussion we will examine the so-called "pink triangle" homosexuals who were interned in concentration camps. The pink triangle, part of a scheme of variously-colored triangles used by the Nazis to identify specific classes of prisoners, was applied to those convicted under Paragraph 175 of the German Penal Code. Homosexuals were one of these classes, but according to Johansson,

[M]any of those convicted under Paragraph 175 were not homosexual: some were opponents of the regime such as Catholic priests or leaders of youth groups who were prosecuted on the basis of perjured testimony, while others were street hustlers from Berlin or Hamburg who had been caught up in a police dragnet (Johansson in Dynes:997).

As many as 6,000 of the approximately 10,000 "pink triangles" died in the work camps, but few, if any, were gassed in the death camps. Some of those who died met their deaths at the hands of homosexual *Kapos* ("trustees") and guards of the SS. At first glance it is difficult to understand why the homosexual leaders of the Nazis would persecute other homosexuals on the basis of their sexual behavior. We alluded, in the matter of the Sex Research Institute, to the fact that the homosexual movement in Germany was divided into two diametrically opposed camps which some have called the "Fems" and the "Butches." These terms are common among homosexuals today, as is the disdain "Butches" feel for "Fems."

A researcher of the homosexual movement Gordon Westwood writes that masculine homosexuals "deplore [effeminate] behavior," many considering effeminate homosexuals "repulsive" (Westwood:87). Another researcher, H. Kimball Jones, reports that reaction to "Fems" is often violent in the general homosexual community. "[They label them] 'flaming faggot' or 'degenerate fag,'" with one homosexual exclaiming, "You know, I loathe these screaming fairies" (H.K.Jones:29). Jay and Young's 1979 examination of the American homosexual movement, The Gay Report, contains numerous personal statements by masculine homosexuals critical of effeminacy. "Fem behavior can be vicious and destructive, demeaning to women and gay men," says one. Another asserts, "To me someone who is 'femme' is a self-indulgent...petty, scheming, gos-

Adolf Brand mocks the effeminacy of Magnus Hirschfeld and the "Fems" of the Scientific Humanitarian Committee in this issue of *Der Eigene* titled "The Auntie."

sipy gay being whose self-image has been warped and shaped by unfortunate family situations" (Jay:294ff).

The most hostile to "Femmes" are precisely those homosexuals who deem themselves the most "masculine." In The Homosexual Matrix, C.A. Tripp writes that "[f]ar to the other extreme, there are a number of utterly masculine, sometimes supermasculine homosexuals....They are obsessed with everything male and eschew anything weak or effeminate....Unquestionably they represent the epitome of what can happen when an eroticized maleness gains the full backing of a value system that supports it" (Tripp:92). Cory and LeRoy, in their detailed discussion of homosexual culture, describe the scene in a typical American "leather bar":

> Here, sturdy swaggering males dressed in tight dungarees, leather jackets or heavy shoes, dark hued woolen shirts, and sometimes motorcycle helmets, aspire toward a super-masculine ideal...Behind the facade of robust exploits, the uniform of pretentious male prowess, the mask of toughness, there sometimes lies a dangerous personality that can express itself physically by substituting violence for erotic pleasure; capable of receiving sexual pleasure only by inflicting pain (or receiving it). The general atmosphere in such places is restless and brooding, and one can never be sure when the dynamite of violence will erupt (Cory and LeRoy:109).

Reading this description, one can imagine oneself looking into Munich's *Bratwurstgloeckl* tavern, where the Brownshirts congregated, and finding the same cast of characters -- only wearing different costumes.

This contrast of homosexual types is not simply a phenomenon of modern society. Greenberg writes about homosexuality among the Germans of the first centuries A.D.:

As war became more important to the Germans, the male warriors and their culture became dominant, and the status of women declined. Effeminacy and receptive homosexuality were increasingly scorned and repressed....The effeminate homosexual...was depicted as a foul monster....this stigmatization did not extend to active male homosexuality. [Later, acceptability of masculine oriented homosexuality declined under Christianity, which] was officially opposed to all forms of homosexuality (Greenberg:249f).

The authors do not wish to imply that all homosexuals fall into one or the other of these two simplistic stereotypes. The terms "Butch" and "Fem" in this study are used loosely to differentiate between two ideological extremes relating to the nature of homosexual identity. Generally in this work the German "Fems" are defined as homosexual men who acted like women. They were pacifists and accomodationists. Their goals were equality with heterosexuals and the "right to privacy," and generally they opposed sex with young children. Their leaders were Karl Heinrich Ulrichs and Magnus Hirschfeld.

The "Butches," on the other hand, were masculine homosexuals. They were militarists and chauvinists in the Hellenic mold. Their goal was to revive the pederastic military cults of pre-Christian pagan cultures, specifically the Greek warrior cult. They were often vicious misogynists and sadists. Their leaders included Adolf Brand and Ernst Roehm. The "Butches" reviled all things feminine. Their ideal society was the *Maennerbund,* an all-male "comradeship-in-arms" comprised of rugged men and boys (Oosterhuis and Kennedy:255). In their view, heterosexuals might be tolerated for the purpose of continuing the species, but effeminate homosexuals were considered to be subhuman, and thus intolerable.

Most of the estimated 1.2 to 2 million homosexuals in Germany at the time of the Third Reich undoubtedly fit somewhere between the two extremes of the movement. This may explain the fact that less than 2% of this population were prosecuted under anti-sodomy laws by the Nazis (Cory and LeRoy estimate that "Fems" make up 5-15% of male homosexuals. Cory and LeRoy:73). Most of those who were prosecuted can be shown to fit the profile of the "Fems." Kurt Hiller, a ranking member of the SHC who later succeeded Hirschfeld, "estimated that 75 percent of the male homosexuals sympathized with the parties of the Right" (Johansson in Friedlander:233).

In his introduction to The Men with the Pink Triangle, the supposed testimony of a former pink triangle prisoner at the Flossenburg concentration camp, translator David Fernbach confirms that the "Butch/Fem" conflict was at the heart of the Nazi hatred of the "pink triangles." He writes,

> Naturally, in the paramilitary organization of the SA, Hitler Youth, etc., even the elite SS, the forms of homosexuality that are characteristic of such all-male bodies were as common as they always are...it was quite fundamental to Nazi ideology that men were to be properly "masculine"...when male homosexuality disguises itself as a cult of "manliness" and virility, it is less obnoxious from the fascist standpoint than is the softening of the gender division that homosexuality invariably involves when it is allowed to express itself freely (Heger:10f).

"One of the ten best books of the year."
—Richard Hall, in The Advocate

The Men with the Pink Triangle

Heinz Heger

The true, life-and-death story of homosexual prisoners in the Nazi concentration camps

This, then, is the explanation for the paradox of the Nazi persecution of homosexuals. It is found in the history of two irreconcilable philosophies linked by a common sexual dysfunction. The roots of this conflict extend back into the eighteenth century and span a 70-year period which saw the rise of homosexual militancy in the movement that gave Nazism to the world.

One final item before we move to the next section. It should by this time be apparent to the reader that lesbians did not have a major part to play in Nazism, but they were not completely absent from the Party. Herzer writes that "Claudia Schoppmann has recently shown that prior to 1933, there were Nazi adherents among the leading lesbians in the homosexual emancipation movement. As an example she names the case of Elsbeth Killmer, a leading editor of the most important lesbian periodical of that time, *Die Freundin*, who was active in the Nazi organization *NS-Frauenschaft* early on" (Herzer:221f).

Karl Heinrich Ulrichs

The "grandfather" of the world "gay rights" movement was a homosexual German lawyer named Karl Heinrich Ulrichs (1825-1895). At the age of 14, Ulrichs was seduced by his riding instructor, a homosexual man about 30 years old (Kennedy in Pascal:15). Observers familiar with the apparently high correlation between childhood sexual molestation and adult homosexuality might conclude that this youthful experience caused Ulrichs to become a homosexual. Ulrichs himself, however, arrived at a hereditary rather than an environmental explanation for his condition. In the 1860s Ulrichs began advancing a theory that defined homosexuals as a third sex. He proposed that male homosexuality could be attributed to a psycho-spiritual mix-up in which a man's body came to be inhabited by a woman's soul (and vice-versa for females). He called members of this third sex "*Urnings*" (male) and "*Dailings*" (female). Since homosexuality was an inborn condition, he reasoned,

it should not be criminalized.

Although Ulrichs was
to be unsuccessful in
changing the laws against
homosexuality, his efforts
did encourage widespread
political activism. One
early follower, a Ger-
man-Hungarian writer
named Benkert (under the
pseudonym, Karoly Maria
Kertbeny), coined the term
"homosexual" in an
anonymous open letter to
the Prussian Minister of
Justice in 1869 (Lauritsen

Ulrichs:

The Life and Works of
Karl Heinrich Ulrichs,
Pioneer of the Modern Gay Movement

Hubert Kennedy

and Thorstad:6). Steakley writes that prior to this, homosexuals were known as sodomites, pederasts, or "'Knaben-
schaender' (literally, 'boy-ravishers')" (Steakley:13). The
first psychiatric study of homosexuality in Germany was
published in 1869 as the result of Ulrichs' efforts. It advocated the decriminalization of homosexuality in favor of
medical treatment (Oosterhuis and Kennedy:13).

Ulrichs' greatest intellectual impact on his own generation came from his invention of the term "Uranians,"
which he introduced in 1862 as a new designation for
homosexuals (both *Urnings* and *Dailings*). He took the
term from Plato's <u>Symposium</u>, in which homosexual activity was said to fall under the protection of the ninth muse,
Urania. In the late 1800s German homosexuals frequently
called themselves Uranians, and a militant homosexual
slogan, "Uranians of the world, unite!" became popular
internationally (Rutledge:41). In the following quote Ulrichs uses the term in his explanation of the "third sex"

theory, and graphically illustrates the mentality of the "Fems":

> Apart from the womanly direction of our sexual desire, we Uranians bear another womanly element within us which, it appears to me, offers proof positive that nature developed the male germ within us physically but the female spiritually. We bear this other womanly element from our earliest childhood on. Our character, the way we feel, our entire temperament is not manly, it is decidedly womanly. This inner womanly element is outwardly recognizable by our outwardly apparent womanly nature (Fee:37).

Ulrichs was publicly opposed to sadomasochism and pedophilia (perhaps because of his own molestation as an adolescent). He wrote against the concept of "Greek love" and considered "sexual attraction to the prepubertal to be a sickness." In his attempts to repeal Paragraph 175 of the German Penal Code, Ulrichs advocated more stringent laws against pedophilia. Ulrichs' condemnation of man/boy sex, however, extended only to prepubescent boys. As the following quote from his publication *Forschungen Ueber das Raetsel der mannmannlichen Liebe* ("Investigation of the Enigma of Homosexual Love") reveals, Ulrichs was not opposed to sex between men and boys who were "sexually mature."

> The Urning is not by a hair's breadth any more dangerous to immature boys than the genuine man is to immature girls. For the rest, I gladly leave the child molester to his deserved punishment by the law. Let the integrity of a will-less minor be sacred to every Urning. I have no defense for whoever touches it. Therefore, let the seduction of immature boys, I grant it completely, be a punishable indecent act (Ulrichs:16).

This distinction between mature and immature boys was lost on many who followed the rise of the homosexual movement in Germany. For example, Friedrich Engels, in a letter to Karl Marx about a book Ulrichs had written, said, "The pederasts start counting their numbers and discover they are a powerful group in our state. The only thing missing is an organization, but it seems to exist already, though it is hidden" (Plant:38). Engels considers Ulrichs a pederast despite his arbitrary age restriction for sex with boys.

Ulrichs' political activities paved the way for a large and powerful homosexual movement which grew both in numbers and in political and social influence in pre-Nazi Germany. Barely a quarter of a century after his death in 1895, homosexuality would become openly widespread in the Germany of the Weimar Republic era. Cities such as Munich and Berlin would become international Meccas for the practitioners of all forms of sexual perversion. As William Manchester observed in The Arms of Krupp "Wilhelmine Kulture's emphasis on masculinity had produced a generation of perverts. Abroad, sodomy was delicately known as 'the German vice'" (Manchester, 1968:232).

Samuel Igra, a German Jew who published *Germany's National Vice* in 1945 (a study of homosexual influences in Germany), commented on the rise of homosexuality after the turn of the century:

> In Germany these unnatural vices became a veritable cult among the ruling classes. In 1891 the well-known German psychiatrist, Krafft-Ebbing, one of the great pioneers in that branch of psycho-pathology, published a book entitled *Psychologia Sexualis* in which he declared that sex perversion in Germany was alarmingly on the increase. Commissioner Hans von Tresckow, who was head of a special branch of the Criminal Police Department in Berlin from 1905 to 1919, has published the following in his memoirs:

I can confirm the statement (made by Krafft-Ebbing) that homosexualist groups have been steadily on the increase in recent decades, especially in the big cities. At the present time in Berlin there are for certain more than one hundred thousand persons who are addicts of this practice. They are closely banded together and even have their own paper, *Die Freundschaft*, which appears regularly and defends their interests" (*Von Fuersten and Anderen Sterblichen*, by Hans von Tresckow, p. 110. F. Fontane & Co. Berlin. 1922) [Igra:27f].

Magnus Hirschfeld and the SHC

Ulrichs' successor Magnus Hirschfeld was a prominent Jewish physician and homosexual. Dr. Hirschfeld, along with two other homosexuals, Max Spohr and Erich Oberg, joined together to form the *Wissenschaftlich-Humanitaeres Komitee* ("Scientific-Humanitarian Committee"). As we

have noted, the SHC was dedicated to two goals: 1) to carry on Ulrichs' philosophy and works and 2) to work for the legitimization of homosexuality by the German public via the repeal of Paragraph 175, the German law which criminalized homosexual conduct (Steakley:23f). Homosexualist historian Richard Plant writes,

Magnus Hirschfeld

It would be hard to overestimate Hirschfeld's importance...He became the leader of several psychological and medical organizations, the founder of a unique institute for sexual research...He also founded the 'Yearbook for Intersexual Variants,' which he edited until 1923 (Plant: 28-29).

Hirschfeld was originally committed to Ulrichs' "third sex" theory but he later abandoned this idea. Still, Hirschfeld remained true to many of the rest of Ulrichs' theories, building upon them through the work of the Scientific-Humanitarian Committee, whose efforts he directed toward the political goal of decriminalizing homosexuality. Hirschfeld coined the term "transvestite," which has become the accepted label for both men and women who compulsively costume themselves as members of the opposite sex (J. Katz:210).

The SHC circulated petitions among German intellectuals and politicians calling for the abolition of Paragraph 175. Due to Hirschfeld's groundwork in creating a positive public image, these petitioning efforts met with increasing success. But for all the appearance of dignity and scientific impartiality which it displayed to German society, the SHC offered a far different perspective to those who saw it from within. Hans Blueher, whose contribution to the German homosexual movement is chronicled later in this study, once visited Hirschfeld at the SHC. The meeting was precipitated by Hirschfeld's offer to write the foreword to Blueher's book describing homosexuality in the *Wandervoegel*. Blueher writes,

> I was led into the study of the "Wise Man of Berlin" (as he was called)...Sitting on a silk-covered fauteuil, legs under him like a Turk, was an individual with bloated lips and cunning, dimly coveting eyes who offered me a fleshy hand and introduced himself as Dr. Hirschfeld...[Later in a meeting of the SHC] the first to greet me was a corporal with a deep bass voice; he was, however, wearing women's clothes... "A so-called transvestite!" commented Dr. Hirschfeld, whose nickname was "Aunt Magnesia," and introduced us...Then a most beautiful youth appeared..."A hermaphrodite!" said Hirschfeld. "Why don't you come to me during my office hours tomorrow, you can see him naked then"...An older gentle-

man in his sixties...recited a poem...to a sixteen year old youth, full of yearning...I turned to Laurent, who was the only kindred spirit in this pack of lemurs, "Tell me, haven't you noticed that we're in a downright brothel here?" (Blueher in Mills:160f).

Blueher's disgust with Hirschfeld and the SHC was representative of the attitude of the masculine homosexual camp. But at this stage of the conflict, the "Fems" were fully in control and enjoyed what support there was in German society for the homosexual political cause. The SHC's "scientific" focus lent an air of legitimacy to its political goals that the masculine group could not achieve. Yet it was a strategy that would ultimately backfire on the "Fems." Sociologist David Greenberg writes that Ulrichs' third-sex theory "was a controversial strategy among German homosexual activists; those in the anti-feminist wing of the movement viewed male homosexuality as an expression of male superiority and considered the Ulrichs-Hirschfeld position insulting" (Greenberg: 410).

Hoping to use the argument that homosexuality is congenital to justify its decriminalization, Hirschfeld tried desperately to legitimize his "third-sex" theory and homosexuality generally (ibid.:410). He formed the Sex Research Institute of Berlin, which opened its doors on July 1, 1919. It's purpose was in part to provide legal services for men arrested for violating Paragraph 175 but also to legitimize the view of homosexuality as a medical condition (Bianco:64). In that same year, Hirschfeld produced the first pro-homosexual film "*Anders als die Andern*" (Different from the Others) in which he appeared briefly (ibid.).

The Sex Research Institute, housed in a Berlin mansion purchased by Hirschfeld, assimilated the SHC's massive collection of books, photographs and medical documents and began a campaign to make itself "respectable" in German society. According to Plant, "attending physicians offered various kinds of sexual counseling...treated people for venereal diseases...[and gave] advice on abortion procedures." The fact that many Nazi leaders were treated at the Sex Research Institute led the Institute's Assistant Director, Ludwig L. Lenz, to conclude that its destruction by the Nazis in 1933 was for the purpose of destroying evidence of Nazi perversions (see above).

For many years the Scientific-Humanitarian Committee was the largest and most influential homosexual organization in the German "gay rights" movement. In 1914, it had one thousand members (Steakley:60). But homosexuality in Germany was much more prevalent than the size of the membership of the SHC would suggest. Not surprisingly, one of the early goals of the SHC was to find out how many homosexuals there were in the German population. In what may have been the world's first survey of its kind, the SHC distributed 6611 questionnaires to Berlin students and factory workers in 1903. The results were published the following year in the *Jahrbuch* ("Yearbook") and showed that 2.2% of the German male population admitted to being homosexual (ibid.:33).

The New Hellenes

At the same time that Ulrichs and Hirschfeld were promulgating their theories of male homosexuality as an expression of femininity, a rival group of homosexuals was reaching into antiquity for its own "masculine" philosophy. As homosexual scholar Hubert Kennedy writes in Man/Boy Love in the Writings of Karl Heinrich Ulrichs:

> Happily, some boy-lovers were already speaking out in opposition to Hirschfeld in Berlin at the beginning of this century...[Der Gemeinschaft] Der Eigene, mostly bisexual and/or boy-lovers, opposed the "third sex" view of homosexuality. Seeing the "love of friends" as a mascu-

Hellenism-inspired statue in the House of German Art is part of a tour of Berlin given to Mussolini by Adolf Hitler in 1937.

line virtue, they urged a rebirth of the Greek ideal (Kennedy:17f).

This "Greek ideal" was a culture of pederastic male supremacy. Male homosexuality, especially between men and boys, was considered a virtue in Hellenic (Greek) society. In several of his Dialogues, Plato serves as an apologist for pederasty, and apparently considered man/boy sex to be superior to heterosexual relations. As author Eva Cantarella notes in Bisexuality in the Ancient World, "Plato makes clear in the Symposium that it was perfectly acceptable to court a lad, and admirable to win him...Pederasty did not lurk in the shadows of Greek life, it was out in the open" (Greenberg:148, 151). Cantarella reviews the literature of the period, including Plato's writings. She writes that Plato developed a theory "of the existence of two different types of love: the love inspired by the heavenly Aphrodite, and the love inspired by the common Aphrodite." Only "pederastic courtship," notes Cantarella, reflected the "heavenly" form of love (Cantarella:59). In his Symposium, Plato expounds this theory:

> [Homosexual] boys and lads are the best of their generation, because they are the most manly. Some people say they are shameless, but they are wrong. It is not shamelessness which inspires their behavior, but high spirit and manliness and virility, which leads them to welcome the society of their own kind. A striking proof of this is that such boys alone, when they reach maturity engage in public life. When they grow to be men, they become lovers of boys, and it requires the compulsion of convention to overcome their natural disinclination to marriage and procreation; they are quite content to live with one another unwed (ibid.:60).

Cantarella writes that "[t]he gender which attracted and tempted Socrates was the male sex" as well. She cites another of Plato's dialogues in which Socrates falls in love with Cydias, a schoolboy, proclaiming "[I] caught fire, and could possess myself no longer" (ibid.:56ff).

Voltaire may have had both of these men in mind when he once remarked of the propensity of classical philosophers, "Once, a philosopher, twice, a sodomite!" (Grant, 1993:28). To be fair, however, the characterizations of Plato and Socrates as pederasts is hotly contested by many historians.

In the defense of the philosophers it must be noted that Plato, whose writings provide our only evidence for speculating on the life of either man, wrote mostly in dialogue. It is thus difficult to know to what extent he agreed with the ideas expressed by his characters. It should also be noted here that in is last work, the Laws, Plato asserted the value of the family and the moral wrongness of homosexuality (Laws: 841A-841D). Still, based on the fact that homosexual pederasty was widely practiced and accepted in Greece and that Plato based The Republic (his vision of "utopian" society -- addressed later in this book) upon the Spartan homosexual military cult, the authors believe that in his earlier life Plato was at least an apologist for pederasty and may indeed have practiced this perversion himself.

What remains most relevant to this study (and is confirmed by Plato) is that the Greek military establishment enthusiastically embraced homosexuality. Here we find the model for the new Hellenes -- an ultramasculine, male supremacist, homoerotic warrior cult. The armies of Thebes, Sparta and Crete were each examples of this phenomenon (as are the modern Islamist terror groups). Cantarella notes that the ancient historian, Plutarch of Chaeronea (50-120 A.D.) wrote of "the sacred battalion" of Thebans made up of 150 male homosexual pairs (Cantarella:72), and of the legendary Spartan army, which inducted all twelve-year-old boys into military service where they were "entrusted to lovers chosen among the best men of adult age." Plutarch also reports of a Cretan military induction ritual in which boys were abducted and sexually enslaved for a period of two months by adult pederasts before receiving their "military kit" (ibid.:7). This last perversion undoubtedly inspired or was inspired by the Greek myth of Ganymede. Author Jason Berry sheds some light on this apparent derivation:

Rembrandt's *Rape of Ganymede* depicts the pederasty of Zeus (in the form of an eagle).

Certain gods practiced man-boy love as did the bi-sexual male aristocracy; the armies of Thebes and Sparta were charged with homosexuality as a fire of the male power drive. Pagans in the late [Roman] Empire adulated gods like Zeus, who abducted and raped Ganymede — a living myth that one philosopher denounced for influencing those men who ran "marketplaces of immorality and...infamous resorts for the young for every kind of corrupt pleasure" (Berry:200f).

It is possible that the term "gay" is derived from this mythical Greek figure, Ganymede, cup-bearer of the gods, who exemplified the concept of man/boy sex to the masculine homosexuals. The British term "catamite," meaning the submissive partner in a male homosexual relationship, is derived from the Roman version of Ganymede, *Catamitus*. The terms "gay" and "lesbian" (the latter derived from the name of the Isle of Lesbos in Greece) eventually re-

Nazi parade features Greek theme.

placed the terms *Urning* and *Dailing* as the names of choice for homosexuals.

In ancient Greece, as in the masculine homosexual faction in Germany, only the masculine form of homosexuality was esteemed and all things feminine were despised. The form of homosexuality which dominated Greek culture was ultramasculine and militaristic. It can be assumed that women, as well as men who identified with womanly traits and thinking, were considered naturally inferior to the elite pederasts. Cantarella writes that Plato, in *Timaues*, went so far as to theorize that women were the reincarnations of men who had "lived badly" in a previous life (Cantarella:58).

As we will see, the revival of Hellenic paganism became a fundamental aspect of the Nazi identity. In <u>Nation-alism and Sexuality</u>, historian George L. Mosse notes its significance: "The Greek youth, an important national symbol in the past, reigned supreme during the Third Reich. Hitler's own taste was influenced by the neo-classical revival...[which often included] pictures of nude youth...not unlike those of boys bathing" (Mosse:172). But the Nazis adopted more than just symbolism from the "boy-lovers" who reasserted the Greek ideal; their ideas and philosophies are indelibly stamped on the Nazi regime.

The influence of the Greek homosexuals on Nazi culture is perhaps explained best by contemporary German psychoanalyst, Wilhelm Reich in his 1933 classic, The Mass Psychology of Fascism:

> Among the ancient Greeks, whose written history does not begin until patriarchy has reached a state of full development, we find the following sexual organization: male supremacy...and along with this the wives leading an enslaved and wretched existence and figuring solely as birth machines. The male supremacy of the Platonic era is entirely homosexual...The same principle governs the fascist ideology of the male strata of Nazi leaders (Bluher, Roehm, etc.). For the fascists, therefore, the return of natural sexuality is viewed as a sign of decadence, laciviousness, lechery, and sexual filth...the fascists ...affirm the most severe form of patriarchy and actually reactivate the sexual life of the Platonic era in their familial form of living...Rosenberg and Bluher [the leading Nazi ideologists] recognize the state solely as a male state organized on a homosexual basis (Reich:91ff).

The Clash of Cultures

A key to understanding the cause of the German social collapse, which culminated in the atrocities of the Third Reich, is found in the conflict of Hellenic and Hebrew (Judeo-Christian) value systems. This war of philosophies, as old as Western civilization itself, pits the homoeroticism of the Greeks against the marriage-and-family-centered heterosexuality of the Jews. Johansson and Percy write of this conflict from the homosexualist perspective:

> While the Greeks cultivated *paiderasteia* as a fundamental institution of male society and attribute of gods and heros, in two centuries, under Persian rule (538-332 B.C.), Biblical Judaism came to reject and penalize male homosexuality in all forms. Jewish religious consciousness deeply internalized this taboo, which became a distinctive feature of Judaic sexual morality, setting the worshippers of the god of Israel apart from the gentiles whose idols they despised. This divergence set the stage for the confrontation between Judaism and Hellenism (Johansson and Percy:34).

In implying that the rejection of homosexuality by the Jews *began* in this time period, Johansson and Percy ignore the Biblical record, but they are correct that the Jews' opposition to homosexuality was a central factor in their hostility to the Greeks. They continue (somewhat bitterly), describing the context in which the first clash of these value systems occurred:

> At the heart of the "sodomy delusion" lies the Judaic rejection of Hellenism and *paiderasteia,* one of the distinctive features of the culture brought by the Greek conquerors of Asia Minor. It is a fundamental, ineluctable clash of values within what was destined to become Western civilization. Only in the Maccabean era did the opposition to Hellenization and everything Hellenic lead to the intense, virtually paranoid hatred and condemnation of male homosexuality, a hatred that Judaism bequeathed to the nascent Christian church (ibid.:36).

In his article "Homosexuality and the Maccabean Revolt," Catholic scholar Patrick G. D. Riley also identifies homosexuality as the focal point of conflict between the Jews and the Greeks. The Greek King, Antiochus, had ordered that all the nations of his empire be "welded... into a single people" (Riley:14). This created a crisis for the Jews, forcing them to choose between faithfulness to Biblical commandments (at the risk of martyrdom) and participation in a range of desecrations from "the sacrificing of pigs and the worshiping of idols, to 'leaving their sons uncircumsized, and prostituting themselves to all kinds of impurity and abomination' (1 Macc. 1:49-51)" (ibid.:14).

The Greeks also built one of their *gymnasia* in Jerusalem, which "attracted the noblest young men of Israel...*subduing them under the petaso*" (emphasis ours -- 2 Macc. 4:12). In the traditional Latin translation the above phrase is rendered "to put in brothels" (Riley:15). The gymnasia were notorious throughout the ancient world for their association with homosexual practices. In fact, Flaceliere concludes from Plutarch's writings that from the beginning of its acceptance in Greece, "the development of homosexuality was connected to the rise of gymnasia...[which usually contained] not only a statue or Hermes, but also one of Eros" (Flaceliere:65).

The tensions which led to the Jewish revolt were exacerbated when the Jewish high priest, a Hellenist himself, offered a sacrifice to Heracles (Hercules), who was a Greek symbol of homosexuality. Riley adds, "The Jewish temple itself became the scene of pagan sacrificial meals and sexual orgies [including homosexuality]." The final insult (for which Antiochus is identified in the Bible as the archetype of the antichrist) "was the installation in the temple of a pagan symbol, possibly a representation of Zeus [Baal], called by a sardonic pun 'the abomination of desolation'" (Riley.:16).

In the ensuing religious revolt, the Maccabees "preserved what would become the moral charter of Christendom, just as in defending marriage they saved what would be the very material of its construction, namely, the family" (ibid.:17). Yet, though they preserved the Judeo-Christian sexual ethic, the Maccabees did not vanquish Greek philosophy as a rival social force. Of the two irreconcilable belief systems, the Judeo-Christian one would prevail, allowing the development of what we know today as Western culture; yet Hellenism survived.

Adolf Brand and the "Community of the Elite"

One of the earliest leaders of the masculine homosexual counter-movement in Germany, himself a Hellenist, was Adolf Brand. In 1896, one year before Magnus Hirschfeld formed the Scientific-Humanitarian Committee, young Adolf Brand began publishing the world's first homosexual

Cover of *Der Eigene* magazine.

serial publication, *Der Eigene* ("The Elite"). [The word *Eigene*, eye'-gen-eh, can be roughly translated "queer," which may shed some light on the derivation of this term in English, but we have chosen the translation used most often by historians because it emphasizes the elitist philosophy of *Der Eigene's* authors.]

Besides being militantly pro-homosexual, *Der Eigene* was racist, nationalistic and anti-Semitic. Mosse writes,

> The use of racism to gain respectability was a constant theme of the first homosexual journal in Germany, Der Eigene...Even before the paper published a supplement called Rasse und schonheit (Race and Beauty) in 1926, Germanic themes had informed much of its fiction, as well as images of naked boys and young men photographed against a background of Germanic nature. One poem, written by Brand himself and entitled, "The Superman," praised manliness, condemned femininity, and toyed with anti-Semitism, apparently because of the poet's quarrel with Magnus Hirschfeld, a rival for leadership of the homosexual rights movement (Mosse:42).

Brand's stated market for *Der Eigene* was men who "thirst for a revival of Greek times and Hellenic standards of beauty after centuries of Christian barbarism" (Brand in Oosterhuis and Kennedy:3).

In 1903 Brand was briefly jailed as a child pornographer for publishing pictures of nude boys in the magazine, but nevertheless *Der Eigene* remained in publication until 1931, peaking at over 150,000 subscriptions during the years of the Weimar Republic [1919-1933] (Mosse:42). In addition to *Der Eigene,* Brand published a satirical journal *Die Tante* ("The Fairy" or "The Auntie") which often ridiculed Hirschfeld and his assistants (Oosterhuis and Kennedy:6).

On May 1, 1902, Brand and two pederasts, Wilhelm Jansen and Benedict Friedlander, formed the *Gemeinschaft der Eigenen* ("Community of the Elite"). Its leading theorist was Friedlander (1866-1908), author of *Renaissance des Eros Uranios* ("Renaissance of Uranian Erotica"), a 1904 publication which featured a picture of a Greek youth on the cover. Friedlander wrote that the Community wanted to carry out the goals of the lesbian and radi-

RENAISSANCE
DES EROS URANIOS

Die physiologische Freundschaft,
ein normaler Grundtrieb des Menschen
und
eine Frage der männlichen Gesellungsfreiheit

In
naturwissenschaftlicher, naturrechtlicher,
culturgeschichtlicher und sittenkritischer
Beleuchtung
von
Benedict Friedlænder.

Buchschmuck von Casberg-Krause.

1904
Verlag „RENAISSANCE"
(Otto Lehmann)
SCHMARGENDORF-BERLIN.

Title page and cover picture from Benedict Friedlander's <u>Renaissance of Uranian Erotica</u>, 1904. The sub-title reads: "Physiological friendship, a normal fundamental drive of men, and a question of male freedom of association in natural science, natural rights, cultural-history and moral criticism.

cal feminist Dr. Helene Stocker who wanted German society to revert to pagan values. Friedlander writes,

> The positive goal...is the revival of Hellenic chivalry and its recognition by society. By chivalric love we mean in particular close friendships between youths and even more particularly the bonds between men of unequal ages (B. Friedlander:259).

According to James Steakley in The Homosexual Emancipation Movement in Germany:

> The Community looked to ancient Greece and Renaissance Italy as model civilizations and argued that Christian asceticism was responsible for the demise of homosexual relations. Friedlander, who was married, advocated pedophile relations combined with family life, and Brand contrasted his journal with Hirschfeld's *Jahrbuch* by saying he wanted to show "more of the Hellenic side of things" (Steakley:43).

Steakley goes on to show how the Community supported the work of Elisar von Kupffer, a "Butch" homosexual and an advocate of "Greek love," who strongly attacked the Scientific-Humanitarian Committee as pseudo-scientific (Steakley:46).

HOMOSEXUALITY
and
MALE BONDING
in
PRE-NAZI
GERMANY

the youth movement, the gay movement
and male bonding before Hitler's rise:
original transcripts from Der Eigene,
the first gay journal in the world

Harry Oosterhuis, PhD
Hubert Kennedy, PhD
Editors

In Homosexuality and Male Bonding in Pre-Nazi Germany, Oosterhuis and Kennedy write that "Kuppfer stated in a letter of 25 December 1925 to Brand that the word 'homosexual' was repugnant to him, because it reminded him of the 'fairies' in Hirschfeld's Committee, and he requested Brand never to mention his name in such a context" (Oosterhuis and Kennedy:34).

Friedlander described heterosexuals and effeminate homosexuals as *Kummerlings* (puny beings). The Ulrichs-Hirschfeld school believed that both homosexuality and heterosexuality were equal and legitimate forms of sexual love. However, the Brand-Friedlander school believed that eros (sexual love) had a rising scale of worth, with heterosexuality at the bottom and pederasty at the top. Steakley writes, "For the Community, however, heterosexual relations were relegated to purely procreative ends and the esthetic superiority of pedophile relations was asserted" (Steakley:46). In other words, heterosexuals were valued only as "breeders."

Friedlander also quoted from Gustov Jager who argued that, in contrast to the "Fems," masculine homosexuals were Uebermaenner (supermen), superior to heterosexuals because they were even more masculine (Oosterhuis and Kennedy:87). Some of the pederasts of the Community of the Elite did not consider themselves homosexuals at all, declaring the "love of friends" and homosexuality two different phenomena (ibid.:86).

Friedlander for a time was a member of both the Community of the Elite and the SHC. A review of his articles written for the SHC reveal that he endeavored to convince the members of the group that they were not going far enough: the SHC simply wanted the "right to privacy," but the Community of the Elite wanted a complete transformation of Germany from a Judeo-Christian society to a Greco-Uranian one. But the leadership of the SHC was never convinced. The two philosophies were just too different. In 1906 Friedlander left the SHC and, hoping to discredit Hirschfeld, strongly hinted that Hirschfeld and other leaders of the SHC had mismanaged the Committee's funds. But this was not the real reason for his departure. Steakley writes,

> The membership of the Community realized that the Committee's petition, which called for the legalization of same-sex relations only between those over the age of sixteen, neglected their interests. They were also affronted by Hirschfeld's personal effeminacy and his sweeping classification of all homosexuals in one category [as "Fems"] (Steakley:47f).

After his falling-out with Hirschfeld and the leaders of the SHC, Friedlander continued to try to sway its members regarding pederasty as well as to attract its financial supporters to the Community of the Elite. In 1907, Friedlander published an article in *Der Eigene* with a long but revealing title: "Memoirs for the Friends and Contributors of the Scientific-Humanitarian Committee in the Name of the Succession of the Scientific-Humanitarian Committee." In the article, Friedlander said that the Greek "love of youth" (pederasty) was the cause of Paragraph 175. He said that the law was not enacted because of men, but rather because of their jealous wives and mistresses who viewed young boys "as a kind of unfair competition" (*Journal of Homosexuality*, Jan.-Feb. 1991). In the same article Friedlander writes,

> Let us just understand that no one can be a good educator who does not love his pupils! And let us not lie to ourselves that in love the so-called "spiritual" element can ever be completely detached from its physiological foundation. It is an eternal verity: only a good pederast can be a complete pedagogue (Friedlander in Ooosterhuis and Kennedy:77ff).

Benedict Friedlander died in 1908 at the age of 42, but his influence on the German homosexual movement endured. In 1934, just one year after Adolf Hitler came to power, a man named Kurt HildeBrandt echoed Friedlander's views in a book titled _Norm Entartung Verfall_ ("Ideal - Degeneration - Ruin"). In 1934 HildeBrandt was a leader in the Society for Human Rights (SHR), a spinoff of the Community of the Elite. He referred to Friedlander as his "master" and asserted that Greek pederasty had led to "an enhancement of masculinity" (Steakley:49). In _Norm Entartung Verfall_, HildeBrandt presents the Brand-Friedlander theory that masculine homosexuals are the ideal; a master race of beings, and that effeminate homosexuals are, in fact, degenerations of the ideal. HildeBrandt declares that the masculine type is the one that "Nature" intended to rule the world, but that the effeminate types were freaks of nature who would bring any Hellenic society to destruction. HildeBrandt writes,

> It is incomprehensible that these forms should be confused with that type of homosexuality about which such a ruckus is made today. The latter arises contrarily in groups of effeminate men; it counteracts military and intellectual manliness...and is certain of ruin (HildeBrandt :207).

In many ways it is Friedlander's theory of homosexuality that we see implemented in the policies of the Nazis. Although there were obvious exceptions made for political reasons, there is evidence to suggest that only the effeminate homosexuals were mistreated under the Nazi regime -- and usually at the hands of masculine homosexuals. (We will consider the internment of "Roehm's Avengers" -- "Butch" homosexuals of the SA interned in the wake of the Roehm purge -- in a later section). Some historians, such as James Steakley, see Friedlander's influence in Adolf Hitler's own philosophy of homosexuality as well. Steakley writes,

> Hitler, on the other hand, was the Nazi visionary...and there is a truly striking affinity between his views on ho-

mosexuality and those of Friedlander and [Hans] Bluher. These male supremacists wanted to create a new Hellas peopled by strong, naked, but chaste men, inspired by heroism and capable of leadership (Steakley:119).

The Rift Widens

It is clear that Adolf Brand's Community of the Elite wanted nothing to do with Ulrichs' theory of *anima muliebris in corpore virili inclusa* ("a female soul confined in a male body"). They perceived themselves as fully masculine and despised everything female and effeminate. For many years, Ulrichs' "Fem" faction had dominated the German homosexual movement. But during this time, the rift between the "Butches" and the "Fems" grew increasingly wider as the revival of Hellenic pagan values began to transform German society.

As early as 1908, Hirschfeld wrote that the scandals and division of opinion between the "Butches" and "Fems" was damaging the homosexual cause in Germany. He criticized the Community of the Elite for being anti-feminist. In 1914, reflecting the increase of tensions, Hirschfeld characterized the Community of the Elite as "exaggerated side-currents" and "fanatics" (Oosterhuis and Kennedy:24f). At this point Hirschfeld still controlled the movement, but somewhere between 1914 and 1920 the "Butches" became a serious political force themselves. In 1920, they formed the Society for Human Rights. The title seems to lay claim to what had become the Scientific-Humanitarian Committee's trademark: political activism under the banner of "gay rights." Two years later the new SHR published the following, now militant, call to arms:

We no longer want only a few scientists [i.e., Hirschfeld et al.] struggling for our cause, we want to demonstrate our strength ourselves. Here we stand, demanding that which is our right — and who would dare challenge us?

For this reason we must work steadily and everyone must take their part in our work. No homosexual should be absent -- rich or poor, worker or scholar, diplomat or businessman. We cannot deprive ourselves of any support. Therefore join us, swell our ranks before it is too late. At Easter we must show whether we have developed into a fighting organization or just a social club. He who does not march with us is against us (Steakley:76f).

Here we can see the militaristic tone of the "Butch" faction and sense its eagerness to wrest control of the movement from the SHC. Jonathan Katz records, in Gay American History, that "[the SHR became] the largest of the Gay groups in Germany during the 1920s, one that aimed at being a 'mass' organization, and it criticized Hirschfeld's scientific approach" (J. Katz:632). Bear in mind that these were also the early years of the Nazi Party, an organization which shared some founding members with the SHR. Increasingly, the Nazi Party became the vehicle with which the "Butches" opposed Hirschfeld. In July of 1927, after a Nazi Party member made a speech attacking the SHC, Hirschfeld wrote in the SHC newsletter, "We further feel obliged to urgently request of our numerous members in the National Socialist German Workers Party...that they vigorously call their delegates [to the Reichstag] to order" (Steakley:91). The rather desperate tone of Hirschfeld's complaint reflects the reality that his faction had by this time lost control.

To some extent, the homosexuals of the SHC may have brought on themselves the later wrath of the Nazis. In the 1920s and 30s the political enemies of the Nazis used the Nazis' homosexual scandals against them, hurting the party's effort to gain legitimacy. Stories were printed in the newspapers containing "inside" information about homosexual activities among the Nazi leaders. The most noteworthy example of this tactic was when documentation of Ernst Roehm's proclivity for boys, in the form of handwrit-

The Nazi Party was repeatedly damaged by disclosures to the newspapers about homosexuality in its ranks. The leaks came from its enemies in the effeminate faction of the German "gay" movement.
Yad Vashem

ten letters from Roehm himself, was leaked to the Social Democrat newspapers (Oosterhuis and Kennedy:239n).

The Social Democrat Party, of course, was the home of many of the effeminate homosexuals, which the Nazis well knew. It is likely that they suspected some of the inside information against them had come from Hirschfeld's camp. This was probably an accurate surmise. Steakley writes that "Hirschfeld was later sorely discredited within the homosexual community of Germany when it was revealed that he at least occasionally 'leaked' information on homosexuals to the press" (Steakley:64).

This may help to explain why the Nazis bore such enmity against the "Fems," and why they targeted certain of these homosexuals for persecution. However, the Nazis needed no special justification for revenge. The fact that the SHC had made opposition to pederasty an essential tenet of their political strategy was enough. Though not a Nazi, the "Butch" homosexual poet, Stefan George, summed up the attitude of the anti-Hirschfeld camp, saying, "It should be apparent that we have nothing to do with those far from charming people who whimper for the repeal of certain laws, for the most revolting attacks against us [pederasts] have issued from precisely these circles" (George in Steakley:49).

As we can see, understanding the "gay rights" movement in Germany is essential to a complete understanding of the formation of the Nazi Party and the policies of the Third Reich. In turn, understanding the German "gay rights" movement requires an appreciation of the rivalry between the two distinct homosexual factions: the Ulrichs/Hirschfeld "Fems" and the Brand /Friedlander/ Roehm "Butches." Their contest for domination of the "gay rights" movement ended when the "Butches" of the Nazi Party came to power in 1933 and began to construct the Third Reich. They had realized their dream of a revived Hellenic culture of ultramasculine militarism, a dream that was to prove a nightmare for all those who fell short of the Nazi ideal.

Hans Blueher and the Wandervoegel

"In Germany," writes Mosse, "ideas of homosexuality as the basis of a better society can be found at the turn of the century within the German Youth Movement" (Mosse:87). Indeed, at the same time that Brand and Friedlander were beginning to articulate their dream of a neo-Hellenic Germany to the masses, a youthful subculture of boys and young men was already beginning to act out its basic themes under the leadership of men like Karl Fischer, Wilhelm Jansen and youth leader Hans Blueher. In Sexual Experience Between Men and Boys, homosexualist historian Parker Rossman writes,

In Central Europe...there was another effort to revive the
Greek ideal of pedagogic pederasty, in the movement of
Wandering Youth [*Wandervoegel*]. Modern gay-
homosexuality also can trace some of its roots to that
movement of men and boys who wandered around the
countryside, hiking and singing hand-in-hand, enjoying
nature, life together, and their sexuality. Ultimately Hitler used and transformed the movement — much as the
Romans had abused the *paiderastia* of the ancient Greeks
— expanding and building upon its romanticism as a basis for the Nazi Party (Rossman:103).

Another homosexualist, Richard Mills, explains in <u>Gay
Roots: Twenty Years of Gay Sunshine</u> how the *Wandervoegel* movement traces its roots to an informal hiking and
camping society of young men started in 1890 by a fifteen-
year-old student named Hermann Hoffman. For several
years the open-air lifestyle of these boys grew increasingly
popular. They developed their own form of greeting, the
"Heil" salute, and "much of the vocabulary...[which] was
later appropriated by the Nazis" (Mills:168). Early in its development, the movement attracted the attention of homosexual men, including the pederasts who belonged to the
Community of the Elite. In 1901 a teacher by the name of
Karl Fischer (who, as we have mentioned, called himself
der Fuehrer) formalized the movement under the name
Wandervoegel (Koch:25, Mills:153).

Hans Blueher, then just seventeen years old, organized
the most ambitious *Wandervoegel* excursion to that date in
1905. It was on this trip that Blueher met Wilhelm Jansen,
one of the original founders of the Community of the Elite.
At this time the *Wandervoegel* numbered fewer than one
hundred young men, but eventually the number of youths
involved in *Wandervoegel*-type groups in Europe reached
60,000.

Wilhelm Jansen became an influential
leader in the *Wandervoegel*, but rumors of his homo-

sexuality disturbed German society. In 1911, Jansen addressed the issue in a circular to *Wandervoegel* parents. Jansen told them, "As long as they conduct themselves properly with your sons, you will have to accustom yourselves to the presence of so-called homosexuals in your ranks" (Mills:167). Hans Blueher further substantiated the fact that the movement had become a vehicle for homosexual recruitment of boys with his publication of The German Wandervoegel Movement as an Erotic Phenomenon in 1914 (Rector:39f). Mills writes,

[T]he Wandervoegel offered youth the chance to escape bourgeois German society by retreating back to nature...But how was this accomplished? What made it possible for the lifestyle created within the Wandervoegel to differ significantly from its bourgeois parent? The answer is simple: the Wandervoegel was founded upon homosexual, as opposed to heterosexual sentiments ...In order to understand the success of the movement, one must acknowledge the homosexual component

> Die deutsche
> Wandervogelbewegung
> als
> erotisches Phänomen
>
> Ein Beitrag zur Erkenntnis
> der sexuellen Inversion
>
> ———
>
> Von
>
> HANS BLÜHER
>
> ———
>
> Zweite verbesserte und vermehrte Auflage
>
> Verlag B. Weise Tempelhof-Berlin 1914

Blueher's The German Wandervoegel Movement as an Erotic Phenomenon advocated pederasty.

of its leaders...Just as the leaders were attracted to the boys, so were the boys attracted to their leaders. In both cases the attraction was sexually based (Mills 152-53).

Like many of the "Butch" homosexuals Blueher had married but only for the purpose of procreation. "Woe to the man who has placed his fate in the hands of a woman," he wrote. "Woe to the civilization that is subjected to womens' influence" (Blueher in Igra:95).

Foreshadowing the Nazi regime, Blueher "saw male bonding as crucial to the formation of male elites," writes homosexualist historian Warren Johansson. "The discipline, the comradeship, the willingness of the individual to sacrifice himself for the nation -- all these are determined by the homoerotic infrastructure of the male society" (Johansson:816). Mills adds that Blueher "believed that male homosexuality was the foundation upon which all forms of nation-states are built" (Mills:152). Blueher called his hypothetical political figures "heroic males," meaning self-accepting masculine homosexuals. It is precisely this concept of the "heroic male" that prompts Steakley to compare Adolf Hitler's views to those of Blueher and Friedlander.

But this is not the only instance in which the views of Blueher and Friedlander coincide. Like Friedlander, Blueher believed that homosexuals were the best teachers of children. "There are five sexual types of men, ranging from the exclusively heterosexual to the exclusively homosexual," writes Blueher. "The exclusive heterosexual is the one least suited to teach young people...[but exclusive homosexuals] are the focal point of all youth organizations" (ibid.:154).

Blueher was also anti-Semitic. In writing about his visit with Magnus Hirschfeld and the SHC, Blueher denigrated Hirschfeld's egalitarian views, complaining that "concepts like rank, race, physiognomy... things of importance to me -- were simply not applicable in this circle." Igra adds that "[a]ccording to Blueher, Germany was defeated [in W.W.I] because the homosexualist way of life *(die maennerbuendische Weltanschauung)* had been considerably neglected and warlike virtues had degenerated under the advance of democratic ideas, the increasing prestige of family life...the growing influence of women "*and, above all, the Jews*" (emphasis ours -- Igra:97).

Importantly, Blueher's hostility towards the Jews was not primarily based on a racial theory but on their rejection of homosexuality. Igra writes,

> Soon after the defeat [of Germany in W.W.I] Blueher delivered a lecture to a group of *Wandervoegel*, which he himself had founded. The lecture was entitled "The German Reich, Jewry and Socialism." He said: 'There is no people whose destiny...so closely resembles ours as that of the Jews.' The Jews were conquered by the Romans, lost their State and became only a race whose existence is maintained through the family. The primary cause of this collapse, he says, was that the Jews had failed to base their State on the homoerotic male community and had staked all on the family life, with its necessary concomitant of women's encouragement of the civic and social and spiritual virtues in their menfolk rather than the warlike qualities (ibid.:97).

Though largely neglected by historians, Blueher was enormously important to Nazi culture. Igra writes that in the Third Reich "Blueher...[was] adopted by the Nazis as an apostle of social reform. And one of his disciples, Professor Alfred Bauemler...[became] Director of the Political Institute at the University of Berlin" (ibid.:75). Writing before the collapse of the Third Reich, he adds that "[Blueher's teaching] has been systematically inculcated by the Nazi Press, especially Himmler's official organ, *Das Schwarze Korps*, and has been adopted in practice as the basis of German social organization. The Nazi élite are being brought up in segregated male communities called *Ordensburgen*. These are to replace the family as the groundwork on which the state is to rest" (Igra:87). The all-male societies of these

Ordensburgen (Order Castles) were fashioned after the *Wandervoegel*.

Through his influence in the *Wandervoegel* and later as a fascist theoretician, Hans Blueher must be recognized as a major force in the reshaping of Germany. This (and the homosexuality of other *Wandervoegel* leaders) is acknowledged by homosexualist author Frank Rector:

> Blueher's case further explains why many Nazi Gays were attracted to Hitler and his shrill anti-Semitism, for many gentile homosexuals were rabidly anti-Semitic...Gays in the youth movement who espoused anti-Semitism, chauvinism, and the *Fuehrer Prinzip* (Leader Principle) were not-so-incipient Fascists. They helped create a fertile ground for Hitler's movement and, later, became one of its main sources of adherents....A substantial number of those Wandervoegel leaders were known homosexuals, and many others were allegedly gay (or bisexual) (Rector:40).

From Boy Scouts to Brownshirts

In the introduction to his book <u>The Pink Triangle</u>, homosexual author Richard Plant writes of his own experience in a *Wandervoegel*-type group called "Rovers." "In such brotherhoods," writes Plant, "a few adolescents had little affairs, misty and romantic sessions around a blazing fire...Other boys...talked openly about 'going with friends' and enjoying it. The leaders of these groups tended to disregard the relationships blossoming around them -- unless they participated" (Plant:3).

Blueher himself described the homosexual quality of the group as follows:

> The Wandervoegel movement inspired the youth all around during the first six years of its existence, without awaking the slightest suspicion...towards its own mem-

bers...Only very seldom might one might notice one of the leaders raising questions of why he and his comrades didn't want any girls....[later] the name Wandervoegel was mentioned in the same breath as the words "pederasty club" (Blueher:23f).

Richard Plant's reminiscences also substantiate that the *Wandervoegel* groups served as a training ground for Nazis. He recalls his friend in the Rovers, "Ferdi, who explained and demonstrated the mysteries of sex to me and my friends." Plant was later shocked, he says, upon returning to Germany from abroad "to see Ferdi wearing a brown shirt with a red, white and black swastika armband" (ibid.:4).

E.Y. Hartshorne, in German Youth and the Nazi Dream of Victory records the recollections of a former *Wandervoegel* member who confirms that the organization was the source of important elements of Nazi culture. Our knowledge of the influence of the Community of the Elite on the *Wandervoegel* may provide us insight into the cryptic comment at the end of the testimony:

> We little suspected then what power we had in our hands. We played with the fire that had set a world in flames, and it made our hearts hot. Mysticism and everything mystical had dominion over us. It was in our ranks that the word *Fuehrer* originated, with its meaning of blind obedience and devotion. The word *Bund* arose with us too, with its mysterious undertone of conspiracy. And I shall never forget how in those early days we pronounced the word *Gemeinschaft* ["community"] with a trembling throaty note of excitement, as though it hid a deep secret (Hartshorne:12).

Indeed, not only did the grown-up former members of the *Wandervoegel* become one of Hitler's main sources of supporters in his rise to power, but the movement itself be-

Hitler Youth meeting, January, 1934 in Munich.

came the core of a Nazi institution: the *Hitler-Jugend*
(Hitler Youth). So rampant had homosexuality become in
the movement by this time that *The Rheinische Zeitung*, a
prominent German newspaper, warned, "Parents, protect
your sons from 'physical preparations' in the Hitler
Youth," a sarcastic reference to problems of homosexuality
in the organization (Burleigh and Wipperman:188). Sadly,
the boys themselves had by this time been completely indoctrinated by their homosexual masters. Waite writes,

> With the exception of Ehrhardt, Gerhard Rossbach, sa-
> dist, murderer, and homosexual was the most admired
> hero of nationalistic German youth. "In Ehrhardt, but also
> in Rossbach," says a popular book on the youth move-
> ment, "we see the Fuehrer of our youth. These men have
> become the Ideal Man, idolized...and honored as can only
> happen when the personality of an individual counts for
> more than anything else"...the most important single con-
> tributor of the pre-Hitler youth movement [was] Gerhard
> Rossbach (Waite, 1969:210f).

Hans Peter Bleuel, in <u>Sex and Society in Nazi Germany</u>, points out that most of the adult supervisors of the Hitler Youth were also SA officers (who were almost exclusively homosexual). Rector states that Baldur von Schirach, leader of the Hitler Youth organization, was reportedly bisexual (Rector:56). In Germany's National Vice, Jewish historian Samuel Igra confirms this, saying Schirach was arrested by the police for perverse sexual practices and liberated on the intervention of Hitler, who soon afterward made him leader of the Hitler Youth (Igra:72). Igra further states that Schirach was known as "the baby" among the inner pederast clique around Hitler (ibid.:74). Rempel reports that Schirach always surrounded himself with a guard of handsome young men (Rempel:88). Psychiatrist Walter Langer in his 1943 secret wartime report, <u>The Mind of Adolf Hitler</u>, also writes of Schirach's reputed homosexuality (Langer:99).

Baldur von Schirach was the head of the Hitler Youth.

In 1934, the Gestapo reported forty cases of pederasty in just one troop of the Hitler Youth. Bleuel writes of the case of one supervisor, a 20-year-old man who was dismissed from the Hitler Youth in 1938. Yet he was transferred to the National Socialist Flying Corps (Civil Air Patrol) "and was assigned to supervise work by members of the Hitler Youth Gliding Association and eventually detained to help with physical check-ups — a grievous temptation. The man was once again caught sodomizing young men, but was not dismissed from the NSFK" (the National Socialist Flying Corps) - Bleuel:119).

Conditions were essentially the same in 1941. Bleuel reports of another homosexual flying instructor involved in "at least ten cases of homosexuality with student pilots of the Hitler Youth" and "a student teacher and student ...[who] had committed twenty-eight proven acts of indecency with twenty boys at Hitler Youth and Young Folk camps" (ibid.:119). He adds that "[t]hese cases were only the tip of the iceberg, for few misdemeanors within the Party became public in later years and even fewer came to trial" (ibid.:119).

The prevalence of homosexuality in the Hitler Youth is also confirmed by historian Gerhard Rempel in his book Hitler's Children: Hitler Youth and the SS:

> Homosexuality, meanwhile, continued on into the war years when Hitler Jugend boys frequently became victims of molestations at the hands of their SS tutors; Himmler consistently took a hard line against it publicly but was quite willing to mitigate his penalties privately and keep every incident as secret as possible (Rempel:51f).

This last quote from Rempel raises two important points which will be addressed at greater length later in the book, but deserve at least some mention here. The first point is that Heinrich Himmler, who is often cited as being representative of the Nazi regime's alleged hatred of homosexuals, was obviously not overly concerned about homosexual occurrences in the ranks of his own organization. The second point is that this homosexual activity continued long after Hitler had supposedly purged homosexuals from the Nazi regime (in 1934) and promoted strict policies against homosexuality (from 1935 on). As we shall see later, these policies were primarily for public relations and were largely unenforced.

An interesting sideline to the story of the Hitler Youth illustrates both the control of the youth movement by pederasts and the fundamental relationship between homosexuality and Nazism. In Great Britain, the pro-Nazis formed the Anglo-German Fellowship (AGF). The AGF was headed by British homosexuals Guy Francis de Moncy Burgess and Captain John Robert Macnamara. British Historian John Rempel relates how Burgess, Macnamara and J.H. Sharp, the Church of England's Arch-deacon for Southern Europe, took a trip to Germany to attend a Hitler Youth camp. Costello writes,

> In the spring of 1936, the trio set off for the Rhineland, accompanied by Macnamara's friend Tom Wylie, a young official in the War Office. Ostensibly they were escorting a group of pro-fascist schoolboys to a Hitler Youth camp. But from Burgess' uproariously bawdy account of how his companions discovered that the Hitler Jugend satisfied their sexual and political passions, the trip would have shocked their sponsors -- the Foreign Relations Council of the Church of England (Costello: 300).

In pre-World War II France, the pro-Nazi faction was represented by the Radical-Socialist Party (RSP) and the Popular Party (PP). The Secretary-General of the RSP was Edouard Pfeiffer. Costello writes of Guy Burgess' visit to Pfeiffer in Paris shortly before the war:

As a connoisseur of homosexual decadence, Pfeiffer had few equals, even in Paris. As an officer of the French Boy-Scout movement, his private life was devoted to the seduction of youth. Burgess discovered all this when he visited Pfeiffer's apartment in Paris and found...[him] with a naked young man...he explained to Burgess that the young man was a professional cyclist, who just happened to be a member of Jacques Doriot's Popular Party (ibid.:315).

Once again we see flagrant sexual perversion in the heart of the Nazi movement -- long after the Roehm Purge. It appears also that the correlation between Nazism and homosexuality disregarded national boundaries. As we have seen, both Hans Blueher and Benedict Friedlander observed that youth organizations are often (in their view, appropriately) led by pederasts. Events in Europe during the first part of the twentieth century, particularly those involving the National Socialists, strongly support this theory.

The revival of Hellenic culture in the German homosexual movement, then, was an integral factor in the rise of Nazism. Right under the nose of traditional German society, the pederasts laid the groundwork for the ultramasculine military society of the Third Reich. The *Wandervoegel* was certainly not a "homosexual organization" per se, but its homosexual leaders molded the youth movement into an expression of their own Hellenic ideology and, in the process, recruited countless young men into the homosexual lifestyle. The first members of the *Wandervoegel* grew to manhood just in time to provide the Nazi movement with its support base in the German culture. As Steakley put it, "[the] Free German Youth jubilantly marched off to war, singing the old *Wandervoegel* songs to which new, chauvinistic verses were added" (Steakley:58).

Rossbach (wearing armband) with SA Stormtroopers, May 1, 1923.

Gerhard Rossbach and the Freikorps Movement

The *Freikorps* movement began during the years immediately following the close of World War I. After the war
and the subsequent socialist revolution in Germany in
1918, tens of thousands of former soldiers of the German
army volunteered for quasi-military service in a number of
independent reserve units called *Freikorps* (Free Corps),
under the command of former junior officers of the German
army. These units were highly nationalistic and became increasingly violent as the social chaos of the Weimar Republic worsened. Rossbach's organization, originally called
the *Rossbachbund* ("Rossbach Brotherhood") exemplified
the German *Freikorps*. As Waite records in <u>Vanguard of
Nazism</u>, "the lieutenants and the captains — Roehm...Ehr-
hardt, Rossbach, Schultz and the rest — formed the back-
bone of the Free Corps movement. And...it was they who
were the link between the Volunteers [anti-communists]
and National Socialism" (Waite, 1969:45). Once again we
see the essential relationship between homosexuality and

Nazism, since many of these "lieutenants and captains" were known or probable homosexuals, some of whom eventually served in the SA. German historian and Hitler contemporary Konrad Heiden writes that "[m]any sections of this secret army of mercenaries and murderers were breeding places of perversion" (Heiden:30). Historian G. S. Graber agrees:

> Many...[*Freikorps*] leaders were homosexual; indeed homosexuality appears to have been widespread in several volunteer units. Gerhard Rossbach...was an open homosexual. On his staff was Lieutenant Edmund Heines who was later to become the lover of Ernst Roehm (Graber:33).

Waite's analysis shows that the *Freikorps* movement was one intervening phase between the *Wandervoegel* movement and the Nazi *Stuermabteilung* — the SA. "The generation to which the *Freikorpskaempfer* ['Free Corps warriors'] belonged," writes Waite, "the generation born in the 1890s — participated in two experiences which were to have tremendous effect on his subsequent career as a Volunteer [in the *Freikorps*]. The first of these was the pre-war Youth Movement; the second, World War I" (Waite, 1969:17). The young men who had been molded by the Hellenic philosophies of the youth movement had come of age just in time to fight in the first World War. There, they were further shaped and seasoned by the hardships and horrors of trench warfare.

It was in the trenches of World War I that the concept of *Stuermabteilung* (Storm Troops) was developed — elite, hard-hitting units whose task it was to "storm" the enemy lines. The tactics of the Storm Troopers proved to be so effective that they were quickly adopted throughout the German army. The Storm Troop system created a tremendous increase in the number of young commanders of a certain breed. Waite writes,

> Only a very special type of officer could be used. He must be unmarried, under twenty-five years of age, in excellent physical health...and above all he must possess in abundance that quality which German military writers call ruthlessness. The result was that at the time of the Armistice Germany was flooded with hundreds of capable, arrogant young commanders who found an excellent outlet for their talents in the Free Corps movement (ibid.:27).

It is not difficult to recognize that the description of the preferred Storm Trooper is a model of the *Wandervoegel* hero: ultramasculine, militaristic, physically conditioned, largely unrestrained by Judeo-Christian morality, and guided by the "Fuehrer Principle" (ibid.:28). It is no wonder, then, that many of these men became youth leaders in their turn (ibid.:210). In the preceding chapter, we learned that homosexual sadist and murderer Gerhard Rossbach was "the most important single contributor to the pre-Hitler youth movement" and a "hero to nationalistic German youth." In the days before Baldur von Schirach developed the Hitler Youth, Rossbach organized Germany's largest youth organization, named the *Schilljugend* ("Schill Youth") in honor of a famous Prussian soldier executed by Napoleon (ibid:210n).

But Rossbach's contribution to the Nazis was far greater than the mere shaping of young men into Nazi loyalists. It was Rossbach who formed the original terrorist organization which eventually became the Nazi Storm Troopers, also known as "Brown Shirts." Both the Rossbach Storm Troopers and the *Schilljugend* were notorious for wearing brown shirts which had been prepared for German colonial troops, acquired from the old Imperial army stores (Koehl:19). It is reasonable to suppose that without Rossbach's Storm Troopers, Adolf Hitler and the Nazis

A *Freikorps* unit marches through a German city.

would never have gained power in Germany. Heiden describes them:

> Rossbach's troop, roaring, brawling, carousing, smashing windows, shedding blood...was especially proud to be different from the others. Heines had belonged to it before joining Hitler; then Rossbach and Heines had formed a center with Roehm; it led the SA while Hitler was under arrest [for leading the Beer Hall *Putsch*] (Heiden, 1944:295).

Rossbach's *Freikorps* was formed almost exclusively of homosexuals. As fascist novelist, Edwin Dwinger, would later declare through one of his characters, Captain Werner, "Freikorps men aren't almost all bachelors for nothing. Believe me, if there weren't so many of their kind, our ranks would be pretty damn thin" (Theweleit, Vol 1:33). Rossbach's adjutant, Edmund Heines, was another pederast and a convicted murderer who later became Ernst Roehm's adjutant in the SA (he was also the sexual partner

Edmund Heines (center) with Bicycle Company.

of Rossbach, Roehm and possibly Hitler as well). During the incident known as "The Night of the Long Knives" in which Hitler killed Roehm and a number of other SA leaders, Heines was surprised in bed with a young SA recruit (Gallo:236). Historian Frank Rector describes Heines:

> Distinguished by a girlish face on the body of a truck driver, Heines was an elegant, suave, and impeccably groomed killer. He liked to shoot his victims in the face with his 7.65 Walther automatic or beat them to death with a club...In addition to Heines' value as a first rate adjutant, gifted administrative executive, and aggressive and adroit SA leader, Heines had a marked talent as a procurer [of boys]...garnering the fairest lads in the Fatherland for...sexual amusement (Rector:89).

Perhaps because of Edmund Heines' special talent, Rossbach assigned him to develop the *Schilljugend.* Igra tells how he profited thereby:

> Edmund Heines, the group-leader of the storm troops at Breslau, was a repulsive brute who turned the Nazi headquarters of the city into a homosexual brothel. Having 300,000 storm troopers under his command he was in a position to terrorize the neighborhood...One of his favorite ruses was to have members of the youth organization indulge in unnatural practices with one another and then threaten their parents that he would denounce these youths to the police...unless he received...hush money. Thus Heines not only indulged in homosexual orgies himself — he was often Roehm's consort in this — but he promoted the vice as a lucrative business (Igra:73).

Ernst Roehm and the Development of the SA

Next to Adolf Hitler, Ernst Roehm was the man in Germany most responsible for the rise of Nazism, indeed of Hitler himself. Rector writes that "Hitler was, to a substantial extent, Roehm's protégé" (Rector:80). A driving force behind the National Socialist movement, Roehm was one of the early founders of the Nazi Party. Both Roehm and Hitler had been members of the socialist terrorist group called the Iron Fist (Heiden, 1944:89).

It was at a meeting of the Iron Fist that Roehm reportedly met him and "saw in Hitler the demagogue he required to mobilize mass support for his secret army" (Hohne:20). With Roehm's backing, Hitler became the first president of the Nazi Party in 1921 (ibid.:21). Shortly thereafter, Rossbach's *Freikorps*, integrated into the Party first under Herman Goering's and then Roehm's authority, was transformed into the dreaded Nazi SA.

In his classic Nazi history, <u>The Rise and Fall of the Third Reich</u>, author William Shirer describes Ernst Roehm

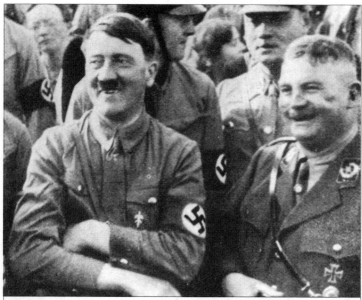

Hitler and Roehm share a laugh in the early days of the party.

as "a stocky, bull-necked, piggish-eyed, scar-faced professional soldier...[and] like so many of the early Nazis, a homosexual" (Shirer:64). Roehm was recruited into
homosexuality by Gerhard Rossbach (Flood:196). Rector
elaborates,

> Was not the most outstanding, most notorious, of all ho-
> mosexuals the celebrated Nazi leader Ernst Roehm, the
> virile and manly chief of the SA, the *du* buddy of Adolf
> Hitler from the beginning of his political career? [Hitler
> allowed Roehm the rare privilege of addressing him with
> the familiar form "thou," indicating intimate friendship].
> Hitler's rise had in fact depended upon Roehm and every-
> one knew it. Roehm's gay fun and games were certainly
> no secret; his amorous forays to gay bars and gay Turkish
> baths were riotous. Whatever anti-homosexual sentiments
> may have been expressed by straight Nazis were more
> than offset by the reality of highly visible, spectacular,
> gay-loving Roehm. If there were occasional ominous

rumblings and grumblings about "all those queers" in the
SA and Movement, and some anti-gay flare-ups, homo-
sexual Nazis felt more-or-less secure in the lap of the
Party. After all, the National Socialist Party member who
wielded the greatest power aside from Hitler was Roehm
(Rector:50f).

Consistent with the elitist philosophies of Benedict
Friedlander, Adolf Brand, and Hans Blueher, Roehm
viewed homosexuality as the basis for a new society. Louis
Snyder, prominent historian of the Nazi era, writes,

> [Roehm] projected a social order in which homosexual-
> ity would be regarded as a human behavior pattern of
> high repute...he flaunted his homosexuality in public and
> insisted that his cronies do the same. What was needed,
> Roehm believed, was a proud and arrogant lot who could
> brawl, carouse, smash windows, kill and slaughter for the
> hell of it. Straights, in his eyes, were not as adept in such
> behavior as practicing homosexuals (Snyder:55).

Under Roehm, the SA became the instrument of Nazi
terrorism in German society. It was officially founded on
August 3, 1921, ostensibly as a "Special section for gym-
nastics and sport," but in his first directive to the group, Hitler defined the SA's purpose as "a means of defense for the
movement, but above all a training school for the coming
struggle for liberty" (Heiden, 1935:82f).

Historian Thomas Fuchs reports that "The principle
function of this army-like organization was beating up anyone who opposed the Nazis, and Hitler believed this was a
job best undertaken by homosexuals" (Fuchs:48f). At first
serving simply to protect the Nazis' own meetings from
disruptions by rivals and troublemakers, the SA soon expanded its strong-arm tactics to advance Nazi policies and
philosophies. In a 1921 speech in Munich, Hitler set the
stage for this activity: "[the] National Socialist movement

will in future ruthlessly prevent if necessary by force all meetings or lectures that are likely to distract the minds of our fellow citizens..." In *Mein Kampf*, Hitler describes an incident (when his men were attacked by Communists adversaries) which he considered the baptismal act of the SA:

When I entered the lobby of the Hofbrauhaus at quarter to eight, I no longer had any doubts as to the question of sabotage...The hall was very crowded...The small assault section was waiting for me in the lobby...I had the doors to the hall shut, and ordered my men — some forty-five or -six — to stand at attention...my men from the Assault Section — from that day known as the SA — launched their attack. Like wolves in packs of eight or ten, they threw themselves on their adversaries again and again, overwhelming them with blows...In five minutes everyone was covered with blood. These were real men, whom I learned to appreciate on that occasion. They were led by my courageous Maurice. Hess, my private secretary, and many others who were badly hurt pressed the attack as long as they were able to stay on their feet (Hitler:504f).

In all actions the SA bore Roehm's trademark of unabashed sadism. Max Gallo describes the organization:

Whatever the SA engage in — whether they are torturing a prisoner, cutting the throat of an adversary or pillaging an apartment — they behave as if they are within their rights, as artisans of the Nazi victory...They are the SA, beyond criticism. As Roehm himself said many times: "The battalions of Brown Shirts were the training school of National Socialism" (Gallo:38).

The favorite meeting place of the SA was a "gay" bar in Munich called the *Bratwurstgloeckl* where Roehm kept a reserved table (Hohne:82). This was the same tavern where some of the early meetings of the Nazi Party had been held (Rector:69). At the *Bratwurstgloeckl*, Roehm and associates — Edmund Heines, Karl Ernst, Ernst's partner Captain [Paul] Rohrbein, Captain Petersdorf, Count Ernst Helldorf — would meet to plan and strategize. These were the men who orchestrated the Nazi campaign of intimidation and terror. All of them were homosexual (Heiden, 1944:371).

Indeed, homosexuality was all that qualified many of these men for their positions in the SA. Heinrich Himmler would later complain of this: "Does it not constitute a danger to the Nazi movement if it can be said that Nazi leaders are chosen for sexual reasons?" (Gallo:68). Himmler was not so much opposed to homosexuality itself as to the fact that non-qualified people were given high rank based on their homosexual relations with Roehm and others. For example, SA *Obergruppenfuehrer* (Lieutenant General) Karl Ernst, a militant homosexual, had been a hotel doorman and a waiter before joining the SA. "Karl Ernst is not yet thirty-five, writes Gallo, he commands 250,000 men...he is simply a sadist, a common thug, transformed into a responsible official" (ibid.:50f). Later, Ernst became a member of the German Parliament (Machtan:185). Gallo writes,

> Roehm, as the head of 2,500,000 Storm Troops had surrounded himself with a staff of perverts. His chiefs, men of rank of *Gruppenfuehrer* or *Obergruppenfuehrer*, commanding units of several hundred thousand Storm Troopers, were almost without exception homosexuals. Indeed, unless a Storm Troop officer were homosexual he had no chance of advancement" (Knickerbocker:55).

Otto Friedrich's analysis in Before the Deluge is similar:

Karl Ernst

> Under Rohm, the SA leadership acquired a rather special quality, however, for the crude and blustering *Oberster* SA *Fuehrer* was also a fervent homosexual, and he liked to surround himself, in all the positions of command, with men of similar persuasions (Friedrich:327).

In the SA, the Hellenic ideal of masculine homosexual supremacy and militarism had finally been realized. "Theirs was a very masculine brand of homosexuality," writes homosexualist historian Alfred Rowse, "they lived in a male world, without women, a world of camps and marching, rallies and sports. They had their own relaxations, and the Munich SA became notorious on account of them" (Rowse:214). The similarity of the SA to Friedlander's and Brand's dream of Hellenic revival is not coincidental. In addition to being a founder of the Nazi Party, Ernst Roehm was a leading member of the Society for Human Rights, an offshoot of the Community of the Elite (J. Katz:632).

The relaxations to which Rowse refers in the above quote were, of course, the homosexual activities (many of them pederastic) for which the SA and the CE were both famous. Hohne writes,

> [Roehm] used the SA for ends other than the purely political. SA contact men kept their Chief of Staff supplied with suitable partners, and at the first sign of infidelity on the part of a Roehm favorite, he would be bludgeoned down by one of the SA mobile squads. The head pimp was a

Emile Maurice, Peter Granninger and Storm Trooper Schiedermeier at a reunion of the Old Guard, March 11, 1934. Maurice was Hitler's homosexual chauffeur. Granninger was a pederast who recruited boys from the local high school.

shop assistant named Peter Granninger, who had been one of Roehm's partners...and was now given cover in the SA Intelligence Section. For a monthly salary of 200 marks he kept Roehm supplied with new friends, his main hunting ground being Geisela High School Munich; from this school he recruited no fewer than eleven boys, whom he first tried out and then took to Roehm (Hohne:82).

Although the original SA chapter in Munich was the most notorious, other SA chapters were also centers of homosexual activity. In <u>Political Violence and the Rise of Na-</u>

zism, Richard Bessel notes that the Silesian division of the SA was a hotbed of perversion from 1931 onward (Bessel:61).

Roehm and his closest SA associates were among the minority of Nazi homosexuals who did not take wives. Whether for convention, for procreation, or simply for covering up their sexual proclivities, most of the Nazi homosexuals had married. Some, like Reinhard Heydrich and Baldur von Schirach, married only after being involved in homosexual scandals, but often these men, who so hated femininity, maintained a facade of heterosexual respectability throughout their lives. As Machtan notes, "That Hitler...encouraged many of them to marry should not be surprising: every conspiracy requires camouflage" (Machtan:24). These were empty marriages, however, epitomized by one wife's comment: "The only part of my husband I'm familiar with is his back" (Theweleit:3).

As we have seen, then, the SA was in many respects a creation of Germany's homosexual movement, just as the Nazi Party was in many ways a creation of the SA. Before we take a closer look at the formation and early years of the Nazi Party, we must examine two other very important movements which contributed to Nazism. These are the occult Theosophical-Ariosophical movement, and the intellectual movement which created the National Socialist philosophy. Both of these movements, which are integral to our understanding of the Nazi Party and its actions, were also heavily influenced by homosexuals.

Chapter Two

HOMO-OCCULTISM

The story of the occult in world history is also a story of homosexuality. By occult, we mean the formalized religious expression of pagan culture as opposed, for example, to the philosophical ideas of Hellenic paganism discussed in the previous chapter. In The Occult Roots of Nazism, historian Nicholas Goodrick-Clarke identifies the roots of occultism in western history:

> Occultism has its basis in a religious way of thinking, the roots of which stretch back into antiquity....Its principal ingredients have been identified as Gnosticism, the Hermetic treatises on alchemy and magic [rooted in Gnosticism], Neo-Platonism, and the Cabbala....Gnosticism properly refers to the beliefs of certain heretical sects among the early Christians that claimed to possess gnosis, or special esoteric knowledge of spiritual matters....The Gnostic sects disappeared in the fourth century, but their ideas inspired the dualistic Manichaean religion of the second century (Goodrick-Clarke:17)

Since occultism is associated primarily with Gnosticism, the association of the Gnostics with homosexuality is of primary relevance to this study. Thus we

found an obscure reference to Hitler as a Manichaean in
Steven Katz's The Holocaust in Historical Context, Vol-
ume 1, of interest. Arthur Evans' Witchcraft and the Gay
Counterculture provides some illumination here. Mani, for

whom Manichaeism
is named, was a third
century Prince of
Babylon who devised
his own form of
Gnosticism. Gnostics
blended pagan sex
rituals and Mother
Goddess worship
with elements of New
Testament Christian-
ity and "rejected Je-
hovah God as an evil
demon."
Manichaeism im-
posed on Gnosticism
a caste system of
leaders (elect) and
followers (hearers).

A Manichaean sect called the Bogomils (later called the
Cathars) arose in Bulgaria and spread across Europe. Homosexuality became so closely associated with these Bul-
garian heretics that the practice became known as
"buggery." Indeed, "the word for Cathar in most European
languages came to be the word for homosexual: in German,
Ketzer, in Italian, *Gazarro*, and in French, *Herite*....Heresy
and homosexuality became so interchangeable that those
accused of heresy attempted to prove their innocence by
claiming heterosexuality" (Evans:51ff).

We probably all take for granted the fact that today our
modern world culture is dominated by the religions based
on the Mosaic law (i.e. Judaism, Christianity and Islam). In

their orthodox forms each of these religions regards homosexuality as an abomination. But pagan cultures have no such prohibition. (By definition, pagans are people who are not Jews, Christians or Moslems). In pagan cultures, homosexuals as a group often hold an elevated position in religion and society. When pagan civilizations ruled the world, homosexuality and pederasty were widely practiced and accepted. Homosexualist author Judy Grahn writes,

Many aspects of shamanism had homosexual content, and many of the gods, spirits, and divinities of the world have been associated with Gayness. In Tahiti there were special divinities for homosexual worship. The ancient Shinto temples of Japan display scenes of sexual ritual orgies similar to those of the Bacchanalia of the Romans...the Great Mother Goddess of ancient China, Kwan-Yin, was worshiped with sexual rites that included homosexuality. When the Spanish conquistadores reached Central America and the Yucatan, they found a prevalence of Gay priests and sacred statues and stone sculpture depicting the homosexual union as a sacred act. In the Yucatan the god Chin is said to have established sacred homosexuality and a Gay priesthood serving in the temples just as was true of the temples of ancient Babylon and Sumeria (Grahn:129).

Christian writer George Grant concurs. He writes that "Rome was a perpetual satyricon. Egypt, Persia, Carthage, Babylon, and Assyria were all steeped in pederastic tradition. And the ancient empires of the Mongols, Tartars, Huns, Teutons, Celts, Incas, Aztecs, Mayans, Nubians, Mings, Canaanites, and Zulus likewise celebrated depravity, degradation and debauchery" (Grant, 1993:24). In Sexuality and Homosexuality, historian Arno Karlen writes of homosexual cults throughout the ancient world: "'male temple prostitutes'—existed among the devotees of Ishtar and Astarte in Syria, the Albanians and Babylonians, the

Canaanite neighbors of the ancient Hebrews, and in Cos,
Crete and Ephesus in the Greek world" (Karlen:6).

The ancient religion of Baal, familiar to students of the
Bible as the set of beliefs and practices which so often corrupted Hebrew society in history, was one such cult. Wor-
shippers of Baal "'built for themselves high places and
pillars, and Asherim (phallic poles used to honor the goddess of fertility) on every high hill and under every green
tree; and there were also male cult prostitutes in the land'"
(quotation from 1 Kings 14 in Karlen:9). Reference to these
practices is found in several places in the Bible, notably
Deuteronomy 23:17-18: "There shall be no ritual harlot of
the daughters of Israel, or a perverted one of the sons of Israel. You shall not bring the wages of a harlot or the price
of a dog [male prostitute] to the house of the LORD your
God for any vowed offering, for both of these are an abomination to the LORD your God" (NKJ).

The Baal cult survived into Roman times and figured
prominently in the infamous debaucheries of the Roman
emperors in the first centuries after Christ. Karlen writes,

> It was in association with such cults that emperors' devi-
> ance became most flagrant. Commodus, who took the
> throne in 180, appeared in public dressed as a woman and
> was strangled by a catamitic [homosexual] favorite;
> Hadrian deified his homosexual lover Antious. But nei-
> ther matched Elegabalus, who began his rule at the age of
> fourteen in 218, after having been raised in Syria as a
> priest of Baal. He entered Rome amid Syrian priests and
> eunuchs, dressed in silks, his cheeks painted scarlet and
> his eyes made up. Various Roman historians say that he
> assembled the homosexuals of Rome and addressed them
> garbed as a boy prostitute; put on a wig and solicited at the
> door of a brothel; tried to get doctors to turn him into a
> woman; offered himself for buggery while playing the
> role of Venus in a court mime; kissed his male favorites'
> genitals in public and, like Nero, formally married one of

"Slaughter of the Prophets of Baal," by Gustave Dore, Old Testament Bible illustration depicting the purging of the Baalist priests from Israel after their defeat in a contest with the Prophet Elijah.

them...Elegabalus erected in Rome the great phallic asherim which the Hebrew kings had kept trying to purge from their land (Karlen:62).

It is relevant to point out that this time period in the Roman empire can be considered the Christians' Holocaust. In 64 A.D. Christians were blamed by Nero for the burning of Rome and were targeted for extermination. Many Christians suffered unimaginable tortures as entertainment for the sadistic homosexual emperors of Rome. Though Rome was less homosexually-oriented than Greece, Roman society was nevertheless heavily influenced by homosexual practices. In Homosexuality, the Torah and Grace, Dwight Pryor reports that 14 of the first 15 Roman emperors were homosexual (tape one). In The Construction of Homosexuality, historian David F. Greenberg writes that "Roman homosexual tastes were so taken for granted that when Antony asked Herod to send his younger brother-in-law Aristobulus to the Roman court, Herod refused because 'he did not think it safe to send him...to the principal man of the Romans, that would abuse him in his amours'" (Greenberg:154f). While there are many differences between the treatment of Christians in Pagan Rome and Jews in Nazi Germany, the prominence of homosexuality among the chief perpetrators of both atrocities cannot be ignored.

As we seek to understand Nazism, it is important to remember that Judaism and its Christian and Islamic offshoots are fundamentally opposed to homosexuality. As we begin to grasp the relationship between homosexuality and occultism on one hand, and between homosexuals and Nazism on the other, the hatred of the Nazis for Jews and Christians may be more easily explained. The Jews were the people responsible for the demise of pagan world domination. Their theology (especially in its Christian form) banished pagan practices, including homosexuality, to a hidden and often reviled subculture. This is not to say that anti-Semitism is strictly a result of occult or homosexual influences. But at its very root there is a spiritual element to the Holocaust that suggests that it was, in some respects, vengeance against the people whose moral laws had relegated pagan sex-religions to obscurity and ignominy.

Yet, while Christianity made great strides in limiting pagan practices, they were not eliminated. Under Judeo-Christian cultural pressure, surviving pagan beliefs and practices, including sexual perversion, were forced from public life, reemerging in secretive and mystical occultic societies.

It is important to our study that we recognize that the Nazis were strongly influenced by pagan occult beliefs and, additionally, that homosexuality is fundamental to many pagan belief systems. As noted by Greenberg this is especially true in relation to "aristocratic warrior societies" (ibid.:111). Indeed, this was true even of the Greeks, whose homosexuality was forced upon them by the Dorian invaders of the twelfth century B.C. "Plutarch (Erotikus, 761 D) states: 'it was chiefly warlike peoples like the Boeotians, Lacedemonians and Cretans, who were addicted to homosexuality'" (Flaceliere:64ff). Author Brian Pronger notes that even the ancient Egyptians exhibited this tendency; their warriors raped enemy soldiers after defeating them in battle (Pronger:138).

It is also important to recognize that homo-occultism has remained a part of pagan cultures throughout the centuries to the present, even though the global predominance of the Judeo-Christian sexual ethic has limited its acceptance in most modern pagan societies such as China and Japan. When Jesuit missionaries arrived in sixteenth century China, for example, they found widespread pederasty (Spence:220) which they quickly moved to erase. And Rossman compares "the institutionalized pederasty of the privileged warrior class of medieval Japan's pederastic military structure" to "Nazi society" (Rossman:23).

Greenberg reports on dozens of mostly primitive modern pagan societies which practice ritual homosexuality, usually pederasty. These societies are found throughout the world, in countries such as Brazil, New Guinea, Morocco, sub-Saharan Africa and Malaysia. Greenberg writes,

> In many societies, male homosexual relations are structured by age or generation: the older partner takes a role defined as active or masculine; the younger, a role de-

fined as passive or female...[In many cases] The homosexual practices are justified by the belief that a boy will not mature [without these attentions] (Greenberg:26ff).

Such modern societies are profiled in The Sambia, by anthropologist Gilbert Herdt, who studied homosexuality in primitive cultures. He writes that "ritual homosexuality has been reported by anthropologists in scattered areas around the world [revealing a]...pervasive link between ritual homosexuality and the warrior ethos....We find these similar forms of warrior homosexuality in such diverse places as New Guinea, the Amazon, Ancient Greece, and historical Japan" (Herdt:203). The process of a boy's homosexual initiation in these societies is horrific: he is deprived of sleep, starved, beaten and raped over several days until he is completely "resocialized" as a homosexual (ibid:179f).

Thus homosexuality in paganism is not a relic of antiquity but an ongoing phenomenon. And the prevalence of homosexuals as occult leaders continues today. In the context of Western culture this may simply be because homosexuals gravitate to philosophies which oppose Judeo-Christian morality. But this would not explain the wide occurrence of homosexual rituals in primitive and pre-Christian pagan cultures.

Homosexualist Laurence J. Rosan writes that "the priests of polytheistic or spirit religions...[are] expected to be 'different'-- unworldly, even eccentric, given to visions, dramatic pronouncements and so on -- an ideal opportunity for both male and female homosexuals!" (Rosan:268f). The Bible, however, offers its own explanation, defining an individual's homosexuality not as an incidental factor in pagan religion but, at least in some cases, as the consequence of "worshiping the creation rather than the Creator." The Book of Romans, Chapter 1, Verses 18-27 reads as follows:

For the wrath of God is revealed from heaven against all ungodliness and unrighteousness of men, who suppress the truth in unrighteousness, because what may be known of God is manifest in them, for God has shown it to them. For since the creation of the world His invisible attributes are clearly seen, being understood by the things that are made, even His eternal power and Godhead, so that they are without excuse, because, although they knew God, they did not glorify Him as God, nor were thankful, but became futile in their thoughts, and their foolish hearts were darkened. Professing to be wise, they became fools, and changed the glory of the incorruptible God into an image made like corruptible man — and birds and four-footed animals and creeping things. Therefore God also gave them up to uncleanness, in the lusts of their hearts, to dishonor their bodies among themselves, who exchanged the truth of God for the lie, and worshiped and served the creature rather than the Creator, who is blessed forever. Amen. For this reason God gave them up to vile passions. For even their women exchanged the natural use for what is against nature. Likewise also the men, leaving the natural use of the woman, burned in their lust for one another, men with men committing what is shameful, and receiving in themselves the penalty of their error which was due (NKJ).

Ironically, the Biblical event which marks the beginning of homosexual practices in the post-flood world is the same one that is misinterpreted by pseudo-Christian white supremacists to justify their racial theories. Christian researcher Dwight Pryor gives the following interpretation (which we have summarized) of a familiar Biblical passage. In Genesis 9, Noah fell unconscious from drinking too much wine and while he was thus incapacitated Ham "saw [or uncovered] his nakedness." This term, used primarily in the book of Leviticus, is a Hebraic euphemism for sexual intercourse. "And Noah awoke from his wine, and knew what his younger son had done to him." As a re-

"Noah Cursing Caanan," by Gustave Dore.

sult of his sexual attack on his father, Ham is cursed by Noah. (In <u>Call of the Torah</u> Rabbi Elie Munk cites Hebrew scholars who also interprets Ham's violation as "an act of pederasty") - (Munk:220). Thus Ham becomes Canaan, for whom the land of Canaan is named. Some generations later the Canaanite cities of Sodom and Gomorrah would be destroyed by God because of homosexuality. White supremacists refer to Ham as the father of the colored races which they call "mud people." But it is homosexual perversion, not skin color, which is associated with the curse of Canaan.

Madame Blavatsky and the Theosophical Society

An examination of the homo-occultic influences on the Nazis must begin with the Russian-born mystic Helena Petrovna Blavatsky (1831-1891), founder of the Theosophical Society and a figure who looms large behind some of the defining actions and beliefs of the Nazi Party. Blavatsky was probably a lesbian, but we have no proof that she actually engaged in lesbian sexual activity. She is described as a very "masculine" woman who dominated her many followers, both male and female (Cavendish:250). She was married twice and maintained a long association with Theosophical Society co-founder Henry Olcott, but these were relationships of convenience. Blavatsky insisted she had never had sex with either husband (Meade:137) and wrote, "There is nothing of the woman in me. When I was young, if a young man had dared to speak to me of love, I would have shot him like a dog who bit me" (ibid.:50).

A world famous occultist, Blavatsky founded the Theosophical Society in 1875 in New York, but soon moved her operation to India where she wrote an influential occult book called The Secret Doctrine in 1888. In The Secret Doctrine Blavatsky expounds the Theosophical theory of creation; a seven-step progression of human evolution in which successive "races" evolve from a lower to a higher form of life. She calls these stages "root races" and identifies our current "root race" as the fifth of seven -- the Aryan race --

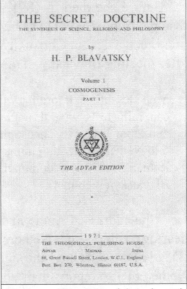

Madame Blavatsky (above) and the title page of her book which based Aryan supremacy on occultic fantasies.

which follows the fourth race, known as the Atlantean. Blavatsky used a variety of esoteric symbols in the book, including triangles and swastikas. She claimed to be the chosen spokesperson for two "exalted masters" who communicated telepathically with her from their secret dwelling place in Tibet (Goodrick-Clarke:18ff). In 1884 the first German Theosophical Society was established. Despite its ludicrous tenets, Theosophy became extremely popular in Germany and Austria. Its Aryan racist elitism appealed to the growing number of ethnic Germans whose *voelkisch*, or nationalist, sentiments demanded a reunited Germany. According to Blavatsky, the Aryans were the most spiritually advanced people on earth, but the Jews had a "religion of hate and malice toward everyone and everything outside itself." This was a message tailor-made for Nazism.

Before she died in 1891, Blavatsky chose her British disciple Annie Besant to be her successor. Besant, who had once been a devout Christian, became a dedicated occultist after meeting Blavatsky. James Webb writes,

> Mrs. Besant's extraordinary transformations from Anglican minister's wife through birth-control propagandist and labor leader to Theosophist ...are...well known...Arthur Nethercot, her biographer, suggests an element of the lesbian in the rapid domination of Mrs. Besant by H. P. Blavatsky (Webb:94).

"She addressed Annie in suspiciously fulsome and endearing terms," writes Nethercot, "'Dearest,' 'My Dearest,' 'Dearly Beloved One,' and signing herself 'Very adoring.'" Nethercot also reports that "she dispatched missives to Annie...and addressed them to 'My Darling Penelope' from 'Your...female Ulysses'" (Nethercot:306).

Besant's "mentor and partner" in running the Theosophical Society was Charles Leadbeater, whom Webb describes as "that type of mildly homosexual clergyman who is as familiar now as he was then" (Webb:95). But Leadbeater's homosexuality was not "mild" enough to keep him

Pederast Charles Leadbeater (left) with Annie Besant and Colonel Olcott.

out of trouble. "From his early days as a Hampshire curate until the close of his life," writes Webb, "he seems to have had an incurable taste for young men" (ibid.:95).

At one point Leadbeater claimed to have discovered the new Messiah -- the returned Christ -- in the person of a young Indian named Jiddu Krishnamurti. Krishnamurti gained international acceptance among followers of Theosophy as the new Savior. The boy's father nearly ruined the scheme for the Theosophists, however, when he accused Leadbeater of corrupting his son. "There was...small doubt that Leadbeater had been up to his old tricks again" (ibid.:102).

Cult figure and author Jiddu Krishnamurti as an adult.

Under Besant and Leadbeater, Theosophy attracted an even

greater following. The writings of both Besant and Leadbeater, as well as Blavatsky, were translated and published
in Germany. An 1892 periodical, *Lotus Blossoms*, featured
Blavatsky's writings and "was the first German publication
to sport the theosophical swastika upon its cover"
(Goodrick-Clarke:25). As time went on numerous other
Theosophy-based occult groups formed in Germany and
Austria. Several of these groups would provide the philosophical framework for Nazism.

Guido von List and the Armanen Order

Guido von List (1848-1919)
was the first to combine German nationalism with the occult teachings of Theosophy.
A bitter critic of Christianity,
especially Catholicism, List
had converted to Wotanism
(worship of Wotan, the ancient German god of storms)
as a young teenager. Years
later List "became a cult figure on the eastern edge of the
German world. He was regarded by his readers and followers as a bearded old patriarch and a mystical nationalist
guru whose clairvoyant gaze had lifted the glorious Aryan
and German past of Austria into full view from beneath the
debris of foreign influences and Christian culture"
(Goodrick-Clarke:33).

Although twice married, List was almost certainly homosexual. His closest associates included occultists Jorg
Lanz von Liebenfels and Harald Gravelle, the former very
probably, the latter avowedly, homosexual. Gravelle, a
leading Theosophist in Germany, also contributed to the

pederast journal, *Der Eigene*. List was also known as the Aleister Crowley of Vienna because he was deeply involved in Hindu Tantrism, a form of black magic that incorporated deviant sexual rituals (J.S. Jones:124). In The Magical World of Alister Crowley, biographer Francis King states that as part of his occultic rituals, Crowley "deliberately humiliated himself by being...the passive partner in act[s] of buggery" (King in Tompkins:421).

In 1908 List formed the Guido von List Society in part to promote his Ariosophist research and writings, which by this time had become viciously anti-Semitic (ibid.:43).

List's occult activities ranged across a wide spectrum. He was an expert on the Rune alphabet and wrote several books on the subject.

Aleister Crowley.

He was particularly infatuated with the dual lightning bolt symbol that would later become the designation for the SS. (J. S. Jones:125). (The single lightning bolt would be adopted by the Hitler Youth.) He was also a self-styled occult master, claiming to be "the last of the Armanist magicians who had formerly wielded authority in the old Aryan world" (Goodrick-Clarke:33).

In 1911, List formed an elitist occult organization called the Hoeher Armanen-Orden ("Higher Armanen Order"). The HAO was a hierarchical priesthood in which he was Grand Master. List claimed this cult was the surviving remnant of an ancient order of priest-kings called the *Armanenschaft*. This group was the source of List's greatest influence on the Nazis. Goodrick-Clark writes,

Bugle corps flies the banner of the single lightning bolt, the occultic symbol of the Hitler Youth.

List's blueprint for a new pan-German empire [based upon a revival of the *Armanenschaft*] was detailed and unambiguous. It called for the ruthless subjection of non-Aryans to Aryan masters in a highly structured hierarchical state. The qualifications of candidates [for positions in the new social order]...rested solely on their racial purity...But List went further still, anticipating the mystical elitism of the SS in Nazi Germany...List's ideal was a male order with an occult chapter (Goodrick-Clarke:64f).

Not only is List's design strikingly similar to the later plans of Heinrich Himmler for the SS-controlled state, but it is also reminiscent of the Brand/Friedlander philosophy of militaristic male supremacy.

Although the Armanen Order was never a large organization, its membership included high-ranking members of Austrian society (ibid.:233n). One devotee of List's writings would become the hub of the Nazi movement: the young Adolf Hitler. After the fall of the Third Reich, a book written by Guido von List was found in Hitler's private library. On the inside cover was written the inscription: "To Adolf Hitler, my dear brother in Armanen," although this is insufficient evidence to conclude that Hitler belonged to the order itself (J.S. Jones:124; Waite, 1977:90).

Jorg Lanz von Liebenfels and Ariosophy

If any occultist can be said to have had more influence on Hitler and the Nazis than List it would be Jorg Lanz von Liebenfels (1874-1954). Lanz was a former Cistercian Monk who had been thrown out of the order "for carnal and worldly desires" (Sklar:19). Since the Cistercian Order was a closed, all-male monastery, it is assumed that Lanz's indiscretions were of a homosexual nature. German writer Friedrich Buchmayr noted the following about Lanz

[F]ollowing his ordination in 1898, as a priest, Lanz was put to use as a teacher of choir boys. In April of 1899, the 24-year-old left the order, stating his reason for this step as "increasing nervousness" and "irritation." In the Chapter Book his departure was accounted to "carnal loves." His later radical hatred of women suggests a failed relationship with women (Buchmayr, *Biographisch-Bibliographisches Kirchenlexikon*, Vol. XVI, 1999)

It was through Lanz that Hitler would learn that many of his heroes of history were also "practicing homosexuals" (Waite, 1977:94f). After being expelled from the monastery, Lanz formed his own occultic order called the *Ordo Novi Templi* or the Order of the New Temple (ONT). The ONT was related to the *Ordo Templi Orientis* or Order of the Temple of the East,

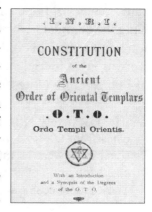

which, like List's organization, practiced tantric sexual rituals (Howard:91).

Hitler was aware that Lanz was a homosexual, according to Frau Elsa Schmidt-Falk of the Nazi Genealogy Office of Munich, as reported by Daim. Schmidt-Falk frequently spoke with Hitler personally in her role as a genealogical researcher whose task was to verify the racial purity of highly-placed Nazis. She did not conclude from her discussions that Hitler was personally associated with Lanz (although he may have been) but she reported that

> Lanz was also mentioned once in the following connection: a convicted homosexual had addressed a plea for clemency to Hitler, in which he designated [Lanz] as a homosexual. Hitler allowed this man to disappear...immediately....[At another time] Hitler mentioned Roehm, Heines, etc. and also Lanz von Liebenfels and his group, about which (group) he (Hitler) at least accepted that it was actively homosexual (Daim:41).

Both List's and Lanz' organizations were modeled on the Teutonic Knights and the Knights Templars, militaristic monastic orders founded in 1118 A.D. to fight in the Crusades (Goodrick-Clarke:60). Following the crusades, the Templars returned to Europe, but did not demobilize. Instead the members established monasteries which became centers of trade and influence. In the early 1300s the Knights Templars were condemned by Pope Innocent III for homosexual perversion and occultic practices. They were brought to trial and disbanded by King Philip the Fair of France. Igra writes,

> [Homosexuality's] morbid history in the German blood dates from the time of the Teutonic Knights...Their personal lives were as infamous as the more widely publicized infamies of their brother Knights, the Templars. These latter became so corrupt that they raised the practice

Jorg Lanz von Liebenfels, "The Man Who Gave Hitler His Ideas."

of their cardinal vice [homosexuality] into a religious cult...There were innumerable public trials where the most revolting details were brought to light (Igra:18).

Others have confirmed the prevalence of homosexuality among the Teutonic Knights. Adolf Brand, writing in *Der Eigene*, said of the Teutons (from whom the Teutonic Knights take their name), that "the Edda [Norse mythology] extols it [homosexuality] as the highest virtue of the Teutons (Brand in Oosterhuis and Kennedy:236f). Nazi leaders, especially Himmler, were infatuated with the Teutons. Sklar writes that "Like List and Lanz, Himmler was obsessed with...the Order of the Teutonic Knights" and that he "saw his Black Guards [the S.S.] as an elite cadre of Teutonic warriors" (Sklar:14ff). Likewise, Frederick the Great, Hitler's personal hero, "revived the vices of the Teutonic Knights" in his army (Igra:19).

Hitler's *Ordensburgen* ("Castles of the Order") were "the highest residential academies for the training of the Nazi elite" and "received their name from the medieval fortresses built by the Teutonic Knights" (Snyder:261). It was fitting, then, that the swastika flag would first be flown over one of these fortresses. On Christmas day, 1907, many years before the swastika would become the symbol of the Third Reich, Lanz and other members of the ONT raised a swastika flag over the castle which Lanz had purchased to house the order (Goodrick-Clarke:109). Lanz chose the swastika, he said, because it was the ancient pagan symbol of Wotan (Cavendish:1983). Wotanism, incidentally, was claimed by List to have been the national religion of the Teutons (Goodrick-Clarke:39).

The journal of the ONT was called *Ostara*, named for the female counterpart to Wotan in the pagan Germanic pantheon. Some of the titles of *Ostara* pamphlets included "The Dangers of Women's Rights and the Necessity of a Masculine Morality of Masters," and "Introduction to Sexual-Physics, or Love as Odylic Energy." Lanz claimed homosexuality was the result of "Odylic" influences (Waite, 1977:93f). Lanz hated women, writing that "the soul of the woman has something pre-human, something

Nr. 1

Die Ostara und das Reich der Blonden

Von J. Lanz-Liebenfels

Als Handschrift gedruckt in 2. Auflage, Wien 1930
Copyright by J. Lanz v. Liebenfels, Wien 1922

Titelblatt des „Ostara"-Heftes 1, 1922, 2. Aufl. 1930

demonic, something enigmatic about it" (Rhodes:108). "Nature herself," wrote Lanz, "has ordained women to be our slaves" (Lanz in Daim:31). He blamed Aryan racial impurities on promiscuous women who were copulating with "men of lower races."

Lanz's occult philosophies, which he dubbed Ariosophy (Aryan Theosophy), were an enlargement upon the ideas of Guido von List. To the foundation of Theosophy and German nationalism, Lanz added the popular theme of social Darwinism, as promoted by Ernst Haeckel and the Monist League. Haeckel is famous today for his debunked theory that "ontogeny recapitulates phylogeny," the idea that the unborn young of all species pass through distinct embryonic stages that recapitulate the evolution of successive phyla. But in pre-Nazi Germany, Haeckel was famous for his application of Darwin's concept of "survival of the fittest" to human society. Cambridge historian and London Times journalist Ben Macintyre writes,

> The German embryologist Haeckel and his Monist League told the world, and in particular, Germany, that the whole history of nations is explicable by means of natural selection: Hitler and his twisted theories turned this pseudo-science into politics, attempting to destroy whole races in the name of racial purity and the survival of the fittest...Hitler called his book *Mein Kampf*, "My Struggle," echoing Haeckel's translation of Darwin's phrase "the struggle for survival" (Macintyre:28f).

Lanz's Ariosophy would fuel the imaginations of the Nazi elite, despite (or perhaps because of) its lunatic qualities. "Lanz fulminated," writes Goodrick-Clarke, "against the false Christian tradition of compassion for the weak and inferior and demanded that the nation deal ruthlessly with the underprivileged" (Goodrick-Clarke:97). Waite reports that Hitler was an avid fan of *Ostara* and developed his anti-Semitic philosophy with the help of racist pamphlets published and distributed by Lanz and Guido von List.

[Hitler] bought some anti-Semitic pamphlets for a few pennies. These pamphlets, which were so important to the formation of Hitler's political thinking, were distributed by a virulently anti-Semitic society called the List-Gesellschaft. The tracts were written by two now-forgotten pamphleteers, Georg Lanz von Liebenfels (1872-1954) and Guido von List (c. 1865-1919). Of all the racist pamphlets available to Hitler during those years, only those written by Lanz and List set forth in explicit detail the ideas and theories that became unmistakably and characteristically Hitler's own. Only they preached the racial theory of history which proclaimed the holiness and uniqueness of the one creative race of Aryans; only they called for the creation of a racially pure state which would battle to the death the inferior races which threatened it from without and within; and only they demanded the political domination of a racial elite led by a quasi-religious military leader. Hitler's political ideas were later developed and reinforced in racist circles of Munich after the war in 1919-1923, but their genesis was in Vienna under the influence of Lanz and List (Waite, 1977:91).

In 1958 Wilhelm Daim, an Austrian psychologist, published a study of Lanz entitled _Der Mann der Hitler die Ideen gab_ ("The Man Who Gave Hitler His Ideas"). In the book, Daim recounts that Lanz had met Hitler in Vienna when the latter was 20 years old. Hitler often visited occult bookstores and he used his contacts in some of them to locate Lanz after having trouble finding back issues of _Ostara_. While he was destitute in Vienna, Hitler "hotly defended Liebenfels' ideas against skeptics" writes Snyder (Snyder:211). In 1932, twenty-three years after that fateful meeting, Lanz wrote, "Hitler is one of our pupils...you will one day experience that he, and through him we, will one day be victorious and develop a movement that makes the world tremble" (Cavendish:1983). This proclamation, however, did not sit well with *der Fuehrer*, and he had Lanz's writings banned in 1933 (Snyder:211).

Lanz's *Ostara* was a focal point for racist and occult figures in Germany. In *Ostara,* Lanz proposed that "unsatisfactory" racial types be eliminated by abortion, sterilization, starvation, forced labor and other means. He also recommended Aryan breeding farms where a master race, destined to control the world, could be hatched (Cavendish:1983). Heinrich Himmler would later create such a breeding program (called *Lebensborn*) during the Third Reich. The close similarity of Lanz's prescription for the elimination of "inferiors" to the views of Benedict Friedlander suggests the possibility of a relationship between The ONT (Order of the New Temple) and the Community of the Elite. One link was Harald Gravelle, a homosexual member of the Guido von List Society who wrote for both *Ostara* and *Der Eigene* (Steakley:67n.34). Gravelle was "the principle theosophist of Lanz's acquaintance, with the exception of Guido List" (Goodrick-Clarke:100).

Although not directly connected to the ONT, the astrologist, Dr. Karl Gunther Heimsoth was another link between the Community of the Elite and the occultists. Heimsoth, a homosexual, was "a close friend and Freikorps comrade of Roehm" and maintained "close contact with several future Nazi big wigs" (Machtan:108f). He wrote a book titled *Charakter Konstellation*, which was devoted entirely to the horoscopes of homosexuals (Rector:81); he was also a contributor to *Der Eigene*. Heimsoth is remembered for coining the term "homophile" (Oosterhuis and Kennedy:188), which was a common American synonym for homosexual in the early decades of the "gay" movement here.

The Thule Society

In 1912, various follow-
ers of List and Lanz formed
an organization called the
Germanen Order. Di-
verging radically from the
purely philosophic and spiritual focus of the groups that
the two "masters" had
formed, the Germanen Or-
der was to take an active role
in fulfilling the goals of
Ariosophist teachings. "The
principle aim of the
Germanen Order," writes
Goodrick-Clarke, "was the
monitoring of the Jews and
their activities by the cre-

Emblem of the Thule Society.

ation of a center to which all anti-Semitic material would
flow for distribution" (Goodrick-Clarke:128). Only Aryans of pure descent were allowed to become members. The
first World War disrupted the organization, but in the after-
math of the war the chapters of the Order began to engage in
direct action against those they considered to be their enemies.

After the war the Order began to be "used as a cover organization for the recruitment of political assassins"
(ibid.:133) who revived the practices of the *Vehmgericht*, a
medieval vigilante society whose only sentence was death
(Waite 1969:216ff). Prominent among these assassins were
Gerhard Rossbach, Edmund Heines and other "Butch" homosexuals who would later help to shape the Nazi Party
(Snyder:92, Waite:222f).

Some 354 enemies of the nationalists were killed over
several years in the campaign of *Vheme* murders, the most

prominent being Walther Rathenau, Foreign Minister of the German Republic during World War I. Ironically, many of the victims were killed for sexual and not political reasons. Waite writes,

> The Feme [Vheme] was often directed against former comrades of post-Free Corps organizations. The very multiplicity of Bunds and secret societies led to competition, quarreling and death....Competition and conflict was intensified by the fact that many of the Freebooters were homosexuals and hence prone to jealousy and "lover's quarrels." The Mayer-Hermann case will serve as an example.
>
> Oberleutnant Mayer was Kreisleiter of the "Arbeitsgemeinschaft Rossbach." He was also, as court testimony euphemistically put it, "an enemy of women," as was his Leader, Gerhard Rossbach and, supported by a wealthy tobacconist, one Kurt Hermann, he founded his own "Arbeitsgemeinschaft Mayer." But Oberleutnant Mayer soon became jealous of a certain Gebauer, a former Baltic fighter, who was also courting Herr Hermann. Mayer charged Gebauer with treason and sent two of his men to Hermann's home. They found the traitor in bed with Herr Hermann -- Frau Hermann was away at the time -- and carried out the sentence of the Feme (Waite 1969:222f).

In 1917, because of the association of the Germanen Order with political terrorism, its Bavarian chapter changed its name to the Thule Society "to spare it the attentions of socialist and pro-Republican elements" (ibid.:144). The Thule Society retained many of the bizarre occult theories originated by Blavatsky and "had close ties to Crowley's organization" (Raschke:339). Historian Wulf Schwarzwaller writes,

> Briefly, the creed of the Thule Society inner circle was as follows: Thule was a legendary island in the Far North, similar to Atlantis, supposedly the center of a lost, high

level civilization. But not all secrets of that civilization had been completely wiped out. Those that remained were being guarded by ancient, highly intelligent beings...The truly initiated could establish contact with these beings...[who could] endow the initiated with supernatural strength and energy. With the help of these energies of Thule, the goal of the initiated was to create a new race of supermen of "Aryan" stock who would exterminate all "inferior" races (Schwarzwaller:66f).

The leader of the Thule Society was a man named Rudolf von Sebottendorf but its chief organizer was Walter Nauhaus, a former member of the *Wandervoegel* movement (Goodrick-Clarke:143). Members of the Thule Society who figure prominently in the rise of Nazism included Hans Kahnert, Dietrich Eckart and Rudolf Hess. In 1919 Kahnert founded Germany's largest "gay rights" organization, the *Bund fuer Menschenrecht* ("Society for Human Rights") which counted SA Chief Ernst Roehm among its members (J. Katz:632n94). Eckart, meanwhile, was a founding member of the German Worker's Party and became Adolf Hitler's mentor (Shirer:65). Like Hitler, Eckart was a subscriber to *Ostara* (J. S. Jones:301n91).

Dietrich Eckart adopted Hitler as his student in 1920. He later stated that he felt "drawn to his [Hitler's] whole being" and that he and Hitler developed an "intimate" relationship in which he referred to the younger man as "my Adolf" (Machtan:117). Eckart never confessed to being a homosexual, but the evi-

Dietrich Eckart

dence suggests that he was. He is alleged by some to have been involved in Tantric occult sex rituals "similar to Crowley's," and even to have initiated Hitler into such activities (Raschke:399). We do know that Eckart was one of the most enthusiastic followers of Otto Weininger, a leading homosexual supremacist whose theories denigrated women (Igra:100). Alfred Rosenberg characterized Eckart as an inveterate misogynist whose "exclusively male company" destroyed his short and childless marriage in 1920 (Machtan:118f).

There is no question at all that Eckart was instrumental in Hitler's early successes. "With Eckart as his mentor," writes Schwarzwaller, "the gauche and inhibited Hitler -- the unsuccessful painter, former PFC, who had not even been promoted to corporal because of 'lack of leadership qualities,' quite suddenly...became an outstanding organizer and propagandist" (Schwarzwaller:68).

Like Roehm and Lanz, Eckart claimed credit for "creating" Hitler. In 1923, shortly before his death, Eckart wrote to a friend, "Follow Hitler! He will dance, but it will be to my tune. We have given him the means to maintain contact with them (meaning the "masters"). Don't grieve for me for I have influenced history more than any other German" (Schwarzwaller:69). Though he would later ridicule many of the occultists and their ideas, Hitler dedicated his book, *Mein Kampf*, to Eckart, and at one time called Eckart his "John the Baptiser" (ibid.:70).

Hitler's next spiritual mentor was Karl Haushofer, who later became Germany's leading theorist on the subject of geo-politics (the scientific study of the influence of geography on political events). A secret member of the Thule Society, Haushofer is credited with training Hitler to think in terms of world conquest and is believed to have virtually dictated Chapter 16 of *Mein Kampf*, which outlines Hitler's foreign policy (Sklar:63f). Haushofer's *Lebensraum* ("living space") theory was later used to justify German expansion, while his familiarity with the Orient allowed him to forge Hitler's alliance with Japan (ibid.). There is evidence to suggest that Haushofer was homosexual as well. In <u>Hitler's Cross</u>, Erwin Lutzer accuses Haushofer of taking Hitler

Karl Haushofer

through the deepest levels of occult transformation until he became a thoroughly demonized being. Hitler was even transformed sexually; he became a sado-masochist, practicing various forms of sexual perversion (Lutzer:61).

More persuasive is the testimony of Ilse Hess, wife of Rudolf Hess, the Thule Society member who would rise the highest in Nazi circles. Hess, a homosexual (his marriage notwithstanding) was one of Hitler's closest friends and a fellow student of Haushofer. Machtan reports that "Ilse Hess...complained that she had gotten no more out of her marriage than a 'girl confirmand' and she even compared herself, where 'the pleasures of matrimony are concerned,' to a 'convent schoolgirl'" (Machtan:149). He adds the following:

Hess had developed a close relationship with Haushofer, who was twenty-five years older than himself. The two of them often spent whole nights sitting together in Haushofer's home, and they also made joint excursions. "He's a wonderful person," Hess enthusiastically told his parents, and Haushofer dedicated to his "young friend Rudolf Hess" a hymn reminiscent of Stefan George [a well-known pederast], which spoke of "his eyes festively illuminating closed doors" just as "a sunset is reflected in a spring." Ilse Hess later confessed in a restrained fashion, that she had "long been almost a trifle jealous" of Haushofer, who seemed to have positively "absorbed" her boyfriend (Machtan:144f).

Hess eventually became the Deputy *Fuehrer* of the Nazi Party. Both Hess and Alfred Rosenberg had "an immense influence on Hitler to whom they preached the gospel of the Thule Society" (Angebert:172). In addition to his involvement with the Thule Society, Hess belonged to yet another offshoot of the Theosophical cult. It was an organization called the Anthroposophical Society, formed in 1912 by Rudolf Steiner. Steiner was a former leader of the German Theosophical Society who split with the group following their "discovery" of the new "messiah." Hess was also a firm believer in astrology (Howe:152).

Hitler was also influenced by other members of the Thule Society. Waite writes,

> In describing his initiation into politics at Munich in 1919, Hitler stressed the importance of a little pamphlet entitled "My Political Awakening" ...[written by] a sickly fanatic called Anton Drexler...Drexler was an adjunct member of the Thule Society, the most influential of the many racist anti-Semitic groups spawned in Munich during the immediate postwar period...By the time of the revolution of 1918, the society numbered some 1500 members in Bavaria and included many of Hitler's later supporters. Hitler himself, it is reported "was often a guest of the Society"...The actual German Worker's Party — which was to become the mighty Nazi movement...differed very little from the discussion groups and activities of the Thule Society or the other racist groups to which all the founders belonged. (Waite, 1977:115).

Homosexual Rudolf Hess became Deputy Fuehrer of the Nazi Party.
Yad Vashem.

SS Chief Heinrich Himmler was the leading occultist of the Nazi Party and may have been a homosexual as well.   Yad Vashem

Yet another prominent Nazi who was strongly influenced by the German occult movement was Heinrich Himmler. Himmler maintained a close relationship with a prominent occultist named Karl Maria Wiligut, who became known as the "Rasputin of Himmler" (Goodrick-Clarke:177). It is not clear if this designation is meant to imply that Wiligut shared the infamous Russian's penchant for sexual licentiousness. Wiligut claimed to have a gift of clairvoyant "ancestral memory," certainly quite useful to the racial purists of the Nazi Party who were concerned with proving their own Aryan heritage. Wiligut was responsible for designing the Death's Head ring worn by members of the SS.

Under Himmler, the SS became a veritable occultic order. Christian names of SS soldiers were replaced with Teutonic names, and all members were required to maintain the strictest secrecy and detachment from the rest of society (Sklar:100). In later years Himmler spent vast sums of money on esoteric research projects such as an expedition to Tibet "to look for traces of a pure Germanic race which might have been able to keep intact the ancient Nordic mysteries" (ibid.:102). (This little-known aspect of Nazi history is, of course, the inspiration for the Steven Spielberg movie, *Raiders of the Lost Ark*.)

Himmler may well have been a homosexual (two sources are cited later in the book), however, his intense obsession with secrecy largely shielded him from disclosure of his private life. He did, however, foster the cult of the *maennerbund* among his men. Some report that SS special forces training required recruits to soap each other's bodies during showers to establish mutual dependency (Reisman, 1994:3). Later, Himmler would make empty threats against homosexuals in public pronouncements, but it is clear that he was completely comfortable being part of Adolf Hitler's clique of pederasts.

In any case, we can see that the occult roots of the Nazi

Party ran deep into German history. It is also apparent that many of the leading occult figures responsible for this legacy were homosexuals. From ancient pagan roots through Blavatsky to List and Lanz, and to Hitler himself, the evolution of homo-occultism gave the Nazis their theories of an Aryan Master Race and their justification for the vicious extermination of "inferior" life.

Chapter Three

THE HOMOSEXUAL ROOTS OF FASCISM

Another area of history we must explore in order to understand the Nazis is the origin of fascism and national socialist ideology. Fascism is a term which eludes easy definition but most would probably agree that in its narrowest sense, fascism is a form of government characterized by three things: one-party dictatorship, centralized government control of finance and industry, and militant nationalism. It is important to emphasize here that fascism is a form of socialism. It is thus inaccurate and misleading to call the Nazi Party "right wing" although this misidentification is nearly universally accepted today.

In his 1964 work, Varieties of Fascism, historian Eugen Weber said "we should do well to remember that Fascism...considered itself a form of Socialism, freed of humanitarian sentimentalism and Marxist dialectic, truer to fundamental Socialist aims in that it tried to adapt itself to a changing historical reality which the old Marxist interpretation no longer suited" (Weber:29).

In seeking the roots of fascism we once again find a high correlation between homosexuality and a mode of thinking which we identify with Nazism. It is interesting that Weber, without noting the homosexual connection, traced "the pattern of the planned totalitarian state back to

Plato's <u>Republic</u>, and the Fascist mentality to the turbulent, unscrupulous Calicles who appears in another Platonic dialogue, <u>Gorgias</u>" (Weber:11).

So here we begin. The inspiration for the fascist state comes from Plato, the male supremacist and apologist for pederasty. Plato is revered as the preeminent classical philosopher, although his apparent advocacy of man/boy sex is not commonly known. A prototypical statement by the philosopher is recorded in George Grant's <u>Legislating Immorality</u>: "Through the nightly loving of boys, a man, on arising, begins to see the authentic nature of true beauty" (Grant, 1993:24). Plato's <u>Republic</u> is his best known work. The following is a summary of the <u>Republic</u> from W.K.C. Guthrie's <u>A History of Greek Philosophy</u>:

> The Republic (c.370 BC) advances many of Plato's principal ideas, notably those concerned with government and justice. Composed as a debate between Socrates and five other speakers, The Republic is best known for its description of the ideal state (based on Sparta), which Plato argues should be ruled by philosopher-kings (Guthrie in Grolier).

As we have noted, the Spartan society was dominated by a pederastic warrior cult that featured mandatory induction of twelve-year-old boys into homosexual partnerships with adult men. Like all such cults, the Spartan military was rigidly hierarchical and elitist. Plato's concept of the "philosopher-king" is that of an autocratic leader appropriate to such a society. The philosopher-king rules over a kind of fascist utopia. Interestingly, Plato's idealized society in the <u>Republic</u> includes the elimination of the family as a social unit and the elimination of private property.

The next figure cited by Weber in the historic development which would culminate in National Socialism is Frederick the Great (1712-1786) "founder of the perfect Prussian bureaucracy" (Weber:11). He writes, "The Nazi

Siegfried [a Teutonic mythological hero] looked back to the equalitarian elitism of Sparta [and] to the barracks of [Frederick's] Prussian army" (ibid.:82). Frederick clearly fit Plato's description of a philosopher-king. He established a strict military order on the Spartan model and used his elite forces to great advantage, expanding his Prussian empire through ruthless lightning strikes against neighboring countries. He was also a homosexual, and, coincidentally, one of Adolf Hitler's greatest heroes (Waite, 1977:112). Homosexualist historian Noel L. Garde writes,

> Frederick's homosexual inclinations, of which Lt. Katte in his youth was the principle object, were attested by many authorities, notably Voltaire and Frederick himself...The other young men besides Katte were...Baron Frederick Trenck, Count Keyserlingk, Count Goerz and an Italian named Barbarini (Garde:448).

In recent years Frederick has been praised as a model of social liberalism and humanitarianism. Another side of this man, however, explains his appeal to Hitler and the Nazis. Igra describes him:

> Frederick hated women, as such. Die Frau was always a Schimpfwort, an expression of contempt, with him...Though he felt obliged by reason of his position to have a queen, which involved the necessity of getting married, Frederick never lived a husband's life. And though [Martin] Luther's Reform inculcated the marriage of the clergy, with a view to stamping out the vices that had characterized celibacy in Germany, and though the same injunction logically applies to soldiers, Frederick forced the majority of his officers to remain unmarried...In his armies he revived the vices of the Teutonic Knights and the Templars. Frederick is rightly looked upon as the founder of modern German militarism, not merely as state policy but as a worship of destruction for its own sake. He despised humanity in general and

looked on human life, even his own life, as a bagatelle. He constantly carried a phial of poison on his person so that he might put an end to his own life at any moment he considered opportune (Igra:18f).

According to Weber, the National Socialist brand of fascism began in the mid-1800s with the radical Universal German Workingmen's Association (UGWA) (Weber:11). The founder of the UGWA was German socialist leader Ferdinand Lassalle, once the chief rival of Karl Marx for leadership of the communist organization First International. While probably not homosexual himself (he was killed by the aggrieved husband of one of his lovers) Lassalle is remembered for his political rehabilitation of the notorious pederast, Jean Baptiste von Schweitzer, after the Social Democrat Party had expelled him. Schweitzer was a talented lawyer who, in 1862, had become editor of the main periodical of the German socialist movement, *Sozialdemokrat*. In August of that year, two elderly ladies, enjoying a quiet stroll in a public park in Mannheim, accidentally came upon Schweitzer and a schoolboy. Schweitzer was sodomizing the boy in the bushes. He was arrested, given two weeks in jail, and disbarred (Steakley:1).

The Social Democrats disowned Schweitzer, but only one year later Lassalle took Schweitzer under his wing (J. Katz:567n.), stating that a person's sexual tastes had "absolutely nothing to do with a man's political character" (Linsert:178). Schweitzer became president of the UGWA, and on September 7, 1867, was elected to the Reichstag (parliament) of the North German Confederation (Steakley:1ff).

Friedrich Nietzsche

Among the several men who have been dubbed "the Father of National Socialism" (including Jorg Lanz von Liebenfels), Friedrich Wilhelm Nietzsche (1844-1900) is probably most deserving of this distinction, being so labeled by Nazi luminaries Dr. Alfred Rosenberg and Dr. Franck (Peters:221). Others have called him the "Father of Fascism" (ibid.:ix). Rabidly anti-Christian and a homosexual, Nietzsche founded the "God

Friedrich Wilhelm Nietzsche

is dead" movement and contributed to the development of existentialist philosophy. Nietzsche's publisher, Peter Gast, called Nietzsche "one of the fiercest anti-Christians and atheists," and described his book, The Antichrist, as a "ferocious curse" on Christianity (ibid.:119). Nietzsche called Christianity and democracy the moralities of the "weak herd," and argued for the "natural aristocracy" of the *Uebermensch* or superman, whose "will to power" was grounded in the material world (Wren in Grolier).

According to Macintyre in Forgotten Fatherland: The Search For Elisabeth Nietzsche, Frederich Nietzsche never married and had no known female sex partners, but went insane at age 44 and eventually died of syphilis. According to Sigmund Freud and Carl Jung, Nietzsche had caught the disease at a homosexual brothel in Genoa, Italy (McIntyre:91f). Nietzsche's unflattering opinion of women was widely known. His works were "peppered with attacks against women," and, like the pederasts of the Community of the Elite, he relegated women to the role of breeders and sexual slaves. Men, on the other hand were to be bred for war (Agonito:265f).

One of Nietzsche's closest friends and another hero of Adolf Hitler was Richard Wagner, the composer. Wagner was the subject of a 1903 book by Hans Fuchs called _Richard Wagner und die Homosexualitaet_ ("Richard Wagner and Homosexuality") in which Fuchs recommends art as a means for homosexual emancipation (Oosterhuis and Kennedy:86). We do not know whether Wagner was homosexual, although Hitler is reported to have identified him as one. In Kurt Ludecke's I Knew Hitler, the Fuehrer said the following when the issue of homosexuality among the Brownshirts was raised: "Ach, why should I concern myself with the private lives of my followers!....I love Richard Wagner's music -- must I shut my ears to it because he was a pederast? The whole thing's absurd" (Ludeke:477f).

Nietzsche's philosophy was grounded in Greek and Roman paganism, and in his writings he called for "a new Caesar to transform the world" (Peters:viii). Years later, Nietzsche's sister and chief promoter, Elisabeth, would enthusiastically dub Hitler the "superman" her brother had predicted (ibid.:220). Indeed, Elisabeth's adulation of Hitler was mirrored by the _Fuehrer's_ admiration for her brother. Hitler and the Nazis were indebted to Nietzsche for his contribution to German nationalism. "It is not too much to say," writes historian George Lichtheim, "that but for Nietzsche the SS — Hitler's shock troops and the core of the whole movement — would have lacked the inspiration to carry our their programs of mass murder in Eastern Europe" (McIntyre:187). And W. Cleon Skousen writes that when "Hitler wrote _Mein Kampf,_ it was as though Nietzsche was speaking from the dead" (Skousen:348).

Had he lived in that era, Nietzsche might not have become a Nazi. His works include numerous condemnations of anti-Semitism and nationalism (and thus were selectively censored by Elizabeth). But the best measure of Nietzsche's contribution and importance to Nazism is not in conjectures about what Nietzsche might have thought about Nazism, but in the actual reverence of the Nazis for him. Nietzsche's most celebrated book, *Also Sprach Zarathustra*, ("Thus Spake Zarathustra") was considered the "bible" of the Hitler Youth and was "enshrined with Hitler's *Mein Kampf* and Alfred Rosenberg's <u>Myth of the Twentieth Century</u> -- in the vault of the Tannenberg Memorial, which had been erected to commemorate Germany's victory over Russia in the First World War" (Peters:221). Hitler and the Nazis often used Nietzschean phrases such as "will to power," "live dangerously," and "Superman," but more significantly, Nietzsche became a hero to the masses as well. Certain German intellectuals canonized Nietzsche through the popular media of the day. Peters writes,

> Germany's intellectual elite, including poets like Stefan George and writers like Thomas Mann, saw in Nietzsche's "aristocratic radicalism" an answer to the decadent democratic ideals of the West. Fervent young men and women met for ritualistic readings from Zarathustra. Hymns were composed to celebrate the new religion, and by the time the body of the sick philosopher was finally put to rest, he was proclaimed a saint (Peters:ix).

The Cultural Elites

Who were these "intellectuals" who popularized Nietzschean fascism in Germany? Stefan George, one of Germany's most popular poets of the time, was a pederast and "a guiding example" to the Community of the Elite. "George and his disciples," write Oosterhuis and Kennedy, "...revivified Holderlin's concept of *Griechendeutschen* (Hellenic Ger-

Stefan George

mans), [and] contrasted in their poetry and lifestyle the 'eternal spring of homoerotic friendship' from the family" (Oosterhuis and Kennedy:91). Homosexualist Ian Young wrote that "In George, aestheticism, Nietzscheanism and homosexual idealism were transmuted into a poetic philosophy" (Young:183).

In 1903, George became infatuated with a 15-year-old boy and made him a figure of worship in a 1907 book called *Der siebente Ring* ("The Seventh Ring"). His last book, *Das neue Reich* ("The New Kingdom"), published in 1928, "prophesied an era in which Germany would become a new Greece" (Miles in Grolier). In 1933, when Hitler came to power, he offered George the position of President of the Nazi Academy of Letters (a post which he turned down) (Mosse:60).

Thomas Mann's identification with Nietzsche may also have had something to do with the latter's homosexuality. Among other works, Mann is famous for a 1912 novella called *Der Tod in Venedig* ("Death in Venice"), in which "an aging writer risks life and reputation in his attempts to gaze on the Apollonian beauty of the 14-year-old Tadzio" (Reiter in Grolier). Homosexualist historian A.L. Rowse called this novella "the most publicized homosexual story of the century" (Rowse:212). A recently published biography, Thomas Mann: A Life, by Donald Prater, establishes the novelist's homosexuality. A review of this book in *The San Francisco Examiner* (December 23, 1995) states that the book is based in part on Mann's private diaries, which reveal a "secret homoerotic life."

Mann was married and had six children for whom he was "a remote and sometimes terrifying figure." The article reveals that two of these children, Klaus and Michael, committed suicide. Two of his children became homosexuals (Rowse:212). Mann confesses in his diary that the character Tadzio, the 14-year-old boy in "A Death in Venice," was actually modeled after a boy on whom Mann "devel-

oped a crush while holidaying in Venice." We must be clear, however, that Mann's contribution to Nazism, his role in popularizing Nietzsche, was unintended. Mann was personally anti-Nazi, and was *persona non grata* with Hitler's government..
    Nietzsche's influence extended beyond the German border. Adapting for its subject "the Nietzschean ecstasy" in the Italian art world, playwright Frank Wedekind's play, *Spring's Awakening,* features a cast of schoolboys whom he "allowed...to experience all forms of sexuality ...[including] masturbation, heterosexual promiscuity and..homosexual love making between the boys" (Mosse:61). Benito Mussolini himself acknowledged a debt of gratitude to Nietzsche during his dictatorship (Peters:212).
    Nietzsche's sister, Elisabeth, figured prominently in pre-Nazi and Nazi Germany. After Nietzsche's death in 1900, she assumed control of his estate and relentlessly promoted her brother's writings, establishing the Nietzsche Archives. During the Weimar Republic the Archives became "the center of a powerful counter-revolutionary current" of German nationalism (ibid.:206). At one point Nietzsche's followers wanted to build a Nietzsche Temple, complete with statues of Apollo and Dionysos (ibid.:200). While the temple was never built, Adolf Hitler himself commissioned a shrine to Nietzsche, a memorial auditorium and library "where German youth could be taught Nietzsche's doctrine of a master race" (ibid.:222). The *Friedrich Nietzsche zum Gedachinis erbaut* ("Friedrich Nietzsche Memorial Building") was opened in August of 1938 (McIntyre:192).
    An interesting aside to this story is the fact that in 1886 Elisabeth Nietzsche and her husband founded a colony in Paraguay, South America called *Nueva Germania* ("New Germany"). After the fall of the Third Reich, *Nueva Germania* sheltered hundreds of fleeing Nazi war criminals, including the infamous Dr. Joseph Mengele

Hitler is greeted by Elizabeth Nietzsche (insert) at the Nietzsche Archive which he sponsored.

(McIntyre: 5,205ff). Another interesting fact is that Rudolf Steiner, who would later found the occultic Anthroposophical Society, was briefly involved with Elisabeth in the management of the Nietzsche Archives.

Frederich Nietzsche's influence on the Nazis is reflected in all they did. "Become hard and show no mercy," Nietzsche taught, "for evil is man's best force" (Peters:227). One wonders whether history might have been different if Germans had been aware that the writings of their fascist "genius" may have been influenced by impaired brain function "caused by...the tertiary phase of cerebral syphilis" (ibid.:35). In 1902, a doctor by the name of P.J. Mobius attempted to warn his countrymen "that they should beware of Nietzsche, for his works were the products of a diseased brain" (ibid.:184). Unfortunately for the world, Mobius's report was squelched by Elisabeth and her powerful friends.

The attraction of fascism for homosexuals appears in the history of other countries as well. As we noted earlier, pro-Nazi fascist organizations in both England and France were headed by homosexuals. In England, the organization was called the Anglo-German Fellowship, and was headed by British homosexuals Guy Francis de Moncy Burgess, and Captain John Robert Macnamara. (As an aside, while we cannot state conclusively that they acted with treasonous motives, it must be noted that homosexual political activists played a major role in the appeasement of Hitler prior to World War II (Noebel:128ff)).

In France, the pro-Nazi fascists were represented by two groups, the Radical Socialist Party headed by Edouard Pfeiffer (Secretary General), and the French Popular Party headed by Jacques Doriot. Pfeiffer was openly homosexual. Less is known about Doriot, but, as we have shown, his organization seems to have to have had an attraction for homosexuals in any case (Costello:300ff.).

The Belgian fascist "Rexist" movement was led by Leon Degrelle "who would come to regard himself as the spiritual son of Hitler" (Toland:410). In Austria, it was Artur Seyss-Inquart, who, after Hitler's ascension to power was "appointed Minister of the Interior, with full, unlimited control of the nation's police

Seyss-Inquart (left) and unknown Nazi official with Hitler.

forces" (ibid.:434). In Norway, it was the infamous Vidkum Quisling, whose very surname became synonymous with "traitor." Igra identifies all of these men as homosexual (Igra:86). A "top leader" of the Nazi Party in Czechoslovakia was also homosexual (Oosterhuis:243).

A connection between homosexuality and fascism in Germany's military allies is implied by historian Mary Beard In The Sex Life of the Unmarried Adult she writes that "the Fascist movement in Germany, as in Italy and Japan, is essentially a dynamic of unmarried males...Adolph Hitler, [is] a bachelor like the majority of the thirty or forty leaders of the Nazi Party...A number of the prominent Nazis are men with records of sexual perversions as well as of military daring" (Beard:158). Homosexualists John Lauritsen and David Thorstad report that in the Soviet Union, homosexuality became known as "the fascist perversion" during the 1930's. They quote the Soviet writer, Maxim Gorky: "There is already a slogan in Germany, 'Eradicate the homosexual and fascism will disappear'" (Lauritsen and Thorstad:69).

Wilhelm Reich, author of The Mass Psychology of Fascism was a prominent German psychoanalyst when Hitler came to power in 1933. He wrote that homosexuality was the breeding ground of fascism. In 1936, fellow psychiatrist Erich Fromm echoed this view and also linked homosexuality with sado-masochism (Oosterhuis:242). This link has been widely recognized in past decades. Oosterhuis writes,

> Dutch liberal anarchist Anton Constandse...claimed that "because most National Socialist organizations are typically all-male societies, homosexuality was inevitable....Everybody knows that the sexual abuse of youths was quite common in Roehm's SA." From this he inferred that "the great danger of male bonding, especially in the military, is indeed homosexuality." The anti-fascist journal *Het Fundament*, published in Holland, also character-

ized homosexuality as typical of fascism.... [F]eminist Maria Antonietta Macciocchi ...[wrote of] the extreme misogyny of "the brotherhood of male chauvinist fascists and homosexual Nazis." Susan Sontag explained the popularity of sadomasochism in the gay subculture...simply as an "eroticizing of Nazism." According to her, "there is a natural link" between homosexual sadomasochism and fascism. The stereotype was also made visible in such films as Luchino Visconti's *The Damned* (1969), Bernardo Bertolucci's *The Conformist* (1971), Pier Paolo Pasolini's *Salo or the 120 Days of Sodom* (1975), and Volker Schlondorff's *The Tin Drum* (1978) - (Oosterhuis:244f).

We can see that the roots of Nazism are fundamentally interrelated with the homosexuality of its philosophers; a fact noted by many prominent writers and thinkers. (Although it may be mere coincidence we are reminded that the Latin root of fascism is *fasces*, "a bundle of rods." A diminutive of fasces is "faggot," a common pejorative for homosexuals.) In the lives of such men as Plato, Frederick the Great, and Nietzsche, whose writings and deeds were foundational to modern fascism, the common denominator is homosexual behavior. Certainly not every fascist has been homosexual, just as not every homosexual has been fascist. But the glaring truth of history is that contemporary German homosexuals bore a disproportionately large share of the responsibility for the rise of Nazism.

We have now looked at three separate and distinct realms of pre-Nazi German society which contributed to the formation and success of the Nazi Party. In the German "gay rights" movement we saw the pederastic origins of the Hellenic revival and its influence on the youth and *Freikorps* movements. We also saw how the rift between the "Butch" and "Fem" factions of the homosexual movement laid the groundwork for the mistreatment of some homosexuals later on in the Nazi regime.

In the realm of pagan religion we saw the importance of homosexuality in occultism and the influence of occultism in the development of Nazi thought. We have noted that many of the prominent occultists who influenced the growth of Nazism were homosexuals, and that a number of the early Nazis themselves were both homosexuals and occultists. Finally, we have seen that homosexuals and pederasts were integral to the creation and development of fascism and National Socialist philosophy.

Now that we have explored the relationship between homosexuality and the aspects of German thought and culture which led to the development of Nazism, we can begin to examine more closely the formation and early years of the Nazi Party itself, as well as the individuals, including Hitler, who led the Nazi movement.

143

Chapter Four

THE FOUNDING AND EARLY YEARS
OF THE NAZI PARTY

What was to become the Nazi Party began as an outgrowth of the Thule Society in late 1918. It started as a nationalist discussion group called the Political Worker's Circle whose goal was to "extend the appeal of the Thule's nationalist ideology for the working classes" (Goodrick-Clarke:150). The discussion group developed the idea of forming a political party in December of 1918, and did so on January 5, 1919, at the *Fuerstenfelder Hof* tavern in Munich. Adolf Hitler became a member of the German Worker's Party in September of that year. Shirer writes,

> There were two members of this insignificant party who deserve mention at this point; both were to prove important in the rise of Hitler...Captain Ernst Roehm...had joined the party before Hitler...A tough, ruthless, driving man — albeit, like so many of the early Nazis, a homosexual — he helped organize the first Nazi strong-arm squads which grew into the SA...Dietrich Eckart...often called the spiritual founder of National Socialism...became a close advisor to [Hitler]...introducing him to...such future aides as Rudolf Hess (Shirer:64f).

In a very short time Hitler and Roehm began to wrest control of the small group from its founders. Within a few months they had forced the resignation of its Chairman, Karl Harrar, and begun to turn the group away from its origins as a secret society and toward a new identity as "a mass party" (Fest, 1975:120). On April 1, 1920, they changed the name of the party to the National Socialist German Worker's Party. Historian Joachim Fest describes the process Hitler and Roehm used in these earliest days of Nazism:

> At the beginning [Hitler] went at things according to a sensible plan. His first task was a personal one, to break out of anonymity, to emerge from the welter of small-time nationalist-racist parties with an unmistakable image...making a name for himself — by unceasing activity, by brawls, scandals, and riots, even by terrorism if that would bring him to the forefront...[but] Ernst Roehm did more for the NSDAP than anyone else. He held the rank of captain as a political advisor on the staff of Colonel Epp and was the real brain of the disguised military regime in Bavaria. Roehm provided the young National Socialist Party with followers, arms, and funds (Fest, 1975:126f).

By August of 1921, Hitler and Roehm had completed their takeover of the party. On the third of that month they founded the SA and began to assemble the cadre of sexual deviants who would form the core of Nazi leadership for years to come. A pamphlet circulated by disgruntled Nazi members prior to the Hitler takeover shows that the homosexuality of his supporters was no secret. Speaking of Hitler they said, "It grows more and more clear that his purpose is simply to use the National Socialist Party as a springboard for his immoral purposes" (Igra:70f). Former high Nazi functionary and close Hitler confidant, Otto Strasser reports,

Hitler did three things to popularize the party and quiet the threatening clash of wounded vanities. He shortened the name from Nationalsozialistische Deutsche Arbeiterpartei to the letters NSDAP; he adopted the brown shirt of Lieutenant Rossbach's veteran organization for the entire party; and he assumed the all-too-familiar swastika from Erhardt's group (Strasser, 1943:34).

Left to right: Rudolf Hess, Adolf Hitler, Ernst Roehm, Heinrich Himmler and Wolf von Helldorf. Each of these top Nazi leaders was a known or reputed homosexual.

Hitler's Clique of Pederasts

As we will see, almost all of the new leadership of the party were sexual deviants. But this fact raises a question that is foundational to our understanding of the Nazis. Who chose these men as Nazi leaders? Roehm, with whose lifestyle we are now quite familiar, was to some historians the true power behind Hitler's throne. As noted above it was primarily Roehm who organized, funded and armed the terrorist military arm of the party, choosing only homosexuals as officers. And it is true that the party met frequently in the *Bratwurstgloeckl* (Fest, 1975:135f), a homosexual bar where Roehm kept a reserved table.

Yet, despite Roehm's importance to the party, Adolf Hitler himself was the central figure of Nazism and increasingly it was he who determined the fate of every member of the party. Despite suggestions to the contrary, Hitler was not anti-homosexual. In fact, like Roehm, Hitler *preferred* homosexual companions and co-workers. In addition to Roehm and Hess, two of his closest friends, Hitler apparently chose homosexuals and other sexual deviants to fill key positions nearest to himself. Heiden reports that in fact Hitler intentionally "surrounded himself with men of... [homosexual] tendencies" (Heiden, 1935:417).

Rector attempts to dismiss sources that attribute homosexuality to leading Nazis, but nevertheless lists them in some detail:

> Reportedly, Hitler Youth leader, Baldur von Schirach was bisexual; Hitler's private attorney, Reich Legal Director, Minister of Justice, butcher Governor-General of Poland, and public gay-hater Hans Frank was said to be a homosexual; Hitler's adjutant Wilhelm Bruckner was said to be
>
>
>
> bisexual;...Walther Funk, Reich Minister of Economics [and Hitler's personal financial advisor] has frequently been called a "notorious" homosexual...or as a jealous predecessor in Funk's post, Hjalmar Schacht, contemptuously claimed, Funk was a "harmless homosexual and alcoholic;"...[Hitler's second in command] Hermann Goering liked to dress up in drag and wear campy make-up; and so on and so forth (Rector:57).

Wilhelm Bruckner

Igra, who confidently asserts that the above men were homosexuals, cites still other Hitler aides and close friends who were known homosexuals. He states that Hitler's chauffeur and one-time personal secretary, Emile Maurice, for example, was homosexual, as well as the pornographer,

Julius Streicher, whom Hitler appointed *Gauleiter* of Nuremberg. Igra writes,

Julius Streicher, the notorious Jew-baiter, was originally a school teacher, but was dismissed by the Nuremberg School Authorities, following numerous charges of pederasty brought against him...His paper, Der Stuermer, was frequently confiscated by the police, even at the height of the Nazi regime, because of the sexual obscenities displayed in the drawings and described in the text" (Igra:72f).

A rare sight (above) as Hitler relinquishes the stage to his close friend, Julius Streicher. The two are caught on camera (below) on a private outing.

Among the homosexuals closest to Hitler, Heiden lists "Heines, Reiner, Ernst, Von Helldorf, Count Spreti [and]

Count du Moulin-Eckhardt, jr" (Heiden, 1935:417).

The evidence for homosexual leanings in another leading Nazi, Joseph Goebbels, is rather thin, but adds further insight to the inner workings of the group. Goebbels, Reich propaganda leader and close aide to the *Fuehrer*, is reported to have had a party in 1936 that degenerated into a violent homosexual orgy. The party featured "torch-bearing page boys in tight fitting white breeches, white satin blouses with lace cuffs and powdered rococo wigs" (Grunberger:70). Grunberger writes that Nazi roughnecks "were so affected

Gregor Strasser (left), Joseph Goebbels and unidentified boy (possibly his stepson).

by the rococo setting that they hurled themselves upon the bewigged page boys and pulled them into the bushes. Tables collapsed, torches were dimmed, and in the ensuing fracas a number of Party old fighters and their comely victims had to be rescued from drowning" (ibid:70).

Goebbels may not have participated in the revelry himself, though Klaus Theweleit writes that "there is a significant moment in Rossbach's account where he contests the right of Goebbels 'of all people' to act as a 'moral arbiter,'" apparently assuming that his meaning is "'common knowledge' on the internal grapevine" (Theweleit, Vol 2:327).

Ralf George Reuth, in Goebbels (Harcourt Brace, New York, 1993), reports that Goebbels was accused by Roehm of pederasty. After Roehm's homosexuality was exposed in the German press, Goebbels [a longtime rival] tried to get him dismissed from the party. "Roehm took revenge by spreading in return all sorts of rumors about Goebbels' relationship with Magda Quandt. He went so far as to suggest that Goebbels was interested less in Magda than in her young son. So along with Roehm's homosexual excesses, people were talking about the "cloven foot's 'impossible (and immoral) relationship'" (Reuth:138f). (Goebbels' club foot apparently gave rise to the epithet.). We also know that homosexual SA figure Wolf von Helldorf escaped assassination in the Roehm purge due only to intervention by Goebbels (Reuth:137).

In his own diaries, Goebbels revealed an animosity toward homosexuals in the party, although that does not prove he did not have such inclinations himself. Diaries are, after all, generally written with one's posterity in mind.

Another close Hitler associate was Albert Speer. An October 30, 1995 book review in Newsweek, titled "Inside a Third Reich Insider" featured the book Albert Speer: His Battle With Truth by Gitta Sereny. The article speaks of a "homo-erotic (not sexual) relationship" between Speer and Hitler that was discussed in a previous book by a German psychoanalyst, Alexander Mitscherlich. Sereny writes that "Speer himself acknowledged that Mitscherlich 'came closest to the truth.'" Although Sereny claims this relationship was non-sexual, he reports that Speer's secretary said Speer gave himself to Hitler "body and soul." Sereny also observes that Speer never told Hitler he was married because of his "romantic" feelings for Hitler. (Sereny:109).

In Albert Speer: The End of a Myth, German historian Dr. Matthais Schmidt commented on an "erotic" element to Speer's relationship with Hitler. While Speer was remodeling Hitler's official residence, Hitler invited him to lunch. "At lunch, Speer sat at Hitler's side. The conversation became personal — and the two men 'fell in love at first sight'" (Schmidt:41f). Aside from these insinuations we have no evidence of an actual homosexual relationship between Hitler and Speer.

Langer writes in the 1940s that "[e]ven today Hitler derives sexual pleasure from looking at men's bodies and associating with homosexuals" (Langer:179). He adds, quoting Strasser, that Hitler's personal body-guard was "almost always 100% homosexuals" (ibid.:179).

It should be remembered that Hitler's greatest hero was

Hitler's personal SS bodyguard.

Frederick the Great, a well known homosexual (Garde:44). Clearly, Adolf Hitler was not anti-homosexual, at least not in his personal lifestyle. Indeed, the evidence of Hitler's apparent preference for homosexuals is so overwhelming that, as have many historians before us, we naturally ask the question, "Was Hitler a homosexual?"

Was Adolf Hitler a Homosexual?

Until the publication of Professor Lothar Machtan's powerful biography The Hidden Hitler in 2001, we were much less confident in stating that Hitler was indeed a homosexual. Machtan, a history professor in Bremen, Germany, set out to prove Hitler's homosexuality and did so most convincingly, drawing upon hundreds of period documents. We shall consider the evidence at length.

One point upon which we remain unconvinced was whether Hitler was exclusively homosexual or whether he had relations with women. Machtan writes,

> [A] small number of contemporaries...were pretty explicit on the subject of Hitler's sex life. These include August Kubizek, Kurt Ludecke, Ernst Hanfstaengl, Rudolf Diels, Erich Ebermayer, Eugen Dollman, Christa Schroder and Hans Severus Ziegler. They are all unanimous in stating, quite positively, that Hitler did not have sex with women. Some of them expressly say that Hitler was homosexual; others convey the same thing obliquely (Machtan:23)

There are at least four women, however, including his own niece, Gely, with whom Hitler is reported to have had sexual relationships. These relationships were not normal, if in fact they occurred. Both Waite and Langer write that Hitler was a coprophile (a person who is sexually aroused by human excrement) and suggest that his sexual encounters with women included expressions of this perversion as

Hitler with the Rubal family. Gely, as an adult, is at far right. She committed suicide in 1931, not long after this picture was taken..

well as other extremely degrading forms of masochism. It is interesting to note that all of these women attempted suicide after allegedly becoming sexually involved with Hitler. Two succeeded (Langer:175f). Hitler contemporary Otto Strasser writes of an encounter he had with Hitler's niece Gely:

> Next day Gely came to see me. She was red eyed, her round little face was wan, and she had the terrified look of a hunted beast. "He locked me up," she sobbed. "He locks me up every time I say no!" She did not need much questioning. With anger, horror and disgust she told me of the strange propositions with which her uncle pestered her. I knew all about Hitler's abnormality. Like all the others in the know, I had heard all about the eccentric practices to which Fraulein Hoffmann was alleged to have lent herself, but I had genuinely believed that the photographer's daughter was a little hysteric who told lies for the sheer fun of it. But Gely, who was completely ignorant of this other affair of her uncle's, confirmed point by point a story

scarcely credible to a healthy-minded man (Strasser, 1940:72).

Langer suggests that Hitler may very well have engaged in homosexual behavior, saying "persons suffering from his perversion sometimes do indulge in homosexual practices in the hope that they might find some sexual gratification. Even this perversion would be more acceptable to them than the one with which they are afflicted." (Langer:179). He reports, for example on the testimony of Hermann Rauschning, a trusted Hitler confidante whom Hitler appointed President of the Danzig Senate in 1932 (Wistrich:240, Snyder:282). He later fell out of favor and fled Germany in 1936 (ibid.). Langer writes,

Rauschning reports that he has met two boys who claimed that they were Hitler's homosexual partners, but their testimony can hardly be taken at face value. More condemning would be the remarks dropped by [Albert] Foerster, the Danzig gauleiter, in conversation with Rauschning. Even here, however, the remarks deal only with Hitler's impotence as far as heterosexual relationships go without actually implying that he indulges in homosexuality. It is probably true that Hitler

Albert Foerster

calls Foerster "Bubi," which is a common nickname employed by homosexuals in addressing their partners. This alone is not adequate proof that he has actually indulged in homosexual practices with Foerster, who is known to be a homosexual (Langer:178). [Significantly, Foerster was Julius Streicher's protégé.]

Waite concurs:

There is insufficient evidence to warrant the conclusion that Hitler was an overt homosexual. But it seems clear that he had latent homosexual tendencies...It is true that Hitler was closely associated with Ernst Roehm and Rudolf Hess, two homosexuals who were among the very few people with whom he used the familiar *du* ["thou"]. But one cannot conclude that he therefore shared his friends' sexual tastes. Still, during the months he was with Hess in Landsberg, their relationship must have become very close. When Hitler left the prison he fretted about his friend who languished there, and spoke of him tenderly, using Austrian diminutives: "Ach mein Rudy, mein Hesserl, isn't it appalling to think that he's still there." One of Hitler's valets, Schneider, made no explicit statement about the relationship, but he did find it strange that whenever Hitler got a present he liked or drew an architectural sketch that particularly pleased him, he would run to Hess — who was known in homosexual circles as "Fraulein Anna" — as a little boy would run to his mother to show his prize to her...Finally there is the nonconclusive but interesting fact that one of Hitler's prized possessions was a handwritten love letter which King Ludwig II had written to a manservant (Waite, 1977:283f). [*Hess was known by other names in the German "gay" subculture. In recent years, long sealed Soviet archives have been opened to the West. In <u>Deadly Illusions</u>, authors John Costello and Oleg Tsarev report of seeing the "so-called 'Black Bertha'*

Hitler, Maurice and Hess in Landsberg Prison (dark-suited man is unidentified).

Adolf Hitler's homosexual chauffeur Emile Maurice is seen here in Hitler's first automobile.

file, named from Hess's reported nickname in Berlin and Munich" (Costello and Tsarev:xix).]

Other writers offer similar assessments. According to Wilfried Daim, Frau Elsa Schmidt-Falk of the Nazi Genealogy Office of Munich observed that Hitler was so enraptured by the '*maennerbuendleische*' (the young male students) on parade, that on this fact alone she concluded that Hitler was at least unconsciously homosexual (Daim:41). Desmond Seward, in Napoleon and Hitler, quotes Italian dictator, Benito Mussolini, who referred to Hitler as "that horrible sexual degenerate" (Seward:148). He also reports that "the files of the Viennese police list him [Hitler] as a homosexual" (Seward:299). Writer Charlotte Wolff, M.D. quotes Magnus Hirschfeld about Hitler in her book Magnus Hirschfeld. (Hirschfeld, you will remember, was Director of the Sex Research Institute of Berlin which was destroyed by Hitler in 1934.

About three years before the Nazis came to power we had

a patient at the Institute who had a liaison with Roehm. We were on good terms with him, and he told us a good deal of what happened in his circle...He also referred to Adolf Hitler in the oddest possible manner. 'Afi is the most perverted of us all. He is very much like a soft woman,

Ironically, Hitler's machismo was a false front to hide an effeminacy of which he was ashamed.

but now he makes great propaganda in the heroic morale'" (Wolff:438).

Adolf, the Boy Prostitute

In Germany's National Vice, Samuel Igra wrote that as a young man Hitler "had been a male prostitute in Vienna and Munich" (Igra:67). Lending credence to this is the fact that for quite a long time Hitler "chose to live in a Vienna flophouse known to be inhabited by many homosexuals" (Langer:192). That "flophouse" was the *Meldemannstrasse* Hostel. Hitler's long-time "gay" friend Ernst Hanfstaengl identified this residence as "a place where elderly men went in search of young men for homosexual pleasures" (Machtan:56). "It was an open secret at the beginning of the 20th century," adds Machtan, "that municipal hostels for homeless males were hubs of homosexual activity...[where many young men] kept themselves afloat by engaging in prostitution. Hitler spent over three years in this environment" (Machtan:51).

This would help to explain Hitler's close relationships to his purportedly homosexual patrons Dietrich Eckart and Karl Haushofer. Rector writes that, as a young man, Hitler was often called *"Der Schoen Adolf"* ("the handsome

Adolf") and that later his looks "were also to some extent helpful in gaining big-money support from Ernst Roehm's circle of wealthy gay friends" (Rector:52).

But Hitler was apparently not involved with homosexuality solely to survive financially. Even in his pre-Nazi years, most of Hitler's reputed homosexual encounters were consensual meetings in which no money changed hands. Machtan suggests that each of Hitler's longer-term relationships in his youth -- with Reinhold Hanisch, August Kubizek, Rudolf Hausler and Ernst Hanfstaengl -- were homosexual "love affairs."

There are numerous other incidents ("one night stands") in which Hitler was purported to have been the solicitor and not the solicited one. Eugen Dollman, former member of Himmler's staff and one-time Hitler interpreter, cited testimonies from the files of the Munich vice squad in which a series of young men identified Hitler as the man who had "picked them up" on the streets for homosexual relations (Machtan:135ff). Dollman himself was also homosexual (ibid.).

Additional allegations addressed homosexual conduct by Hitler during the first World War. The so-called "Mend Protocol," a document prepared by German military intelligence under Admiral Canaris, contains the testimony of Hans Mend. Considered highly credible, Mend had this to say about Hitler:

> Meanwhile, we had gotten to know Hitler better. We noticed that he never looked at a woman. We suspected him of homosexuality right away, because he was known to be abnormal in any case. He was extremely eccentric and displayed womanish characteristics which tended in that direction....In 1915 we were billeted in the Le Febre brewery at Fournes. We slept in the hay. Hitler was bedded down at night with "Schmidl," his male whore. We heard a rustling in the hay. Then someone switched on his electric flashlight and growled, "Take a look at those two

Ernst Schmidt (left) and Hitler (right) during World War I.

nancy boys." I myself took no further interest in the matter (Ibid:68)

Hitler and "Schmidl" (Ernst Schmidt) were, in Schmidt's words, "always together" during their war years. They remained very close friends and were occasional housemates for over thirty years (ibid.:89ff).

A year or so after the incident described by Mend, Hitler supposedly "posed nude for a homosexual officer named Lammers -- a Berlin artist in civilian life -- and subsequently went to bed with him" (ibid.:100). This may be the incident to which Rauschning referred when he later told U.S. Investigators "that Lance Corporal Hitler and an officer had been charged with engaging in sexual relations" (ibid.).

The homosexual connection certainly helps to explain how Hitler became involved with the nationalists generally, and Ernst Roehm specifically, after the war. It is likely that Roehm's homosexual inclinations were the reason that Colonel Ritter von Epp, the Freikorps commander, chose

Roehm as his adjutant. "There are many indications that the relationship between Roehm and Epp was homoerotic," writes Machtan,"and Hitler once let slip in later years that Roehm's homosexuality first became known around 1920" (ibid.:106f). Roehm, in turn, brought Hitler into the homoerotic Freikorps brotherhood.

The Bayreuth Connection

We have mentioned above that Hitler allegedly identified his favorite composer, Richard Wagner, as a pederast. We are not certain that this is true. What is certain is that Wagner's Bayreuth was "a notorious international rendezvous for prominent homosexuals" whose absorption with Wagner achieved "a cultlike quality" (ibid.:39). One factor in this attraction may have been that Wagner's sons Richard and Siegfried were homosexuals. Richard later committed suicide (ibid.:254). Siegfried, pressured to have an heir, married a woman much younger than himself and had several children but surreptiously continued his homosexual affairs (Wagner:p.197).

Hitler was very close to the Wagner family and spent a great deal of time in Bayreuth. He made numerous private visits there between 1925 and 1933, often with male homosexual companions (ibid.:253ff). One common companion was Julius Schreck, whose photograph hung beside that of Hitler's beloved mother in his (Hitler's) private quarters (ibid.:174f). Machtan cites one incident, however, in which he and Schreck failed to keep an appointment to vacation with their Bayreuth hosts. Instead, Schreck and Hitler turned aside at the *Bad Berneck* health resort, some 20 miles away, where they spent Christmas alone -- the only guests at the inn (ibid.:174).

Hitler may have had yet darker motives for visiting the Wagner home. Only recently revealed is the accusation by Wagner family members "that Hitler sexually abused the

Hitler with Siegfried and Winifred Wagner and their sons (Richard Wagner's grandsons) Wolfgang (left) and Wieland.

young Wieland [Wagner's grandson, now past 75] during the '20s." These allegations came to light in a *Time* magazine interview with American author and former diplomat to Germany, Frederic Spotts, whose research for the book Bayreuth (about the Wagnerian opera festival of the same name) included interviews with the Wagner family (*Time*, August 15, 1994:56).

"Spotts says that his original source was one of Wieland's own children...Now a respected academic, Spotts says it was while he was researching "Bayreuth" that he interviewed his source -- who, he insists, is totally reliable and has no reason to lie. Spotts writes:

This family member told me Hitler sexually abused Wieland in the 1920s when the boy was a preadolescent'...Hitler, who idolized Richard Wagner's supernationalistic operas (as well as his anti-Semitism), had become a close friend of Wieland's mother's. Winifred Wagner gave him the run of the child's nursery. Far from being revolted by what allegedly happened to him, Wieland avidly collaborated with his right-wing family during World War II (*Penthouse*, undated:32).

Weiland later became Hitler's protégé (Wagner:228) and was exempted from military service by Hitler's personal intervention (ibid.:105). The weight of the evidence indicates that Hitler was deeply involved in a series of short and long-term homosexual relationships. Even more certain is that he knowingly and deliberately surrounded himself with practicing homosexuals from the time he was a teenager. His later public pronouncements against homosexuality were designed to hide the life-long intimacy -- sexual and/or homoerotic -- which he maintained with the various men he knew and accepted as homosexuals.

Finally, in our look at Adolf Hitler, the man, we turn to Samuel Igra, a Jew who fled Germany in 1939 after twenty years of observing Hitler and the Nazis:

> For the purposes of the present investigations Hitler is important for what he has represented...when he embarked the German people on the policy that brought about the world catastrophe. He was the central figure around which a number of men grouped themselves, from the 1920's onwards, in a movement to gain supreme control of the German people. As the movement developed they were aided and abetted and supported financially as well as politically by the industrial capitalists of the Rhineland; but the initiative did not come from the latter. It came from Hitler as the condottiere [leader] of a band of evil men who were united together by a common vice [homosexuality] (Igra:26).

While the Nazis promoted a hypermasculine ideal, Herman Goering (seen here in rouge and make-up) was reputedly a transvestite.
Yad vashem

The Nazi Rise to Power

Through the 1920s, Hitler continued to capitalize on the political unrest of the German people to build the Nazi organization. The party's public image was greatly enhanced by the recruitment of Hermann Goering, a former World

War I fighter ace who was revered as a war hero. Goering was probably not a homosexual though he was said to have been very fond of "painting his nails and putting rouge on his cheeks" (Fuchs:160). He joined the party after hearing a speech by Hitler in which he vowed to rebuild Germany's military and throw off the yoke of the Treaty of Versailles. Hitler immediately set him to the task of training the SA as a military organization (Toland:123), an accomplishment that further increased Nazi power.

By the fall of 1922, Hitler had become the symbol of renewed German nationalism to many in Germany, although the average citizen had little knowledge of Hitler's personal life or the lives of the Nazi leaders. At this point Hitler believed he would ultimately assume power in Germany through military strength, and he was not terribly concerned with portraying an image of morality. "The Party newspaper," writes Edouard Calic, "explained that Hitler wanted to organize the movement on a military basis to achieve power, and that if it was necessary he would lead an uprising to renounce the Versailles Treaty" (Calic:33). However, his attempt to implement his plan in the infamous Beer Hall *Putsch* proved so disastrous that Hitler was forced to develop a different strategy.

On November 8, 1923, Hitler attempted to take advantage of a period of political turmoil to seize control of the government of Bavaria. This ill-fated maneuver (later dubbed the Beer Hall *Putsch*) not only failed militarily, it put Hitler in prison for nine months, thus nearly ending the party. When he was finally released from Landsberg prison on December 20, 1924, he announced that thereafter the Nazi Party would seek power through legitimate political means (ibid:64). This decision put the actions and goals of the party to the test of public opinion. Immediately, Hitler was confronted with this challenge. Shirer describes the internal condition of the party:

...in those years when Hitler was shaping his party to take over Germany's destiny he had his fill of troubles with his chief lieutenants who constantly quarreled not only among themselves but with him. He, who was so monumentally intolerant by his very nature, was strangely tolerant of one human condition -- a man's morals. No other party in Germany came near to attracting so many shady characters...pimps, murderers, homosexuals... Hitler did not care, as long as they were useful to him. When he emerged from prison he found not only that they were at each other's throats but there was a demand from the more prim and respectable leaders such as Rosenberg and Ludendorf that the criminals and especially the perverts be expelled from the movement. This Hitler frankly refused to do. (Shirer:173).

Rudolf Hess (far right) and other early Nazis upon their release from prison after serving time for involvement in the Beer Hall *Putsch*.

Hitler learned that public opinion was not with him in the matter of homosexuality, despite Germany's international reputation as a haven for homosexuals. Incriminating letters which had been stolen from Roehm by a male prostitute (Plant:60) became a public matter when Roehm took the matter to court (Hohne:81). This, of course, exacerbated the conflict among Hitler's lieutenants, and led Hitler to initialize the first in a series of public relations efforts to hide Nazi perversions from the German people. The greater part of these conflicts, interestingly, were between the homosexuals themselves who, according to Shirer "quarreled and feuded as only men of unnatural sexual inclinations, with their peculiar jealousies, can" (Shirer:172). He writes,

By 1926...the charges and countercharges hurled by the Nazi Chieftains at one another became so embarrassing that Hitler set up a party court to settle them and prevent his comrades from washing their dirty linen in public. This was known as the USCHLA from Untersuchung-und-Schlichtungs-Ausschuss — Committee for Investigation and Settlement. Its first head was a former general, Heinemann, but he was unable to grasp the real purpose of the court, which was not to pronounce judgment on those accused of common

Hitler's personal attorney, Hans Frank, was also a homosexual.

crimes but to hush them up and see that they did not disturb party discipline or the authority of the Leader. So the general was replaced by...Major Walter Buch, who was given two assistants. One was Ulrichs Graf, the former butcher who had been Hitler's bodyguard; the other was Hans Frank, a young Nazi lawyer...This fine judicial triumvirate performed to the complete satisfaction of the

Fuehrer. A party leader might be accused of the most ne-
farious crime. Buch's answer was, "Well, what of it?"
(ibid.:174).

Obviously, the act of assigning Buch, Graf and Frank to
this intra-party "court" rendered it a complete sham (at
least in regard to homosexual crimes), since all were homosexuals. The only purpose of this and later efforts ostensibly designed to address charges of sexual perversion among
the Nazis was to hide the truth from the public. Here is the
root of Nazi "anti-homosexual" policies.

As Nazi power grew, Hitler became increasingly
dependent on the support of the German population. And,
understandably enough, the German people were at the
same time growing increasingly disgusted with the debaucheries taking place in German cities. This twofold influence on Hitler led him to take ever more hard-line public
stands against homosexuality in order to cover up the truth
about the party. The severity of his public reactions to each
new scandal (especially the later ones) mitigated the impact
of rumors which constantly circulated in German society
about Nazi leaders. Hitler's strategy regarding all moral issues was to craft his rhetoric carefully "in order not to of-
fend the sensibilities of the people" (Mosse:159).

Roehm, of course, presented a particularly difficult
problem for the Nazis because of his militant support for
what we know today as "gay rights." His SA men began to
be referred to by the anti-Nazis as the "Brown Fairies"
(Rector:56). Some time after Roehm's exposure as a
homosexual (in his 1925 trial against the male prostitute,
Herman Siegeseites,) he left Germany to take a post in the
Bolivian Army. It is unclear whether he made this move in
response to a personal sense of disgrace about the
publicizing of his pederastic activities, or whether Hitler
had convinced him to get out of the public eye for the good

Roehm's SA troops, seen here leafletting prior to an election, became known as the "Brown Fairies."

of the party. In any case, Roehm's absence was only temporary. Plant writes,

> In 1929 a party squabble threatened to tear the SA apart; a rebel group under Captain Walter Stennes had started a mutiny. Stennes taunted Roehm's stalwarts at a rally, dismissing them as "sissies in frilly underwear who couldn't order their boys around." As the rebellion grew more serious, Hitler ordered his old friend to return to Germany. Roehm did not hesitate to heed his Fuehrer's call and his armed squads quickly and ruthlessly suppressed the mutineers (Plant:60f).

While Roehm was away, the Nazis had been fairly successful at keeping their perversions out of sight. Most of the Nazis remained "in the closet," or at least out of situations that their political enemies could use against them. This, of course, changed when Roehm returned. Once again, stories of Roehm's exploits were passed along the grapevine. It would be old news, however, that hurt the Nazis again when Roehm's damaging letters were published by the newspapers belonging to the Social Democrats. These, along with articles on the homosexual practices of subordinate SA leaders, were published on the occasion of Roehm's appointment to head the SA (Oosterhuis and Kennedy:239n). "Social Democrats and Communists," write Oosterhuis and Kennedy, "suggested [in their newspapers] that nepotism and abuse of power in the SA and the Hitler Youth had contributed to making homosexuality an essential characteristic of the fascist system" (ibid.:251). Herzer comments that the press campaign against Roehm "invoked the possibility that 'large segments of German youth' could be led to homosexuality through abuse of military authority by SA members, most of whom were teenagers" (Herzer:225n). He writes:

> The prospect of Roehm's exploiting his military authority over young Nazis for his "private" interests was the target of such headlines in the leftist press as "Captain Roehm Abuses Unemployed Young Workers," "Fox Guards Chicken Coop," or Physical and Moral Health of German Youth at Stake." It could scarcely go unremarked...that regulations otherwise rigorously implemented were suspended precisely in the Nazis private army, that the professional proscription of homosexuality that applied to every teacher, every officer, and every church functionary

Reunion of the "Old Fighters" who had been with Hitler in the early days of the Nazi movement.

did not apply among the Nazis (Herzer:214).

Hitler, confronted with this threat to the Nazi image, responded with a dual strategy. He first offered a limited defense of Roehm, saying, "His private life cannot be an object of scrutiny unless it conflicts with basic principles of National Socialist ideology" (Bluel:98). Hitler also attempted to draw a distinction between the party and the SA by portraying Roehm's proclivities as an aspect of military society. "[The SA] is not an institute for the moral education of genteel young ladies, "said Hitler, "but a formation of seasoned fighters" (Bluel:98). The implication seems to have been that homosexuality was an odd quirk of military life that should be overlooked in light of the value of these soldiers' mission and experience. Furthermore, he promised expulsion from the party for anyone who continued to engage in "tongue-wagging" and "letter-writing" (Koehl: 43).

Homosexuality was clearly not limited to the SA, however. Attorney and Hitler contemporary Erich Ebermayer, also a homosexual, observed in his diary that

> During its time of struggle, the National Socialist movement -- and not just the Roehm clique -- was a fraternity such as Blueher portrayed in his books, its motive force being homoeroticism...My exceedingly trustworthy sources of information about these confidential matters...have hitherto...*proudly* stressed the homoerotic orientation of the Fuehrer and his inner circle (emphasis in the original. Machtan:232).

Secondly, Hitler strengthened his rhetoric against homosexuality in German society at large. An article that appeared in the official Nazi newspaper went so far as to threaten homosexuals with extermination. Once again this was empty rhetoric. Adolf Brand, whose openly homosexual magazine, *Der Eigene*, was by this time widely read in

Germany, responded to the Nazi article with one of his own. Brand writes,

> Men such as Captain Roehm, are, to our knowledge, no rarity at all in the National Socialist Party. It rather teems there with homosexuals of all kinds. And the joy of man in man, which has been slandered in their papers so often as an oriental vice although the Edda frankly extols it as the highest virtue of the Teutons, blossoms around their campfires and is cultivated and fostered by them in a way done in no other male union that is reared on party politics. The threatened hanging on the gallows, with which they allege they want to exterminate homosexuals, is therefore only a horrible gesture that is supposed to make stupid people believe that the Hitler people, in the matter of male-to-male inclinations, are all as innocent as pigeons and pure as angels, just like the pious members of the Christian Society of the Virgin...The public threat against the homosexuals has in the meantime not frightened any youth-friend or man-friend into deserting this party. One knows perfectly well that all those public threats are only paper masks (Brand in Oosterhuis and Kennedy:236f).

Power and Abuse

Despite Brand's protestations, Hitler's ruse was quite successful in regard to the Nazis' political fortunes. As Machtan notes, "What would now be rightly condemned as discriminatory disparagement of a minority was then still regarded as a criminological fact: that homosexuals make exceptionally skillful liars" (Machtan:103). The

Communist graffitti: "Death to Fascism."

party fared well in the elections of 1932, and on January 30, 1933, Adolf Hitler was appointed Chancellor of Germany. The Nazi Party had finally come to power. However, the elections following Hitler's appointment, called by Hitler himself, were even more critical to the Nazis. Hitler was demanding the power of authoritarian rule over Germany, but public support for his plan was ambiguous

The Reichstag was torched by the Nazis.

(Toland:288). The greatest threat came from the Communists who had significant power and support of their own. The Nazis' diabolical solution to this problem involved the burning of the German Reichstag (another famous incident in Nazi history which is tied to the homosexuals in the party). Carroll Quigley, in <u>Tragedy and Hope</u> writes,

> [I]t was evident a week before the election that the German people were not convinced [that the Nazis should gain the increased power they sought]. Accordingly...a plot was worked out to burn the Reichstag building and blame the Communists. Most of the plotters were homosexuals and were able to persuade a degenerate moron from Holland named Van der Lubbe to go with them...Most of the Nazis who were in on the plot were murdered by Goering during the 'blood purge' of June

30, 1934" (Quigley:437f). Van der Lubbe was executed for the crime.

Van Der Lubbe was homosexual as well. Oosterhuis quotes a 1933 book prepared by the World Committee for the Victims of German Fascism:

> Enquiries in Leyden have definitely established the fact that he [Van Der Lubbe] was homosexual. This is of great importance for his later history....Van Der Lubbe's homosexual connections with the National Socialist leaders and his material dependence on them made him obedient and willing to carry out the incendiary's part (Oosterhuis:253).

In The Life and Death of Hermann Goering, authors Ewan Butler and Gordon Young list the Reichstag fire conspirators. "The camarilla which finally drew up plans for the 'frame-up' against the Communists consisted, besides Captain Goering, its originator, of Goebbels, Roehm, Heines, Count Helldorf, leader of the Berlin S.A., Karl Ernst, a certain StandartenFuehrer (regimental commander) of the S.A. named Sander and two other members of the S.A., Fiedler and von Mohrenschild" (Butler and Young:111).

The strategy succeeded. The people, perceiving the Nazis as saviors in a time of crisis, gave the party complete control of German government. Not everyone in Germany, however, was pleased with Hitler's ascension to power. Former Chancellor Kurt von Schleicher gave voice to an inner fear that foreshadowed his own death: "This pack of scoundrels, these criminals, these filthy boy streetwalkers! Well, they better not come near me" (Rector:64). Schleicher was killed in Munich by Hitler's murder gang during the Roehm Purge (Fest, 1975:465).

Once the party had come to power several homosexuals in the Nazi leadership believed they could act with

"Party Comrades, Heed Discipline," pleads this sign at the Brown House, headquarters of the SA.

impunity in regard to their homosexual exploits. This attitude would lead to severe consequences for these few men and indirectly dictate Hitler's official policy regarding homosexuality.

By the spring of 1934, Ernst Roehm's homosexual activities had become more flagrant than ever, to the extent that Himmler himself made a special trip to plead with Roehm to be more discrete. Roehm pretended to accede but, as Gallo reports

> The next morning Himmler's agents report that one of the most fantastic orgies they had ever seen took place the night before at Roehm's headquarters. Bottles thrown from the windows smashed on the pavements below, and the sound of raucous laughter echoed in the street. Roehm himself had been an all-night participant, with his *Lustknaben*, his male prostitutes. Himmler is furious. (Gallo:68).

Roehm's exploits also began implicating the more genteel homosexuals in the party. Roehm's entourage now

Ernst Roehm with aide-de-camp Count von Spreti.

included "young sons of the nobility, who form a brilliant staff with the faces of perverse angels: Baron von Falkenhausen, Count von Spreti, the Prince von Waldeck: all aides-de-camp to Captain Roehm" (Gallo:46). (Waldeck was the first member of the old nobility to join the Party and had been recruited by Himmler, himself -- Snyder:371).

At this same time Edmund Heines was appointed Chief of Police of Breslau. Gallo writes,

> His staff resembles Roehm's -- they are the objects of its chief's amorous passion. The homosexual Engels is OberstuermbannFuehrer (Lieutenant Colonel), and the

young Schmidt is aide-de-camp. This twenty-year-old is Heines' latest folly. Whatever that handsome young blonde does, he is protected by his lover. Once, in a moment of drunkenness, he publicly kills a drinking companion with his sword, but the Chief of Police forbids the public prosecutor to intervene....Beside this couple, the depraved Engels, a watchful intriguer, plays the part of Heines' evil genius. He is one of those who use the SA organization and the Hitler Youth to recruit participants for his erotic games (ibid.:70).

Samuel Igra also noted the increasingly public nature of the Nazi leaders' activities:

It was not merely that these men practiced their vices in private and among their own clique; but they made a system, almost a cult, of their moral corruption, and used their positions of power to molest with impunity innocent boys and girls whose features and physique they fancied. When Kube and his staff visited the vil-

Wilhelm Kube, *Gauleiter* of Ostmark and founder of the anti-Christian "German Faith Movement."

lages of his district, *Kube ist da* was the warning passed from mouth to mouth among the people, whereupon parents hid their boys and girls in the cellars or in the back kitchens. The scoundrel needed so much money for his filthy orgies that he had his accomplices appointed to positions in the local savings banks and borough treasurers' offices, where they systematically robbed the tills. In Frankfort-on-Oder, for instance, Kube's accomplices robbed the Post Office Savings Bank of 180,000 marks (about £15,000), and though the case was proved against him in court, he was dismissed only for a while and reinstated in the Party again.

These incidents divided the Nazi elite as no other issue had. Amoral scoundrels all, the majority were nevertheless practical men who knew the importance of discretion, even for dictatorial tyrants. The unquenchable arrogance of these SA leaders forced Hitler into an untenable position -- one which Roehm's enemies within the party would soon exploit. Hitler first would soon be compelled by Roehm's powerful enemies to assassinate the worst offenders in his ranks. Second, to counter the public impression that his party was rife with homosexuality, Hitler would be forced to publicly take a harder line against sexual deviance.

Chapter Five

THE PERSECUTION OF HOMOSEXUALS

Homosexualist revisionists assert that Hitler's ascension to the Chancellorship marked the beginning of a homosexual Holocaust in Germany. For example, as early as 1978, homosexual political activists claimed that "[m]any thousands and hundreds of thousands [of homosexuals] were...imprisoned in concentration camps where they died" (ONE Letter, May, 1978). Over the years the story has assumed ever more fantastic proportions. In 1986 Plant wrote, "After years of frustration...Hitler's storm troopers now had the opportunity to smash their enemies: the lame, the mute, the feebleminded, the epileptic, the homosexual, the Jew, the Gypsy, the Communist. These were the scapegoats singled out for persecution. These were the 'contragenics' who were to be ruthlessly eliminated to ensure the purity of the 'Aryan race.'" (Plant:51). Rector writes, "Hitler's homophobia did not surface until 1933-1934, when gays had come to affect adversely his New Order designs -- out of which grew the simple solution of murdering them en masse" (Rector:24).

Unsupported assertions such as these have allowed the theory of a "Gay Holocaust" (in which homosexuals are portrayed alongside the Jews as victims of a campaign of

Cover of Richard Plant's popular revisionist history, <u>The Pink Triangle</u>.

extermination) to gain currency in the United States. The evidence does not support this theory. Unfortunately, the portrayal of homosexuals as Nazi victims has assumed a kind of "untouchable" status among supporters of "gay rights," probably because the success of the movement depends so heavily on public sympathy. Thus, today we see active suppression of information linking homosexuals to the Nazis and misrepresentation of homosexuals' experience in the Third Reich. A few "gay" academics are more forthright. For example, homosexualist scholar Manfred Herzer admits:

> As far as the scope of homosexual men's support of the Nazis is concerned, we face a self-imposed void in our knowledge that has taken on the dimensions of an ideologically motivated taboo. Within gay historiography, even such a repugnant figure as the Nazi leader Ernst Roehm has repeatedly been consigned to the role of victim, first of leftist and then of Nazi "homophobia," for only by doing so has it been possible to perpetuate a slanted account of history that persistently portrays homosexuals as persecuted martyrs and passive victims (Herzer:199).

Homosexualists Johansson and Percy promote the use of "outing" (exposing public figures, past and present as "gay") to influence public opinion about homosexuality and the "gay" agenda. They advise that "[a]ctivists should clearly not out a notorious criminal or mass murderer as they would a famed medical missionary or celebrated inventor" (Johansson and Percy:284). They acknowledge that "[a]pologists generally prefer to deny that homosexuality was widespread among Nazi leaders after the purge of Roehm and his associates....[although Italian "gay" activist] Massimo Consoli has reversed this tendency by dwelling at length on the homosexuality of the early followers of the NSDAP (National Socialist Party). (Consoli is, however, a leading proponent of the "Gay Holocaust" public relations ploy -- Grau:5).

Then we have the problem of simple error in claims such as that made by homosexualist Claudia Schoppmann. She has claimed that German "gay rights" leader Martin Radszuweit was murdered in a concentration camp (Herzer:226). Herzer states authoritatively that Radszuweit did *not* die in a concentration camp: "...he died in the 1980s in his house in Berlin-Kopenick" (ibid.:226).

The Harvard Gay and Lesbian Review (Summer 1995) contains an admirably candid review of the book Hidden Holocaust? by Gunter Grau (in which Schoppmann was a minor contributor):

> Grau and Schoppman conclude that there was no "holocaust" of gays — hence the question mark in the book's title. This assessment is based on the wide range of contemporary documents...Grau discounts the current wild estimates of the number of gays killed by the Nazis, suggesting a figure closer to 5,000...How, then are we to read the widely quoted incendiary statements by Nazis like SS leader Himmler, who consistently called for the 'eradication' of homosexuals?...Much of this rhetoric, Grau says, was propaganda meant for public consumption... Gays were never the subject of pogroms, and never faced

The success of the "Gay Holocaust" myth has encouraged homosexual political activists to equate opposition to their agenda with Nazism. This March, 2000 cover of *Outworld* uses Nazi imagery to malign a pro-marriage ballot measure in California.

the danger that the Jews did in Germany and occupied Europe.

Dr. Judith Reisman, in "The *Pink Swastika* and Holocaust Revisionist History," wrote this comparison of the fate of the two groups under the Nazis:

Were homosexuals treated like Jews, 2-3 million out of 2-3 million German homosexuals should have lost their businesses, their jobs, their property, their possessions and most would have lost their lives. Homosexuals would have been forced to wear pink triangles on their clothing in the streets, they would have had their passports stamped with an "H," been barred from travel, work, shopping, public appearances without their armbands, and we would have thousands of pictures of pink triangle graffiti saying "kill the faggots," and the like. If German homosexuals were not Nazis, these 2-3 million men would have been homeless, walled in ghettos, worked as a mass labor pool, then gassed and their abuse recorded in graphic detail, as were the millions of Jews. And, if Germany's several million "gays" were not Nazi victims, they were Nazi soldiers, collaborators or murderers (Reisman:*Culture Wars*, April 1996).

Lest we forget:

"HOMOPHOBIA and ANTISEMITISM are part of the same DISEASE."

-- *Rabbi Bernard H. Mehlman*

In a small park near the Freedom Trail, a monument is being built in memory of the six million Jews exterminated by the Third Reich. To be dedicated on October 22nd, the NEW ENGLAND HOLOCAUST MEMORIAL will encourage millions of visitors to recall the Shoah – the Holocaust – and consider its many bitter lessons.

Carved in the Memorial's black granite path, alongside six haunting towers of steel and glass, is this horrible reminder of near-history:

"German homosexuals were early victims of Nazi persecution. Many were imprisoned, some were castrated or used in medical experiments. Thousands died in concentration camps."

NEW ENGLAND'S GAY AND LESBIAN COMMUNITY proudly joins a select group of generous corporations and civic leaders as a Cornerstone Benefactor of Boston's newest addition to the Freedom Trail.

Thank you to all who contributed.

New England Holocaust Memorial

Public Dedication Ceremony featuring Elie Wiesel
Sunday, October 22, 1995 at 11:00 am
Congress Street between Faneuil Hall and City Hall
For more information, call (617) 338-▓▓▓▓

Remember

Gay and Lesbian Committee of the New England Holocaust Memorial Committee

Newspaper ad exploits the Holocaust to advance the cause of homosexual legitimization.

The fact is that relatively few homosexuals died in concentrations camps. They were never murdered "en masse" or "ruthlessly eliminated" by the Nazis. Yet many homosexuals were jailed and some did die in Nazi work camps. (Of course, those who were jailed were males; there was never a systematic prosecution of lesbians -- Grau:15). What is the truth about Nazi persecution of homosexuals?

There are several incidents in Nazi history which are most often cited as evidence of their persecution of homosexuals. This list includes (1) the sacking of the Sex Research Institute of Berlin, (2) a series of increasingly harsh public pronouncements and policies against homosexuality by Hitler and Himmler, (3) the Roehm Purge (also known as "The Night of the Long Knives"), and (4) the internment of homosexuals in work camps. We will look at each of these issues in turn.

The Path of the Paranoid

One overarching factor must be kept in mind as we examine the history of Nazi persecution of homosexuals: the paranoia of Adolf Hitler. Hitler was deathly afraid that his own homosexuality would be exposed to the German people, undoing all that he had worked for in his ascension to power. Indeed, Lothar Machtan argues convincingly that the entire Nazi campaign against homosexuality, from the initial anti-sodomy policies to the Roehm purge to the internment of homosexuals in the camps, was orchestrated to prevent the truth about Hitler from coming out. Machtan writes

> Hitler's determination to destroy anything that might have provided an insight into his private life is well documented. He got rid of anything he could, and his arm was long, even before 1933. Those privy to his secrets were bribed, sworn to secrecy, blackmailed or killed....Hitler's...homosexuality...was the secret from his past that threatened at any time to rear its head as he rose politically....and he defended that secret by all available means (Machtan:20f).

One of Hitler's greatest problems was blackmail. Blackmail of homosexuals by estranged partners and prostitutes was a simple fact of life in Germany. "[H]omosexuals were particularly vulnerable to blackmailers, known as *Chanteure* on the homosexual scene," write Burleigh and Wippermann. "Blackmail, and the threat of public exposure, resulted in frequent suicides or suicide attempts" (Burleigh and Wipperman:184).

Police Commissioner Hans von Tresckow, who served in Berlin during the years that Hitler was on the streets in Munich and Vienna, wrote the following in his memoirs:

VON FÜRSTEN UND ANDEREN STERBLICHEN

ERINNERUNGEN EINES KRIMINALKOMMISSARS

VON

HANS VON TRESCKOW

1922
F. FONTANE & Co.
BERLIN

Memoirs of Berlin Police Commissioner Hans von Tresckow.

One of the worst features of homosexualism is that it gives rise to an enormous amount of male prostitution. Many persons who are perfectly normal find it a lucrative though disgraceful trade. In Berlin there are many centers where homosexualists make the acquaintances of accomplices who will serve their requirements. And there are many cafés and taverns which are frequented almost exclusively by such people. The police are powerless to put down this practice, because they require legal authorization to interfere. My experience is that male prostitution has been steadily increasing for some decades past and cases of blackmail are becoming more numerous accordingly; for a person who goes in for this profession is almost always a blackmailer. (Treschow in Lively:18).

For Hitler, the list of blackmailers included numerous political opportunists. Igra reports that Heinrich Hoffman, the official Nazi photographer, gained his position by using information about Hitler's perverse abuse of his (Hoffman's) daughter, Henny, to blackmail the future *Fuehrer* (Igra:74). (Henny Hoffman was later married off to reputed homosexual Baldur von Schirach, probably to quell rumors about his exploits with Hitler Youth boys). Heiden relates another story in which Hitler bought an entire collection of rare political writings to regain possession of a letter to his niece in which he openly revealed his "masochistic-coprophil inclinations" (Heiden, 1944:385).

Even more dangerous than the political opportunists were the political enemies who could not be bought off. As early as 1923, Hitler's enemies were relying on their proof of his perversion to secure an advantage, even if that advantage were only their own self-preservation. Eugen Dollman recorded his experience at a dinner meeting with General Otto von Lossow at the Bavarian war ministry.

Since November 9 [said Lossow], Hitler and his supporters have been well aware that any attempt on my life or those of my officers would cause a European scandal. I have some good friends in this world, and Adolf would lose that game just as he did on November 9 [date of the failed "Beerhall Putsch"]....The general produced from a desk drawer a police file containing secret reports and depositions about the private life of Herr Adolf Hitler dating from the time that he again turned up after the war -- all from the vice squad or police headquarters on Ettstrasse....What a dangerous weapon Otto von Lossow had forged during the years when he was at the height of his authority in Munich (Machtan:135).

Lossow would in fact survive unscathed until his death in 1938, despite "Hitler's well-documented hatred of the 'traitor Lossow'" (ibid.:137).

Others without benefit of hidden documentation of Hitler's sexual sins did not fare as well, even those with whom he had been intimate. Sklar writes that "Hitler attempted to bury all his earlier influences and his origins, and he spent a great deal of energy hiding them...[In this campaign to erase his past] Hitler ordered the murder of Reinhold Hanish, a friend who had shared his down and out days in Vienna" (Sklar:21). Hitler was enraged that Hanish had collaborated with Konrad Heiden, the Hitler biographer who had aired the Nazis dirty linen (Machtan:52).

Until Hitler and his crew finally gained power in Germany, their methods for dealing with those privy to Nazi secrets were limited in form and scope. Afterwards, however, there were more and better ways to solve these kinds of problems and to punish their enemies at the same time.

The Sacking of the Sex Research Institute

The Nazis' hunt for incriminating evidence was obvious in the attack on Magnus Hirschfeld's Sex Research Institute on May 6th, 1933. As noted previously, the Sex Research Institute of Berlin had been founded by Hirschfeld in 1919 as a center for the "study" of homosexuality and other sexual dysfunctions. For all intents and purposes, it served as the headquarters for the effeminate branch of the German "gay rights" movement. For this reason alone, the "Butch" homosexuals of the Nazi Party might have destroyed the Institute. Indeed, throughout the preceding years the Nazis had increasingly harassed Hirschfeld personally.

Victor Robinson, editor of an autobiographical sketch by Hirschfeld, wrote in 1936 that "[a]lthough the Nazis themselves derived great profit from Hirschfeld's theories

Adolf Hitler speaking to the German parliament. Once he had taken power, Hitler quickly fashioned a political climate in which he could control, jail or kill all potential blackmailers.

(and called on him personally for help) they continued his persecution relentlessly; they terrorized his meetings and closed his lecture halls, so that for the safety of his audiences and himself, Hirschfeld was no longer able to make public appearances (Haeberle:368). Homosexualist James Steakley acknowledges the "Butch/Fem" aspect of the incident, saying that some German homosexuals "could conceivably have approved of the measure, particularly if they were Nazi sympathizers or male supremacists" (Steakley:105). Ignorance of the "Butch/Fem" conflict in the German "gay" subculture left many contemporary writers puzzled as to why the Nazis would attack Hirschfeld. An obituary for Hirschfeld written in 1934 exemplifies this confusion:

> There is a darker and more savage irony in the fact that the Nazis should have treated him as an archenemy; for the Nazi ranks are notoriously honeycombed with all degrees of homosexuality, and Hirschfeld is indisputably the man to whom it is mainly due that the right of these 2 percent of sexual abnormals in the masses of the European populations to exist and to function on their own lines is now a matter for public discussion and public agitation (Herzer:221).

The attack against the Institute, however, was not motivated solely by the Nazi enmity against effeminate homosexuals. It was also an attempt to cover up the truth about rampant homosexuality and other perversions in the Nazi Party. Hitler also knew that Hirschfeld's facility had extensive records that could be damaging to himself and his inner circle. This was the reason for the raid, according to Ludwig L. Lenz, the assistant director of the Sex Research Institute, who was in charge on the day of the raid. His description of the situation, part of which was quoted previously, is given here at greater length.

> [O]ur Institute was used by all classes of the population and members of every political party...We thus had a great many Nazis under treatment at the Institute. Why was it then, since we were completely non-party, that our purely scientific Institute was the first victim which fell to the new regime? The answer to this is simple...We knew

too much. It would be against medical principles to provide a list of the Nazi leaders and their perversions [but]...not ten percent of the men who, in 1933, took the fate of Germany into their hands, were sexually normal...Many of these personages were known to us directly through consultations; we heard about others from their comrades in the party...and of others we saw the tragic results: I refer here especially to a young girl whose abdomen was covered with pin scratchings through the sadism of an eminent Nuremberg Nazi; I refer also to a thirteen year old boy who suffered from a serious lesion of the anal muscle brought about by a senior party official in Breslau and to a youth from Berlin with severe rectal gonorrhea, etc., etc....Our knowledge of such intimate secrets regarding members of the Nazi Party and other documentary material — we possessed about forty thousand confessions and biographical letters — was the cause of the complete and utter destruction of the Institute of Sexology (Haberle:369).

Burleigh and Wipperman report that the ransackers had "lists" of materials they were looking for (Burleigh and Wipperman:189) and that they carted away two truckloads of books and files. The materials taken from the Institute were burned in a public ceremony, captured on film, on May 10th (Steakley:105). The spectacular and oft-replayed newsreel footage of this event has caused the burning of books to become synonymous with Nazism. What information went up in smoke on that day will never be known, but we can be sure that the pile of burning paper contained many Nazi secrets. According to homosexual sources who were in Germany at the time, the Nazis destroyed twelve thousand books and thirty-five thousand photographs.

The building itself was confiscated from the SHC and turned over to the Nazi Association of Jurists and Lawyers (ibid.:105). This may perhaps be interpreted to mean that it remained in the hands of homosexuals. We know that at least Hans Frank, Hitler's private lawyer, and the Nazi party's star attorney Dr. Alfons Sack were homosexuals (Machtan:219).

Anti-Homosexual Policies

Whenever the Nazis arrested homosexuals and raided even the homes of their supporters they were looking for incriminating evidence against themselves. Machtan writes:

> Hitler was mortally afraid of the obscurity of the homosexual milieu, which he himself had experienced firsthand in Vienna and Munich. He knew that this demimonde could at any time yield up disreputable secrets -- even some, perhaps, that might affect him personally....Although not interested in a policy of repression toward "ordinary" homosexuals, he was doubly so in cases where definite interests were involved (Ibid.:226).

However, there were also old scores to settle with the effeminate homosexuals who had opposed the Nazi rise to power. What developed, then, was a policy designed primarily to prevent embarrassment to Hitler in which all things homosexual were closely scrutinized by Himmler's secret police. But action was taken only when the Nazi nets caught enemies of the party or of the regime. These activities occurred independently of normal police functions in which violators of German anti-sodomy and anti-pederasty laws continued to be processed through the courts.

The law against homosexual conduct had existed in Germany for many years prior to the Nazi regime as Paragraph 175 of the Reich Criminal Code, to wit: "A male who indulges in criminally indecent activity with another male, or who allows himself to participate in such activity, will be punished with imprisonment" (Burleigh and Wipperman:188). When Hitler came to power he used this law as a means of tracking down and punishing those homosexuals who, in the words of one victim, "had defended the Weimar Republic, and who had tried to forestall the Nazi threat" (ibid.:183). Later he expanded the law and used it as a convenient tool to detain other enemies of the regime.

In February of 1933, Hitler banned pornography, homosexual bars and bath-houses, and groups which promoted "gay rights" (Plant:50). Ostensibly, this decree was a blanket condemnation of all homosexual activity in Germany, but in practice it served as just another means to find and destroy anti-Nazi groups and individuals. Indeed, it is likely that Hitler had been a patron of some of the homosexual-oriented businesses that he shut down. The Berlin "Eldorado" club, for example, was a favorite haunt of the Berlin SA under Captain Paul Rohrbein, a close friend of Roehm and Karl Ernst (Machtan:185).

Was Hitler truly opposed to pornography and "gay" bars? Hitler's close personal friend was the pornographer, Julius Streicher (center), seen here in March, 1934 with some Brownshirted "gay" bar regulars.

The "masculine" homosexuals in the Nazi leadership enforced the new policy selectively, "employ[ing] the charge of homosexuality primarily as a means to eliminate political opponents, both inside his party and out" (Oosterhuis and Kennedy:248). Revisionst Frank Rector also admits that the decree "was not enforced in all cases" (Rector:66). Oosterhuis and Kennedy write that "Although he was well known as a gay-activist, [Adolf] Brand was not arrested by the Nazis" but nearly all of his files were confiscated (Ooosterhuis and Kennedy:7) .

The Washington Blade, the newspaper of the homosexual community in Washington D.C., reported on the research of John Fout, a "gay" history professor at Bard College in New York:

> The Nazis shut down the two or three active Gay political organizations that had been operating in German (sic) as soon as Hitler took power in 1933. However, according to Fout, Gay bars and bathhouses remained open until the late 1930s.... 'The Gay urban subculture survived the Nazi period,' said Fout (Researcher says Nazi persecution not systematic, *The Washington Blade*, May 22, 1998).

Jewish homosexual Gad Beck, Director of Berlin's Jewish Adult Education Center, also challenges "gay" dogma on the degree to which homosexuals were persecuted in Germany. In his book, <u>An Underground Life: Memoirs of a Gay Jew in Nazi Berlin</u>, Beck claims "There was no problem be[ing] a homosexual Jew. Everyone turned a blind eye to whatever we boys were up to with each other" and cited only one case of the Nazi's persecuting a homosexual man (Beck in "Fearless under the Fuhrer,"*The Advocate*, October 26, 1999).

In 1935, Paragraph 175 was amended with Paragraph 175a which broadened the scope of the law restricting homosexual conduct (Burleigh and Wipperman:190). (Interestingly, the new criminal code addressing homosexuality deleted the word "unnatural" from the definition --

Reisman, 1994:3). This new law provided the Nazis with an especially potent legal weapon against their enemies.

It will never be known how many non-homosexuals were charged under this law, but it is indisputable that the Nazis used false accusations of homosexuality to justify the detainment and imprisonment of many of their opponents. "The law was so loosely formulated," writes Steakley, "that it could be, and was, applied against heterosexuals that the Nazis wanted to eliminate...the law was also used repeatedly against Catholic clergymen" (Steakley:111). Kogon writes that "The Gestapo readily had recourse to the charge of homosexuality if it was unable to find any pretext for proceeding against Catholic priests or irksome critics" (Kogon:44).

The charge of homosexuality was convenient for the Nazis to use against their political enemies because it was so difficult to defend against and so easy to justify to the populace. Since long before the Nazis assumed power, homosexuals generally lived clandestine lives, so it was not unusual for revelations of their conduct to come as a surprise to their communities when it became a police matter. This is not to say that actual homosexuals were not prosecuted under the law. Many were. But the law was used selectively against the "Fems." And even in this case, many effeminate homosexuals, especially those in the arts community, were given protection by certain Nazi leaders (Oosterhuis and Kennedy:248). Plant writes,

> The most famous example is that of the actor Gustaf Grundgens...Despite the fact that his homosexual affairs were as notorious as those of Roehm's, Goering appointed him director of the State Theater...[And] On October 29, 1937...Himmler advised that actors and other artists could be arrested for offenses against paragraph 175 only with his personal consent, unless the police caught them *in fla-grante* (Plant:116).

Even the most visible "Fems," however, were treated far differently than were the Jews. Kurt Hiller, successor to Magnus Hirschfeld in the "Fem" faction of the German "gay" movement, was interned in a concentration camp but released (battered but alive) after nine months (Steakley:103). An unknown percentage of homosexual prisoners were arrested not for sex offenses at all, but for political reasons. A document from the Buchenwald archive states,

> In the spring of 1942 a Berlin writer called Dahnke was sent to the camp as a homosexual. The main reason for his internment, however, was political statements which had brought him to the attention of the Gestapo (Grau:267).

A study of the Hitler Youth offers more examples that expose the meaninglessness of the Nazi's harsh rhetoric against homosexuals. We have already noted Koehl's observation that Himmler "mitigated his penalties privately" and tried to keep every incident of homosexual molestation of the Hitler Youth boys by the SS "as secret as possible" (Koehl:51f). But Koehl goes on to cite the records of the RJF, the security division of the Hitler Youth administration. "[D]uring the first six months of 1940," he writes, "[there were] 10,958 crimes committed by Hitler Youths, the most common were theft (5,985), [and] homosexuality (901)" (ibid.:84). When he compared the number of homosexual offenses to the list of expulsions from the organization (an absurdly mild punishment for a supposed capital crime), however, Koehl found a low rate of expulsions for homosexuality:

> Since the RJF Report listed 900 cases of homosexual crimes during a six month period alone, and only a third of that number were expelled during a twenty-five month period by court action, it suggests that the RJF was more

Hitler Youth were frequent targets of the sexual predators in the SA and SS.   Yad Vashem

hesitant to uphold Article 175 of the Criminal Code than its official propaganda would have the public be- lieve...[One] young delinquent with a record of minor thefts, for which he had spent eight weeks in jail, was not expelled from the HJ [Hitler Youth]. In September 1940...[officials] surprised him and several prison workers in a wild homosexual orgy in broad daylight on a roadside. With sensational evidence like this in hand, the...leader then sought to have the culprit expelled from the HJ. But it took some time before this occurred, suggesting that the enforcement of Article 175 was lax (Koehl:85ff).

The increasing indifference of Hitler Youth officials toward homosexuality was an attitude reflected in the larger society as well. In 1937 the Reich Minister of the Interior issued a change of policy regarding Paragraph 175. Under the new ruling only four-time repeat offenders could be jailed or sent to camps for homosexual offenses. This was reaffirmed in 1940 by Himmler (S. Katz:146).

The Roehm Purge

The event in history most frequently cited as evidence of Nazi persecution of homosexuals is known variously as the Blood Purge, the Night of the Long Knives, and the Roehm Purge. Steakley writes that "[t]he indisputable beginning of Nazi terror against homosexuals was marked by the murder of Ernst Roehm on June 28, 1934, 'the night of the long knives'" (Steakley:108). It was on this night (actually over an entire weekend), that Adolf Hitler's closest aides orchestrated the assassinations of hundreds of his political enemies in one bloody sweep. Included in this purge were Roehm and several of the top officers of the SA.

We have emphasized that the leadership of the SA was mostly, if not entirely homosexual. The fact that SA leaders were the primary targets in the massacre could therefore be construed as a sort of "moral cleansing" of the Nazi ranks, which, in fact, Hitler claimed it was. But Hitler lied. The Roehm Purge was driven by political, not moral concerns. Hitler feigned disgust and outrage about the homosexuality of the murdered SA leaders to justify himself

Ernſt Röhm

Die Geſchichte
eines Hochverräters

Verlag Frz. Eher Nachf., G.m.b.H., München 2, NO.

Perhaps anticipating a shortened life, Ernst Roehm published his autobiography <u>History of a High Traitor</u> in 1928 while in South America.

to the German people; it was a tactic he had used previously to allay public suspicions about the sexual deviancy of his inner circle. The importance of this fact is asserted in many leading works by both mainstream and homosexualist historians. The following are excerpts from four different historians who have examined the issue:

> Hitler eliminated his closest friend Roehm and certain SA leaders as potential rivals. The strictly political motivation of this ruthless power play was initially too obvious to be entirely denied, but later it was conveniently obscured by charges of homosexual depravity (Haberle:369f).

> The formal accusations against Roehm and those arrested with him centered on their homosexual activities, which Hitler had of course known about for fifteen years and shrugged off, it being alleged that these activities disgraced the party. For those victims without any homosexual background, "the Great Blood Purge" continued all over Germany, as Nazi leaders got rid of all their most hated enemies, as well as the inevitable "mistakes" (Garde:726f).

> Ernst Roehm wasn't shot because the Nazi Party felt outraged by the abrupt discovery that he was "having" his storm troopers — that had been known for ages; but because his sway over the SA had become a menace to Hitler. In the Hitler Youth the "dear love of comrades" was evilly turned into a political end. And if the Nazi hierarchy was well larded with homosexuals, so was Wilhelm II's court and so was the Weimar Republic (Davidson:152).

> Hitler himself, of course, had been well aware of Roehm's sexual orientation from the earliest days of their long association....So strong was Roehm that the Wehrmacht [German Army High Command] was con-

cerned that he might seize control of the army. In 1934, Hitler became fearful that the Wehrmacht was plotting a coup against him to prevent such a takeover. To forestall this danger, Hitler had Roehm and about one thousand other men murdered one weekend in June 1934, the famous "Night of the Long Knives" (Crompton:79f).

There is some dispute among historians about whether Roehm had planned a coup against Hitler after Hitler's refusal to replace the regular army with Roehm's troops. This takeover of the army had apparently been part of the Nazis' original plan for the maximization of their political strength. Upon his appointment as Chancellor, Hitler was confronted with new and different challenges which required new and different alliances. For some time it appeared that Hitler would remain true to his pact with Roehm. From the time Hitler assumed control of the German government in January of 1933, until the spring of 1934, he allowed the SA to grow from 300,000 to over 3 million members (Plant:54). During this period of rapid growth, Roehm's rivals within the Nazi inner circle grew increasingly alarmed, as did the powerful industrialists and military leaders.

Tension between the SA and the army increased. General Walther von Brauchitsch, speaking for the majority of his fellow officers, said, "[t]hat gang of homosexuals, thugs and drunks should be allowed no part of [German re-armament]" (Gallo:87). For their part, the SA taunted the regular army soldiers, singing "The grey rock will be drowned in a sea of brown" (ibid.:87), meaning that the grey uniformed army would be swallowed up by the Brownshirts. Strasser writes,

At a meeting of the Cabinet, to which he belonged, [Roehm] demanded the incorporation of the Brown Shirts into the regular army, the Brown Shirt officers to retain their ranks. In other words he demanded supreme command of the Reichswehr, the S.S., and the S.A.. He confidently believed that he had Adolf's support...but Hitler remained silent...Blomberg, the Minister of National Defense, suddenly declared that the only course open to President Hindenberg would be to refuse outright. "The discussion is closed," Hitler then said, without daring to look his old friend in the face. Roehm, speechless with fury, walked quickly from the room. After June 30, General von Reichenau declared in an interview with the *Petit Journal* that Roehm's death sentence was virtually signed that day (Strasser, 1940:178).

As the conflict came to a head, SA conspirators created a "hit list" of Army officers who were to be killed (ibid.:218) and allegedly selected *Standartenfuehrer* Julius Uhl to assassinate Hitler himself (ibid.:237). It may be, however, that these allegations were invented as part of a fall-back rationale for the purge. It is well known that Himmler, Goering and Himmler's deputy, Reinhard Heydrich, worked behind the scenes to limit Roehm's power; and it has been reported by some sources that they generated rumors of a Roehm plot to drive a wedge between Roehm and Hitler. In any case, the Roehm Purge was not motivated by the homosexuality of its victims. The great majority of victims were not homosexuals at all. Otto Strasser, a high Nazi functionary whose brother, Gregor, was murdered that night, lists some of the casualties in Hitler and I:

> Klausener and several other Catholic leaders were executed, as well as [Vice Chancellor] von Papen's secretaries. At Hirschberg, in Silesia, all the Jews, all the members of the Stahlhelm, and a few communists were arrested...beaten with rifle butts...and eight people were murdered...[V]on Kahr, an old man of sixty three...was taken from his bed, taken to Dachau, and tortured to death...His crime had been his failure to support the Munich *putsch* in 1923. Ballerstaedt...who had been in-

strumental in Hitler's being sentenced to three months imprisonment, was murdered by a special killer squad. [And] death was the penalty paid by Father Staempfle for having edited *Mein Kampf*, and therefore being familiar with the author's weaknesses (ibid.:200).

Gregor Strasser was murdered during the Roehm Purge

Igra provides us with a long and detailed account of the power struggle which led to the purge, beginning with a refutation of the idea that it represented a policy of extermination of homosexuals by Hitler:

> We shall find that, far from eliminating the sex perverts from his party, Hitler retained most of them, and that he moved against those whom he did eliminate only with the greatest reluctance and after he had been relentlessly pushed by outside forces and circumstances. On June 14 and 15 Hitler was in Venice to see Mussolini. It soon became common knowledge that the German Dictator and his entourage had made an unfavorable impression upon the Italians...Mussolini was never a stickler for puritan morality, to say the least, but there was one vice which the Italians particularly loathe; they call it *il vizio tedesco*, the German vice. The conduct of some members in Hitler's entourage at Venice disgusted the Italians. Mussolini protested against the moral character and political unreliability of the leading personnel in the Nazi Storm Troops and warned Hitler that he would have to sacrifice his favorite colleagues if he wished to save his own personal prestige and that of his regime. Among those colleagues, Roehm, Heines and Karl Ernst were mentioned.
>
> What chagrined [Hitler] the most was that he knew Mussolini had been prompted...by...[German] President

Hindenberg...On June 21, Hitler went to Neudek, Hindenberg's country seat...[He] was literally dumbfounded when confronted on the steps of the Hindenberg family home by General Blomberg and Goering, both in uniform. They informed him that the President would not receive the Chancellor, and that if the heads of the SA were not dismissed martial law would be declared, whereupon Goering would take over civilian control as Chief of Police, and Blomberg, as Minister of War, would take over military control.

Hitler was still recalcitrant and conceived the idea of rallying the Storm Troops around him, as a gesture of defiance against those gentlemen of the right...But an event occurred...which led Hitler to change his plan...He was summoned to Krupp's headquarters and there was received by Goering, and the heads of the Krupp firm and other industrialists...[T]hey delivered their ultimatum: Either Hitler should get rid of his companions or the Goering-Krupp-Blomberg combination would withdraw their support for the regime. Hitler accepted the alternative, but in his own way. He would double-cross Roehm, but he would also double-cross his taskmasters to the Right. He would eliminate a few of the elements that had proved objectionable to the Right, but he would maintain the bulk of them. Besides, he would take the opportunity of the general massacre to remove those against whom he had a grievance -- General Streicher, General Bredlow, Gregor Strasser, etc.(Igra:77f).

Lothar Machtan's analysis, benefitting from an additional fifty years of hindsight, adds another important perspective on this critical event. His study emphasizes that while the German powers were forcing their will upon Hitler, the Fuehrer was confronted with one unescapable truth: the very men he must betray were the ones who held his own darkest secrets in trust. These were already hinting at blackmail due to the increasing tensions in the party. Machtan writes:

THE HIDDEN HITLER

LOTHAR MACHTAN

Roehm was not only acquainted with the shady beginnings of Hitler's political career, he was one of the very few people who knew about his homosexuality. It must have been Hitler's nightmare that he would one day launch a smear campaign....Roehm's friend Edmund Heines [once threatened in 1933] "Adolf hasn't the slightest reason to open his trap so wide -- one word from me, and he'll shut up for good"....As Hitler himself put it, he was faced with "a crisis that could only too easily have had truly devastating consequences for the foreseeable future." His political instinct for self-preservation, if nothing else, compelled him to escalate matters. At the same time, he was urged on by the prospect of concealing his own homosexuality forever by the elimination of dangerous witnesses (Machtan:211f).

Edmund Heines was an especially dangerous threat if former Freikorps soldier Peter Martin Lampel is to be believed. In his unpublished memoirs *Niemandes Knecht*, Lampel claimed to know "a lot about Hitler's homosexuality," including specific knowledge of a liaison with Heines (ibid.:138). Roehm, too, was alleged to have been a sex partner of Hitler, although these rumors were considered "highly exaggerated" by one-time Hitler favorite Putzi Hanfstaengl (ibid.:113).

Pushed to the wall, Hitler chose the Nietzschean path of merciless self-interest. Machtan writes:

Hitler could defend himself only by going to extremes, so the few people who knew that he, too, was homosexual had to be either murdered or thoroughly intimidated. This is revealed by a closer look at the individual victims...Roehm, Ernst and Heines...Gregor Strasser... Karl-Gunther Heimsoth and Paul Rohrbein...senior civil servants privy to potentially explosive evidence about Hitler, for instance, [Prussian Police officials] Erich Klausener...and...Eugen von Kessel; Reichswehr Minister...Kurt von Schleicher and his right hand man, Ferdinand von Bredlow, the Munich police chief August Schneid-huber, the ex-premier of Bavaria, Gustav Ritter von Kahr....the attorneys of Roehm, Strasser, Ludecke and other senior Nazis...the Munich journalist Fritz Gerlich...and....Karl Zehnter [of the "gay" bar] *Bratwurstglockl*.

It may readily be inferred from these few examples that the operation carried out on and around June 30 was....a carefully planned campaign against people who knew, or were suspected of knowing, too much about Hitler (Machtan:216ff).

The Roehm Purge, then, was not a "moral" cleansing of the Nazi ranks, but a political one. Equally it was a realignment of power behind the German government which

Hermann Esser

was primarily forced upon Hitler by powerful political elements, whose support he needed to maintain control. Igra points out that not only did the majority of the SA homosexuals survive the purge, but that the massacre was largely implemented by homosexuals. He cites Strasser that the "Chief Killers of Munich [were] Wagner, Esser, Maurice, Weber and Buch." These men

Walter Buch

"were all known to be sex perverts...of one type or another," concludes Igra (ibid.:80). Plant records that the larger campaign of assassinations across Germany was orchestrated by Reinhard Heydrich, also a homosexual (Plant: 56). Igra addresses Hitler's justification for the purge:

In his defense before the Reichstag a week later Hitler talked of "traitors." That was his alibi...In his speech to the Reichstag he admitted that one of the motives for ordering the massacre was to get rid of the moral perverts in his party and that they were traitors because they practiced homosexualism. But under the dictatorship it was not possible for anyone to put Hitler a question. Nobody asked him to explain how it was that, if his purpose was to get rid of homosexuals, he really didn't rid himself of them but used them as the instruments of his own murder lust and still retained most of them as members of his personal entourage, as well as in key positions of the party organization and the government. Otto Strasser, in his book, The German St. Bartholemew's Night (which has not been published in English), mentions sixteen of these highly placed homosexualist officials who survived the massacres of June 30 and retained their posts (Igra:82).

Following the purge, Hitler received a telegram from Hindenberg "expressing his 'profoundly felt gratitude.'" "'You have saved the German people from a grave peril,' the President wired" (Fest, 1975:470). Likewise, "Defense Minister von Blomberg congratulated Hitler for the successful completion of the 'purge.' (ibid.: 470). The army, too, was pleased by Hitler's move. Only a week after the purge an anti-Nazi Reichswehr officer told the French military attaché in Berlin that the army was 25% pro-Nazi before the purge, but 95% pro-Nazi after the purge (Gallo:312).

Hitler with German President Hindenberg.   Yad Vashem

After the Purge

While it is certainly true that several of the most prominent homosexuals in the Nazi regime were killed on the "Night of the Long Knives" the fact of history is that Adolf Hitler did not purge his regime of homosexuals in this incident or at any subsequent time. On the contrary, a simple review of the historic record reveals that Hitler continued not only to surround himself with homosexuals, but to place them in key positions in the Third Reich.

Judith Reisman notes that "Kazimierz Mocazarski, a Polish resistance fighter, confirmed that homosexuals 'remained party members...got promotions...were protected by the top [Nazi] brass' and served on the battlefield and in prisons" (Reisman, 1994:3). Of the thirteen corps commanders of the SA, all known or suspected homosexuals, only seven were killed in the Roehm Purge (Gallo:16). The rest, along with the probable thousands, perhaps tens of thousands of homosexuals remaining in the SA, were quickly reassigned by Hitler, who put the entire SA under the authority of Heinrich Himmler's SS. Many of these sadistic, brutal men had been useful to Hitler since the beginning, and he made certain that their talents would remain available to him. It is likely that some of these SA survivors were among the participants in Goebbels' dinner-party-turned-orgy in 1936 (Grunberger:70).

Not all SA homosexuals remained loyal to Hitler, however. Snyder records that at least 155 SS leaders were killed in late 1934 and 1935 by a group called "Roehm's Avengers" who "identified their unit on a slip of paper pinned to the body of each victim" (Snyder:298). These assassinations help to explain why Himmler's "antihomosexual" policies were initially strictly enforced, but later (after the Roehm loyalists had been arrested) were much less rigorously applied.

Aside from the SA, Hitler retained all of the sexual deviants of his inner circle, including Goering, Streicher, Frank, Maurice, Schaub, Wagner, Brueckner, Weber and Karl Kaufman, gauleiter of Hamburg. Hess was to remain until 1941, when he left (whether of his own accord or as an emissary of Hitler is still unknown) on his ill-fated "peace" mission to England. As an aside, the loss of Hess must have been very difficult for Hitler. As Ebermayer noted, Hess "was for many years the Fuehrer's [homosexual] partner, especially during their joint detention in Landsberg" (Ebermayer in Machtan:232).

Hitler later openly rewarded some of these men with top jobs in the government. Rector, for example, writes that "Hitler knew about [Walther] Funk, a 'notorious' homosexual, when he appointed him Reich Minister of Economics on February 5, 1938" (Rector: 63). SS

Lieutenant-General Albert Foerster, the homosexual who is mentioned in Langer as a possible sexual partner of Hitler (Langer:178), and whose "black record of atrocities against the Poles" earned him a death sentence in later war trials, was appointed Reich Regent of the Danzig Free State just prior to World War II (Wistrich:178). And Graf von Helldorf, one of Rossbach's original homosexual Brownshirts (Strasser, 1940:26), was appointed by

Hitler's personal financial advisor Walther Funk

Hitler to the post of police president of Berlin in 1935 (Snyder:145).

As he had turned on Ernst Roehm, several of the homosexuals in his inner circle eventually turned on Hitler himself. Johansson and Percy write,

> One gay scholar, Ricard Dey, for years has with others collected data computerized into what he dubs the Encyclopedia Homophilica. Recent publicity about Deputy Fuehrer Rudolf Hess's homosexuality has led him to conclude that the tragically unsuccessful plot to assassinate Hitler in 1944 carried out by Colonel Count von Stauffen berg was masterminded by Admiral Canaris and backed by a *network of other conspirators, like them, rightest homosexuals* (emphasis ours. Johansson and Percy:285).

Discretion would be the watchword for Nazi homosexuals after 1934, however. In light of its public stance following the Roehm purge, the Party could no longer protect flagrant homosexuals in leadership positions. A case in point is mentioned by Oosterhuis. He writes that "[i]n

1937, a top leader of the Nazi movement of the *Sudeten Germans* in Czechoslovakia was arrested for a homosexual offense, once again embroiling the party in a scandal that resembled the Roehm affair" (Oosterhuis:243). In response to this incident, newspaper reporter Walther Bartz (undoubtedly at great personal risk) wrote a series of articles in *Die neue Weltbuehne* on "the homosexual roots of Nazism" (ibid.:243).

One additional incident must be mentioned here which, aside from exposing homosexuals in the post-Roehm party, has great historical significance in its own right: the assassination of Austrian Chancellor Englebert Dollfuss, July 25, 1934. Dollfuss opposed *Anschluss* (the Nazi plan to annex Austria) and Adolf Hitler personally. Igra writes,

> A few days after the murder of Dr. Dollfuss in Vienna (July 25, 1934) the semi-official Italian newspaper, *Il Popolo di Roma*, published the comment:

> *Pederasts and assassins rule in Berlin.*

> By intimating that the authors of the Vienna crime were directly associated with the 'pederasts and assassins' who ruled in Berlin, Mussolini's paper made a grave accusation against the German government at a time when friendly relations existed between the two countries. Under ordinary circumstances the publication of such a statement would have given rise to a diplomatic protest and demanded an explanation. Yet, as far as is known, Hitler made no such protest. Moreover, Mussolini backed up his accusation by ordering the mobilization of Italian troops on the Austro-Italian frontier, as a gesture against Hitler's designs on Austria. But Hitler made no counter-move.

> The explanation of Hitler's silence and inactivity in the face of the Italian challenge may be, and probably is, that he was cowed by Mussolini's blackmail. Mussolini knew that the murder of the Austrian Chancellor had been ordered by Hitler and that this was not done from political

motives exclusively. He knew that personal revenge against Dollfuss was the chief motive working in the dark recesses of Hitler's mind. For Dollfuss had come into possession of an authentic affidavit which connected Hitler directly with the moral scandals I have spoken of....he had certified copies of the affidavit made and entrusted to the diplomatic representatives of [several] governments in Vienna. That is the account which has been

Austrian Chancellor
Englebert Dollfuss

given me, and I have every reason to believe it to be at least substantially true. Among others Dr. Hermann Rauschning assured me that he had seen a copy of such a document, which was in the hands of a foreign government. *It declared that Hitler had been a male prostitute in Vienna at the time of his sojourn there, from 1907 to 1912, and that he practiced the same calling in Munich from 1912 to 1914.* Mussolini obviously knew of the existence of this document, and had a copy of it at his disposal when he charged Hitler with pederasty and murder at one and the same time (Igra:66f).

Igra goes on to relate that the "leader of the gang who murdered Dr. Dollfuss and who actually fired the shots into the Chancellor's body was a certain criminal named [Otto] Planetta who was also a well-known sex pervert" (ibid.:78). Hitler failed to take control of Austria at this time. That would occur in 1938 when Hitler forced the resignation of Dollfuss' successor, Kurt von Schuschnigg in favor of Artur Seyss-Inquart (leader of the Austrian Nazis and also a homosexual -- ibid.:86, Snyder:8).

A few additional words are in order about the extent to

which Hitler's personal fear of disclosure dictated Nazi policy about homosexuality after the purge. Machtan writes:

The violent imposition of a "state of emergency" was intended to enable the authorities to gain possession, at a stroke, of documents considered dangerous by Hitler...His principle motive for taking action against "Roehm and associates" was fear of exposure and blackmail. What additionally confirms this is that the mountains of confiscated documents were not to be used in trials of any kind....Only six months after the Roehm murders, the so-called Malicious Practices Act came into force. This act penalized any remark that might "seriously prejudice the welfare of the Reich"....most of the remarks...related to Hitler himself and his homosexuality....from 1943, remarks to the effect that the "Fuehrer" was homosexually inclined were punishable by death (Machtan:220ff).

It is in this context that we must examine Hitler's instruction to Himmler to clamp down on homosexuality in the nation: "He wanted to get such a grip on the "problem" of homosexuality that it could never again present a threat to his position of power" (ibid.:225). For this reason he required a system of complete control over the homosexual community. The fact that he gained such control and did not use it beyond what was necessary to protect himself (and punish his enemies) is testament to his continued sympathy for his fellow "gays." Indeed, there was really never a campaign to eliminate homosexuality from German society, despite Nazi rhetoric to the contrary.

Heinrich Himmler and the SS

Heinrich Himmler is an extremely important figure in Nazi history. He joined the Nazis in the early years of the party and "participated in the Munich Beer-Hall *Putsch* of November 1923 as a standard-bearer at the side of Ernst

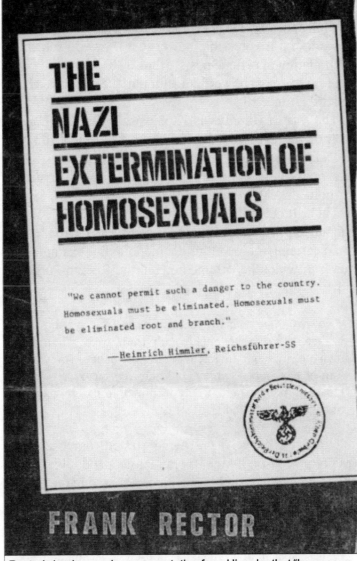

THE NAZI EXTERMINATION OF HOMOSEXUALS

"We cannot permit such a danger to the country. Homosexuals must be eliminated. Homosexuals must be eliminated root and branch."

—Heinrich Himmler, Reichsführer-SS

FRANK RECTOR

Rector's book cover bears a quotation from Himmler that "homosexuals must be eliminated" but the author fails to distinguish rhetoric from reality in Nazi policies.

Roehm" (Wistrich:138). After holding a number of mid-level positions in the party he was appointed "head of Hitler's personal bodyguard, the black-shirted Schulzstaffel

(SS), at that time a small body of 200 men" (ibid.:138). Over the next dozen years Himmler's "astonishing capacity for work and irrepressible power-lust showed itself in his accumulation of official posts" (ibid.:138), eventually winning him the most powerful position in the Third Reich under Hitler himself.

The role of Himmler is also critically important to the assertions of homosexual revisionists. "Heinrich Himmler, Reichsfuehrer SS and head of the Gestapo," writes Steakley, "richly deserves a reputation as the most fanatically anti-homosexual member of the Nazi leadership" (Steakley:111). Indeed, if one were to accept Himmler's public pronouncements against homosexuality at face value, he would certainly deserve this distinction. For example, in a speech in which he commemorated the Roehm Purge, he said:

> Two years ago...when it became necessary, we did not hesitate to strike this plague with death, even within our own ranks...in our judgment of homosexuality — a symptom of degeneracy which could destroy our race — we must return to the guiding Nordic principle: extermination of degenerates" (ibid.:111f).

However, as we have demonstrated, homosexuality was not the reason for the Roehm Purge. And if we look at other evidence we find that Himmler's practice regarding homosexuals was far different than his rhetoric would imply. Grau notes in Hidden Holocaust? that

> In these speculations about a supposed "final solution" to the problem of homosexuality, there is clearly a failure to differentiate what was said in Nazi programmes from what was actually carried out. If Himmler's eradication rhetoric is thought to reflect the fate of individual homosexuals, then obviously the Nazi's policy will be seen as a drive to exterminate them all in the literal sense of the

term. But things appear in a different light once we distinguish between anti-homosexual propaganda for public consumption and the reality on the ground....what he had in his sights was the *homosexual type*. (Grau:6, emphasis ours).

What the Nazis considered the "homosexual type" was the effeminate homosexual male who showed no interest in sexual relations with women. Let us recall the Friedlander distinction between "Butches" and "Fems." Remember that Friedlander, together with the masculine homosexuals of the Community of the Elite, referred to effeminate homosexuals as "degenerates." Clearly, in his speech, Himmler rhetorically lumped the masculine Roehm with all homosexuals, but it is probable that the distinction would have been lost on this particular audience anyway.

Himmler's opposition to homosexuality was directly proportionate to the attitudes of homosexuals about procreation. For him, the individual's highest duty to the state was the improvement of the race through proper breeding.

Just as women in Nazi Germany were valued primarily for procreation, the fate of male homosexuals in Nazi custody hinged primarily on their willingness to rejoin the breeding pool.

Himmler was obsessed with creating a race of "supermen." But in his view, some of the most perfect specimens of Aryan manhood were being lost to this effort due to homosexuality. Himmler felt this "loss" more keenly in light of the fact that Germany had lost two million men in World War I. He also believed there were two million homosexuals in the population. "This meant," write Burleigh and Wippermann, "that Germany's 'sexual balance sheet' had gone into deficit because 'four million men capable of sex' had either died or had 'renounced their duty to procreate' on account of their sexual proclivities" (Burleigh and Wipperman:192).

Himmler's solution to this problem was, logically enough, not the extermination of the delinquent males. Instead he placed great hope in the use of medical "treatments" to reclaim homosexuals for the race. One experiment involved implanting artificial glands in homosexual subjects to introduce additional male hormones to the body. Other efforts paired homosexual prisoners with female prostitutes (ibid.:195f). While the idea of forced medical experiments is abhorrent, the fact that Himmler invested time and resources in such projects shows that he had a very different view of homosexuals than of other prisoners, even of those effeminate homosexuals who were held in such contempt by the Nazi "Butches." Himmler was determined to rehabilitate rather than dispose of them.

Was Himmler a Homosexual?

Himmler may himself have been a homosexual. Filmmaker Walter Frenz, who worked closely with the Nazi elite (including a stint as Hitler's private filmmaker), is reported to have traveled to the Eastern front with Himmler "whose pederastic proclivities he captured on film" (*Washington City Paper*, April 4, 1995). We also know that Gauleiter Helmut Bruckner of Silesia, upon being de-

Roehm and Himmler.

nounced as a homosexual by a Himmler underling in the
month after the Roehm Purge, sent a veiled blackmail threat
via Hess and Goering to expose Himmler's alleged homosexual tendencies (Machtan:226).

Himmler began his Nazi career as an aide to Ernst
Roehm, a fact which clearly refutes the idea that he was a
priggish anti-homosexual zealot. On the contrary,

Himmler's service to Roehm was not performed grudgingly. Himmler voluntarily wrote his own oath of loyalty to Roehm and repeated it ceremoniously each year in Roehm's presence. Gallo records a portion of a letter written to Roehm by Himmler: "As a soldier and a friend, I wish you all you could desire in obedience and loyalty. It has been and always will be my greatest pride to be counted among your most faithful followers" (Gallo:57). For many years Himmler had been pleased to serve the most brazen and outspoken homosexual in the Nazi Party.

It must be noted that even though Himmler helped to orchestrate the Roehm purge, the homoerotic components of his personality had not substantially changed. Herman Glaser, in The Cultural Roots of National Socialism, writes,

> [Even after]...the murder of Roehm and the leading SA personalities...in a certain sense the sodomite romanticism continued to assert itself. The virtually manic search for beautiful male figures perpetrated by Heinrich Himmler, for example, could not just be explained by the delusions of the breeder; it was also compensation for a repressed physical inferiority complex, which especially in people with homosexual tendencies gives rise to neuroses" (Glaser:132).

Himmler, like Hitler, was closely associated with homosexuals throughout his adult life. His path to Nazi leadership, however, was not, like that of so many others, through the German "gay rights" movement. Instead it was through the occult movement, and his Nazi career was defined by his passion for the occult. We have seen how Himmler was profoundly influenced by Guido von List and Jorg Lanz von Liebenfels, the homosexual gurus of nationalistic and anti-Semitic occultism. It was List's dream of a hierarchical male supremacist social order which formed the blueprint for the SS. And it was from List that Himmler appropriated the *"SS"* symbol. From Lanz, Himmler adopted other occult themes. Wistrich writes,

> For him, the SS was at one and the same time the resurrection of the ancient Order of the Teutonic Knights with himself as Grand Master, the breeding of a new *Herrenvolk* aristocracy based on traditional values of obedience, courage and loyalty, and a vast experiment in modern racial engineering (Wistrich:140).

Lanz originated both the revival of the Teutonic Knights theme and the plan for German racial engineering. The latter idea manifested itself in Germany in 1936 as the "State-registered human stud farm known as *Lebensborn* [meaning "fount of life"], where young girls selected for their perfect Nordic traits could procreate with SS men" (ibid.:138). By 1945 over 11,000 births had resulted from the program (Conway:273), which Himmler was later to claim as his greatest contribution to the Third Reich. But the plan, down to some of its details, must be attributed to Lanz. Goodrick-Clarke writes,

> The similarity between Lanz's proposals and the latter practices of Himmler's SS Lebensborn maternity organization... indicate the survival of these mental reflexes over a generation. Lanz's advocacy of brood mothers in eugenic convents (Zuchtkloster), served by pure-blooded Aryan stud-males (Ehehelfer), was revived in the Third Reich (Goodrick-Clarke:97).

Despite his homoerotic inclinations, Himmler was dedicated to the fantasy of an Aryan super race through eugenics, which necessitated heterosexual breeding as a cultural priority. As long as a man performed his procreative duties to the state, Himmler had no problem with his other sexual practices. This attitude is easily recognized in the case of his second-in-command, Reinhard Heydrich, whose own contribution to the Third Reich deserves special attention.

The homosexual Gestapo leader Reinhard Heydrich was one of the most feated men in Germany.   Yad Vashem

Reinhard Heydrich: "The Blonde Beast"

In an organization which exemplified evil, Reinhard Heydrich was considered the quintessential member. "Tall, slim, blonde-haired, with slanting, deep set blue eyes," writes Wistrich, "Heydrich with his military bearing and ice-cool hardness seemed to epitomize the 'Nordic-Aryan type' of Nazi mythology" (Wistrich:134). Himmler selected Heydrich as his right hand-man in 1931, and within a few short years he was feared by everyone but Hitler himself (Rector:61). Wistrich describes him well:

...ruthless, cold and calculating, without any compunction to carrying out the most inhuman measures, Heydrich made himself indispensable to the masters of the Third Reich...His cynicism and contempt for human beings led him to exploit the basest instincts...in weaving his gigantic spider's web of police surveillance in the Third Reich. He filed extensive dossiers, not only on enemies of the Party but also his rivals and colleagues. The 'Blonde Beast,' who controlled the sole intelligence service after 1935, specialized in devious methods of blackmail alongside weapons of open terror and persecution. His hand was most probably in the Tukhachevsky Affair — which led to the purge of Red Army generals in the Soviet Union — and he fabricated the scandalous intrigue which brought down the leading German generals von Blomberg...and von Fritsch...[He] masterminded the mock attack on the Gleiwitz radio transmitter which provided Hitler's excuse for invading Poland...[But] The most satanic consequence of this accumulation of power was revealed in Heydrich's implementation of the order for the wholesale extermination of European Jewry (Wistrich:134f).

Like so many of the Nazis, Heydrich had been a member of the *Freikorps* and "was strongly influenced in his early years by the racial fanaticism of the volkish circles" (ibid.:134). Heydrich also shared the sexual vice that marked Hitler's circle of power. Stevenson created a profile of Heydrich taken directly from the BSC (Allied Intelligence) profile of Heydrich.

[Reinhard Heydrich] was the protégé of Heinrich Himmler, Reich Commissioner for Consolidation of German Racial Stock. Heydrich was fanatical in his hatred of Jews, having himself some Jewish blood. For this reason, Himmler considered him safe. It was always useful to have the means of blackmailing one's colleagues.... "Nobody," Heydrich declared in his anxiety to reach the top, "has greater contempt for Jews than myself. I intend to eliminate the strain."

The fate of "sub-humans" herded into Germany's new mercy-killing centers to be executed on the strength of a physician's oath that the victim was no use to society, the preparations that moved inexorably forward to redesign Europe's entire railroad system to serve the future death camps, all such obscenities before war were made tolerable by the pretense that if you could not actually see them, they could not be happening. In this atmosphere, Heydrich moved with single-minded purpose to a position so close to the Fuehrer that none dared touch him except perhaps Admiral Canaris, who directed the German High Command intelligence service (HICOMINTEL). But even Canaris lost control over young Heydrich. The Admiral had a dossier on Heydrich's homosexual activities after he had been cashiered from the navy, but Heydrich had also become expert at ferreting out embarrassing information about colleagues and superiors...

Heydrich's career was guided and dominated by his relationship with an older friend, Freidrich Karl von Eberstein, son of Count Ernst von Eberstein, Heydrich's godfather. Freidrich von Eberstein was Heydrich's senior by ten years and had served in the navy during World War I. More importantly, Eberstein was one of the original Nazi leaders in the SA and was a personal friend of Adolf Hitler (Calic:33). Historian Callum MacDonald writes,

> While Heydrich was serving on the Naval staff in Kiel, von Eberstein had been leader of the Nazi Stuermabteilung or SA, in Munich and upper Bavaria...In 1931, however, von Eberstein joined another organization, the Schutzstaffel or SS...On the recommendation of von Eberstein, now an officer on Himmler's staff, Heydrich became a member of the Nazi Party, number 544,916, in June 1931. He joined the SA in Hamburg and was soon involved in bloody street battles against the communists and other opponents of the Nazis. He took this step on the understanding that his association with the beerhall brawlers was to be purely temporary and that von Eberstein would use his influence to secure a speedy transfer to the SS...[Later, Hitler] began to look for someone capable of organizing the SS intelligence service on a professional basis and was handed Heydrich's file by von Eberstein (MacDonald:16f).

Outside of his involvement with the early SA we have little evidence to conclude that von Eberstein was homosexual, but we strongly suspect that he was. Other of Heydrich's close associates were known homosexuals. In 1931, when Ernst Roehm was faced with accusations of homosexuality under Paragraph 175, it was Heydrich who came to his defense (Lombardi:12). Heydrich's mentor in the navy, Admiral Wilhelm Canaris, was also alleged to be homosexual -- by Heydrich's successor in the position of Chief of the SD-SS, Ernst Kaltenbrunner (Rector:62). Rector questions this allegation because Kaltenbrunner "once said that 80% of the Abwehr [German Military Intelligence] were sexually perverted" and believed it "to be a center of every form of vice" (ibid.:62). This allegation, however, seems quite consistent with what we have come to know of certain segments of the German military, though the specific statements are perhaps exaggerated. Heydrich and Canaris were very close during Heydrich's tenure in the navy (MacDonald:12), but Canaris later came to fear the man he had trained in intelligence tactics, and kept a dossier on Heydrich's homosexuality as insurance to protect his own career (Stevenson: 349). Much later Canaris was discovered to be a leader in the attempt to assassinate Hitler and was executed at Flossenberg concentration camp on April 9, 1945.

Heydrich's loyalty to Hitler never wavered. Rector writes that "Hitler considered him the ideal Nazi, and Nazi inner circles regarded Heydrich as a likely successor to Hitler even though Hermann Goering was officially slated for the post of Fuehrer" (Rector:62). Hitler's support gave Heydrich nearly unlimited power. As Snyder writes, "Heydrich could order immediate arrests and preventative detention, and he could send any persons to concentration camps at any time. He was the absolute master of life and liberty in the Third Reich" (Snyder:317).

The Grynszpan Affair — Kristallnacht

Perhaps the single most infamous incident orchestrated by Heydrich was the November 9, 1938 *pogrom* known as *Kristallnacht* ("Crystal Night"), in which hundreds of Jews were killed and synagogues and businesses were destroyed across Germany. "In fifteen hours," writes Snyder, "101 synagogues were destroyed by fire, and 76 were demolished. Bands of Nazis systematically destroyed 7,500 Jewish-owned stores. The pillage and looting went on through the night. Streets were covered with broken glass, hence the name *Kristallnacht*" (ibid.:201). Michael Berenbaum, in The World Must Know, adds that ninety-six Jews were killed and thirty thousand were arrested and sent to the camps. Jewish cemeteries, schools and homes were destroyed. As a final insult, the Jews were held responsible for the damage and collectively fined one billion Reichsmarks (Berenbaum:54).

The Nazis characterized this wave of terror as the German people's spontaneous response to the assassination of German Embassy Councilor, Ernst vom Rath. While the "spontaneous" rioting was actually a calculated act of terrorism, the incident that allegedly sparked it was not

Herschel Grynszpan

planned. Ernst vom Rath's murder was a legitimately spontaneous occurrence which the Nazis exploited to justify an attack on the Jews which they had undoubtedly been planning for some time. Interestingly, however, the one common element in the story of the assassination and the story of *Kristallnacht* is homosexuality.

Ernst vom Rath was a high-level SA official who had received a diplomatic posting to the German embassy in Paris. While serving there he had taken up with a seventeen-year-old male prostitute by the name of Herschel Grynszpan, a Polish Jew (Read and Fisher:33). In partial payment for his services, Grynszpan had extracted a promise from vom Rath that his parents would be spared the consequences of a recent law that "revoked the citizenship of Polish Jews who had been living abroad for more than five years and who still retained Polish citizenship" (Rector:57). But vom Rath apparently failed to keep his promise; Grynszpan's family, along with thousands of others "were herded into camps in a no-man's land along the border region of Zbonszyn in freezing weather" (ibid.:58). In retaliation, Grynszpan shot vom Rath on the night of November 7, 1938. Two days later the Nazis staged the "Night of Broken Glass."

Grynszpan was seized by the Gestapo in 1940 (ibid:58).

When at last they had him in their possession, however, their planned high-profile courtroom prosecution went up in smoke. "At the last moment the trial was canceled on Hitler's orders: Grynszpan had threatened to reveal a homosexual relationship with Rath" (ibid.:58). The Nazis were furious. "Vom Rath had been sold to the world as an official martyr, shot down in the service of the Fuehrer. He had even

Joseph Goebbels.

been given a state funeral at which Hitler himself had been a mourner. Was he now to be portrayed in the world's press as a queer with a taste for seventeen-year-old boys?" (Read and Fisher:252).

Of course, the Nazis claimed that the confession was a lie, but apparently there must have been enough evidence to support the story, or the prosecutors could have easily refuted it. Instead, they delayed the trial. Read and Fisher explain:

> The delay gave Goebbels the time to create a new myth about the late Ernst vom Rath, and he set about it in a highly ingenious manner. He arranged for the letters of French prisoners of war to be specially vetted by one of his men, who seized the more passionate and erotic messages. The letters were then doctored to make it appear that they had all been written to vom Rath by various mistresses, with the aim of producing them in court as written evidence of his heterosexuality. At one stroke, Goebbels would have created a new Don Juan, a German womanizer irresistible to Frenchwomen (ibid:253).

Clearly the Nazis could produce no legitimate evidence that vom Rath was a heterosexual. But even their falsified evidence went unused because, in the meantime, the Justice Ministry had obtained additional information that made a public trial impossible. "[A] story had been circulating in public that Herschel had in fact been vom Rath's male whore and procurer for some time in 1938, and that vom Rath had been known in Parisian homosexual circles as 'the ambassadress' and 'Notre Dame de Paris'" (ibid.:253). Additionally, it was learned that vom Rath's brother "had been dismissed from the service for homosexual offenses" (ibid.:253). This was too much for even Hitler's propaganda machine to overcome, so the trial was again postponed.

To be fair, we must acknowledge that Read and Fisher concluded that the allegations of a homosexual affair between vom Rath and Grynszpan were untrue, merely the creation of Grynszpan's lawyer. A review of all the evidence, however, including much which was apparently unknown to Read and Fisher, compels us to conclude that the incident occurred as we have described it herein. Our conclusion is further bolstered by the fact that the Nazis had placed pederastic homosexuals in other foreign posts. The German consul in Casablanca, Morocco, Dr. Theodor Auer, was homosexual as well. His "affair with the son of a local sheikh and his 'behaviour' with Arab, French and Jewish 'bumboys' were detailed by the British Secret Operations Executive (SOE) ("How sex became a weapon of war," *Daily Telegraph*, July 23, 1998).

Grynszpan's young life began and ended in tragedy associated with homosexual perversion. His home town of Hanover (perhaps not coincidentally the birthplace of Karl Heinrich Ulrichs) "was a center of homosexuality," according to Read and Fisher:

There were no fewer than 500 male prostitutes on the police books in 1918, and the chief criminal inspector put the number of homosexuals in the city at about 40,000, out of a total population of 450,000. The Grynszpan's neighborhood earned particular notoriety during the early year's of Herschel's childhood through the activities of one Fritz Haarman, known as "the Butcher of Hanover," who picked up his victims, mostly adolescent boys, in the railway station, and took them home...When he had finished with them, he strangled them, butchered their corpses, and sold the flesh as meat. He was executed in 1925 (ibid.:33).

Grynszpan never did go to trial, though he remained in Nazi custody. Interestingly, the organization which came to his aid during this time was called the Society for Human Rights (ibid.:245). [We are not certain if this was the same "homosexual rights" group which had once boasted Ernst Roehm as a member, but it may have been.] Victor Basch, then head of the SHR "had pleaded for 'liberty or judgment'" in an effort to get him freed, but to no avail (ibid.:245). After 1942 Grynszpan just disappeared, probably killed secretly by the Gestapo.

Kristallnacht, the "spontaneous" incident which Grynszpan's act had supposedly sparked, has also been described as being defined by homosexuality. As all of Europe struggled to understand the cause for this horror, an answer was offered by British Consul-General, R.T. Smallbones. Smallbones was a "self-confessed Germanophile" who had served in Germany, from 1932 to 1939 and "had developed great admiration and respect for the sterling qualities of the people" (ibid.:127). "His opinion, therefore," writes Igra, "rests on first-hand experience of the German people for a long period of years" (Igra:7). He continues:

Victims of the Lidice massacre.

[Smallbones authored] a British White Paper, "Concerning the treatment of German Nationals (including the Jews) in Germany," in which the following statement is made: "The explanation of this outbreak of sadistic cruelty may be that sexual perversion, and, in particular, homosexuality, are very prevalent in Germany. It seems to me that mass sexual perversion may offer an explanation of this otherwise inexplicable outbreak"...I am convinced that this explanation is the correct one [writes Igra]. For, as a matter of fact, the widespread existence of sexual perversion in Germany...at the time the Hitler movement rose to power...is notorious. And authorities on criminal sociology are agreed that there is a causal connection between mass sexual perversion and the kind of mass atrocities committed by the Germans (ibid:7).

Heydrich, the man most responsible for this atrocity, met his death in May, 1942, at the hands of two Czechoslovakian resistance fighters. A bomb was tossed into his car, shattering his spine. He died on June 4, 1942. In retaliation "the Germans took savage revenge, after the manner of the old Teutonic rites, for the death of their hero" (Shirer:1288f). Over 1,500 people were immediately executed and thousands more followed, including the entire population of Lidice (ibid.:1289). The Lidice massacre was orchestrated by Heydrich's replacement, Kurt Daluege, formerly a unit leader in Rossbach's notorious homosexual *Freikorps* (Wistrich:43).

As for the official legal resolution of the *Kristallnacht* affair, that matter was handed to homosexual Walter Buch. A former early SA leader, now President of the Nazi Party Supreme Court, Buch concluded that the Nazi rank and file who had participated in the murderous pogrom were innocent of any crime (ibid:33f).

Chapter Six

HOMOSEXUALITY IN THE
CONCENTRATION CAMPS

We have now arrived at one of the most sensitive topics in our discussion of homosexuality in Nazi Germany. As we have noted, revisionists have attempted to define homosexuals as a class of people who were "targeted for extermination" by the Nazis. One homosexual group went so far as to stage a high-profile "pilgrimage" to the Yad Vashem Holocaust Memorial in Jerusalem in May of 1994. They were met by a delegation of Jewish Holocaust survivors who were so overcome with outrage that some of them had to be restrained from physically assaulting the contingent of (mostly American) political activists. One man cried, "My grandfather was killed for refusing to have sexual relations with the camp commandant. You are desecrating this place..." (*The Jerusalem Post*, May 30, 1994).

Yet, as we have noted, some homosexuals did in fact die in Nazi concentration camps. We do not diminish the tragedy of any life lost under the Nazi reign of terror; however, we must reject the implication that homosexuals as a class should be given moral equivalency to the Jewish people and other victims of genocide. There are five reasons why we must reject this claim of the revisionists.

First, we know that regardless of Himmler's anti-homosexual rhetoric, homosexuals as a class were never targeted for extermination, as their continued role in the Third Reich demonstrates.

Second, those homosexuals who died did so primarily as the result of mistreatment and disease in slave-labor camps -- not in the gas chambers. As reported in the Washington Blade

> John Fout, professor of history...said his research shows that about 50,000 men were imprisoned for homosexual related "offenses" by the Nazis between 1933 and 1945. Most of them, he said, were imprisoned for relatively short sentences and in regular German prisons, not concentration camps as has been generally believed (Researcher says Nazi persecution not systematic, *The Washington Blade*, May 22, 1998).

Third, though we cannot condone the form of punishment meted out by the Nazis, homosexual sodomy was a legitimate crime of long-standing for which individuals were being jailed both before and after the Nazi Regime (and in this country during the same time period). Indeed, Fout acknowledges that rather than being arrested indiscriminately simply for "being" a homosexual, "the overwhelming majority of those arrested...were charged with engaging in sex in public places, such as parks and public restrooms" (ibid). This is in contrast to the internment of Jewish people, whose ethnicity is morally (and in pre-Nazi Germany, legally) neutral.

Fourth, the *actual* number of homosexuals in the camps was a tiny fraction of both the estimated number of homosexuals in Germany and the estimate of the camp population. The camp homosexual population, estimated at 5,000-15,000 by Fout and by Joan Ringelheim of the US Holocaust museum (Rose:40), contained an undetermined percentage of non-homosexuals falsely labeled as homo-

Dachau Concentration Camp was the first to open.

sexuals (see section titled "Anti-homosexual Policies" above). Homosexuals who died were "a small fraction of less than 1 percent" of homosexuals in Nazi-occupied Europe (S. Katz:146), compared to more than 85 percent of European Jewry. To be more specific, Buchenwald was the camp with the highest number of supposed homosexual prisoners. According to Grau, it's annual population count of "pink triangles" peaked at just 189 in 1944, with fewer than 100 such prisoners in the years prior to 1942. "The figures were small in comparison with the total number of prisoners there -- well below one percent in every year" (Grau:264).

Fifth and last, many of the guards and administrators responsible for the infamous concentration camp atrocities were homosexuals themselves, which negates the idea that homosexuals *in general* were being persecuted and interned.

The Nazi system of concentration camps began with Dachau in 1933, but by the fall of the Third Reich the number of sites which had held prisoners in German occupied territory surpassed 10,000 (Parshall:57). It is not generally known that only six of these camps were the notorious "death camps." In his introduction to Jean-Francios Steiner's Treblinka, Terrence des Pres addresses this distinction:

The first Nazi camps, which were set up soon after Hitler came to power in 1933, were designed as places of detention and as training grounds for the SS. Dachau and Buchenwald were among the most notorious, and although we cannot forget that thousands of people perished in these places, we should keep in mind that camps of this kind were not intended or equipped to be instruments of genocide...however, as the Nazi policy of extermination took shape with the Jews as primary target, the major "killing centers," as they came to be called, began to operate...The great killing centers were six: Auschwitz-Birkenau, Sobidor, Chelmno, Belzec, Maidenek, and Treblinka (Steiner:x-xi).

We make this point simply to show that the internment of homosexuals in the concentration camps was not equivalent to that of Jews and other racial groups who were, under Nazi policy, targeted for extermination. As terrible as life could be in the work camps, it offered better chances than being herded into gas chambers or shot in front of mass graves.

An additional point that deserves mention here is that the uniform pattern of brutality for which the camps are known was established as a deliberate and calculated policy by the SA under Ernst Roehm in 1933. Heiden writes that "[t]he S.A. had learned...that the will of an imprisoned mass must be broken by the most loathsome cruelty" (Heiden, 1944:565). He later adds that "[f]rightening reports also trickled through from the concentration camps, and the public began to realize that the Fuehrer's picked troops had organized artificial hells in Dachau...Roehm admitted publicly that these things seemed unbearable to many people, but said he saw no reason for stopping them" (ibid.:732f). Though Roehm was soon killed, his system of mass torture and degradation endured.

The Guards and Kapos

There is one aspect of life in the concentration camps that is seldom noted by historians, yet is profoundly significant in this discussion. That aspect is the unique status of homosexuals in the camps. For while any prisoner could be chosen as a *Kapo* (a slave overseer), none other of the interned groups *except* homosexuals had counterparts among the Nazi guards and administrators (for example, there were no Jewish guards or administrators). Stephan Ross, founder of the New England Holocaust Museum, estimates that "about 20 percent of those guarding Jewish prisoners were homosexuals." Ross was himself interned for five years in Nazi camps as a child and was repeatedly sexually abused by the guards. "[T]hey would beat you and make you do that [perform oral sex]" he said. "To this day I am very angry about it" ("Holocaust Survivor: Molested by Guards," *The Massachusetts News*, April 5, 2000).

Examples of the homosexuality of the concentration camp guards can be found in many of the personal accounts of Holocaust survivors. Elie Wiesel, sent to the Buna factory camp in the Auschwitz complex, for example, acknowledges this in his book <u>Night</u>:

The head of our tent was a German. An assassin's face, fleshy lips, hands like wolf's paws. He was so fat he could hardly move. Like the leader of the camp he loved children...(Actually this was not a disinterested affection: there was a considerable traffic in young children among homosexuals here, I learned later) (Wiesel:59).

In Treblinka, the narrative account of the Treblinka uprising, Steiner records the story of another Nazi administrator, taken from interviews with survivors:

> Max Bielas had a harem of little Jewish boys. He liked them young, no older than seventeen. He had a kind of parody of the shepherds of Arcadia, their role was to take care of the camp flock of geese. They were dressed like little princes...Bielas had a little barracks built for them that looked like a doll's house...Bielas sought in Treblinka only the satisfaction of his homosexual instincts (Steiner:117f).

Walter Poller, a German political prisoner who was interned in the Buchenwald concentration camp, also noted the homosexuality of certain guards. In <u>Medical Block Buchenwald</u> Poller describes the camp practice of mass beatings, and reports on the perverse pleasure these guards derived from the torment of the prisoners:

> If the camp doctor happened to pass by after a mass whipping, and knew that a certain type of homosexual Schar-Fuehrer [platoon leader] and SS officer stood at a certain gate, he arranged a little special entertainment for them, which he called a medical examination (Poller:103).

Poller leaves the details of these "medical examinations" to our imagination. But this brief glimpse into the ranks of the SS guards reveals much about the camps. Poller's distinction between "types" of homosexual SS officers, for example, implies that there were more than a few such guards. Furthermore, their homosexuality was a matter of public knowledge. Both of these inferences are supported in another passage which tells of the retaliation against the Jewish prisoners following the attempted assassination of Hitler in July, 1944:

> Two Scharfuehrer came along the empty camp roads at about nine o'clock. One of them was...an Oberscharfuehrer [commander of platoon leaders] known to the prisoners by the nick-name of "Anna," because of his undisguised homosexuality. They entered one of the Jewish barracks, and there indiscriminately chose five Jews and brought them outside. From a second barracks they brought out eight more. From a third they selected another seven...the twenty Jews were ...[marched] off under Anna's orders...Some time later we heard a burst of firing from the direction of the stone quarry. It was now clear that the earthly existence of our...Jewish comrades had ended (ibid.:136f).

Plant, though a revisionist, admits that "a few SS guards were homosexual" and that they "made some younger inmates, usually Poles or Russians, their 'dolly boys' (Pielpel)" (Plant:166). These homosexual antics were not carried out in secret. Plant writes that such guards would "occasionally compete with *Kapos* for these teenagers. They even drew lots to determine who should go to whom" (ibid.:166). Primo Levi, in <u>Survival in Auschwitz</u> notes that "young attractive homosexuals" had a much higher survival rate than average prisoners (Levi:81).

Younger children were not spared from abuse, but in fact many suffered more harshly. Dr. Judith Reisman writes that Nazi industrialist Alfried Krupp maintained a "children's concentration camp"called *Buchmannshof* where very young children were used in sexual experiments.

> Infants and children under six years of age were torn from their Krupp enslaved mothers and interned in Buchmannshof for their brief lives. Buchmannshof children died at the rate of some 50 per day for years, newly born or taken from parents brought to the Krupp slave camps. Krupp's older slave children were called "slave youth" and little is known about their lives (Reisman, Kinsey: Crimes and Consequences:311).

Reisman believes that the Krupp camp was one source of the appalling "child orgasm" statistics cited in Table 34 of the 1948 Kinsey report (ibid.). Krupp, an exceedingly ruthless and cruel man, was tried and convicted at Nuremberg, but not for his involvement with *Buchmannhof*. The existence of the camp was never mentioned in the Krupp indictment (Manchester:537). (Significantly, Alfried was the grandson of Fritz Krupp, the notorious pederast who committed suicide when his sexual abuse of boys became public knowledge in Germany. The Krupp scandal exposed a powerful and corrupt homosexual clique in the government and led to high-profile courtroom trials between 1907 and 1912. For more on this chapter of German history see Lively, "Germany's National Vice Revisited," in The Poisoned Stream, 1997).

Although homosexuals constituted one of the smallest numerical minorities in the camps (Plant:153), they apparently were appointed in disproportionally large numbers as *Kapos* (roughly the equivalent of "trusties" in our penal system). Psychoanalyst and medical doctor Edmund Bergler writes that "[i]t is...well known that the *capos* in Hitler's concentration and extermination camps were only too frequently recruited from the ranks of homosexual criminals...I had firsthand information on this point from a patient who had spent six years in the infamous camp at Dachau (Bergler:279). Jan D. (who wishes to remain anonymous), in Auschwitz and Gross Rosen from 1940-1945, comments on the role of these prisoners: "The most cruelty inflicted on the Concentration Camps prisoners was done by the '*Capos*' (work detail supervisors), mostly German criminals and homosexuals" (Private letter).

Alfried Krupp

In Hidden Holocaust?, Gunter Grau includes a report from the Buchenwald archives. It reads,

The kapo, Herzog, was a former member of the foreign legion, extremely brutal, apparently homosexual-sadistic and with a frightening tendency to become frenzied; if someone was beaten by him it was all over (Grau:268).

These testimonies are supported by Raul Hilberg, author of The Destruction of the European Jews and a member of the (U.S.) President's Commission on the Holocaust. Rector cites a December 10, 1979 *Village Voice* article in which Hilberg said "that homosexuals were highly valued prisoners [relative to the Jews], and that many kapos — inmates who administered the barracks and dispensed instant discipline (beatings and killings were common) were gay" (Rector:139).

There seems to have been a great dichotomy between the experiences of homosexuals in the camps. While on the one hand, Plant claims that homosexuals were treated more harshly than the members of other groups, citing Kogon's Dachau memoir, The Theory and Practice of Hell, other researchers refute this. Shelly Roberts, one of the Shoah Foundation's researchers posted the following comment on the World Wide Web, March 6, 1997.

I am one of the privileged who is interviewing holocaust survivors for the Spielberg video history project....I have encountered at least half a dozen survivors who offer fragments and indications and scraps of information that some German lesbians and international homosexual men were in fact treated better (a really relative term here) than the average Jewish prisoner....This is separate to any Nazi officer who collected young boys to keep in his private collection (read harum [sic]). These boys were not given any options.

If the information I am hearing from these nice Jewish survivors, who don't appear to have any axes to grind, is true, than [sic] it WOULD seem that (some?most?all?) homosexuals...may have been given some kind of favored status.

Roberts, interestingly, is no fan of <u>The Pink Swastika</u>, which she (or he) characterizes as "a spite-filled revisionist document on the net that purports to be a reality-based treatise on privileged gays" (ibid). In any case, there are conflicting claims about the status of homosexuals relative to other prisoners in the camps. To some extent this may simply reflect the differences between camps and the philosophies of their administrators. But the enduring "Butch/Fem" conflict clearly had a substantial bearing on the treatment of homosexuals.

Plant writes of one survivor who reported that "the guards lashed out with special fury against those who showed 'effeminate traits'" (Plant:172). And Rector records a statement from an interview with a former Pink Triangle named Wolf (a pseudonym) in which the issue of effeminacy was raised. "The ones who were soft, shall I say, were the ones who suffered terribly" (Rector:157).

Rudolf Hoess, the infamous commandant of Auschwitz, defined "genuine homosexuals... [by their] soft and girlish affectations and fastidiousness, their sickly sweet manner of speech, and their altogether too affectionate deportment toward their fellows" (Hoess in ibid.:137f). These "genuine homosexuals" were considered incorrigible and held in special barracks, while many non-effeminate homosexuals were released (ibid.:137). It is probable that Hoess was homosexual. He had been a member of Gerhard Rossbach's homosexual *Freikorps* and a close friend of Edmund Heines (Snyder:301), the procurer of boys for Roehm's pederastic

Rudolf Hoess

orgies.

Wolf's testimony about the homosexual behavior of the SS guards also reveals the sadistic characteristic of the "Butches." "In the cell next to mine was a young male prostitute from Steglitz who the SS forced into [sexual acts]" (Rector:156). He also described a game the SS played each evening. "There were holes in the walls and they would reach through the holes and play with the genitals of the men sleeping close to the holes. Then they would say that they had caught them jacking off, and they would beat them" (ibid.:156). During his imprisonment, Wolf was also forced to witness an execution of six political escapees who had been recaptured by the guards. "They were stripped naked, tied to the table spread-eagle face up, and beaten to death with clubs, one by one, " he reported. "You could see that the SS executioners became sexually stimulated while beating the screaming prisoners to death" (ibid.:157).

This extreme savagery exhibited by the "Butch" homosexuals of the camps was not rare, but some accounts of brutality are more gruesome than others. At Auschwitz, for example, *Kapo* Ludwig Tiene became the most prolific mass murderer of all time by strangling, crushing and gnawing to death as many as 100 boys and young men a day while he raped them (ibid.:143). Incidentally, the second most prolific serial killer in history was also homosexual, the infamous "Bluebeard." The man believed to be the legendary mass killer, Bluebeard, is Gilles De Rais, born in Machecoul, Brittany, in 1404. In The Gay Book of Days, Martin Greif, reports that after being arrested on charges of blasphemy, Gilles de Rais "confessed to having killed some 150 boys 'for the pleasure and gratification of my senses'...He decided that sodomizing his victims would satisfy both his needs and the Devil's, and so more and more boys disappeared into his castle, never to be seen again" (Greif:21).

Perhaps the most grotesque story of all, however, is told by Rector in his chapter on the camps, grotesque not because it is bloodier, but because it reveals how widespread and acceptable these extremes of perversion had become among the Nazi elite. He writes,

As for the SS, their behavior was typical among those who engaged in sexual bestiality. An example is a film, in color with a sound track, that was secretly made for the pornographic enjoyment of a select coterie of Nazis showing a wild drunken orgy of beautiful boys and handsome young men being whipped, raped and murdered by the SS (Rector:144). (Note: Rector adds that this film is still today "very discreetly and very privately shown to only an inner circle of certain homosexuals in Europe").

No study of homosexuality in the Nazi concentration camps would be complete without mentioning a book called The Men with the Pink Triangle. In recent years this book has become a standard text for revisionists because it is purportedly the only autobiography written by a former pink triangle prisoner. The book itself, however, written by Heinz Heger, cannot be considered reliable. It is presented as an autobiography, yet translator David Fernbach admits in his introduction that Heger's account is *not* his own but is the story of "an anonymous victim of the Nazis, an Austrian" (Heger:9). And though it contains quite a number of anecdotes about homosexuality among the SS guards which would otherwise be useful in this discussion, these stories all have a distinct quality of sexual fantasy. We are asked to believe that nearly every male authority figure whom "Heger" encounters requires him to perform oral sex, for example.

Other ostensibly true-life histories of camp survivors are sober chronicles of enslavement and degradation, but "Heger's" account is almost whimsical in places and includes numerous implausible scenes, such as one in which

"Heger's" *Kapo* lover countermands an order to punish "Heger" which comes from the camp commandant himself. For this reason we will not credit the many examples of homosexual sadism reported in this work. Before we leave the subject of guards and *Kapos*, we must mention one of the few accounts of lesbians in Nazi history, again in connection with the prison system. In Paris Under the Occupation, Historians Perrault and Azema describe the activities of the French Gestapo. They identify "Sonia Boukassi, a drug addict, and Violette Morris, onetime French weight-lifting champion, both lesbians, [as] the chief women's interrogators" in the notorious torture chambers of *La Carlingue* (Perrault and Azema:38).

The Prisoners

Homosexual prisoners did not integrate well into the prison populations, writes Eugen Kogon. The prisoners ostracized "those whom the SS marked with the pink triangle" (Kogon:44). Kogon attributes this dislike to the fact that the homosexual population included "criminals, and especially blackmailers...Hostility toward them may also have been partly rooted in the fact that homosexuality was at one time widespread in Prussian military circles, as well as the SA and the SS" (ibid:44).

Kogon implies that the prisoners associated homosexuality with their tormentors and thus saw the "pink triangles" as objects of fear and hatred. Plant supports this view, noting that "homosexual prisoners were often tainted by the crimes of the homosexual guards—even though they themselves were often the victims" (Plant:167). There is evidence, as well, that the homosexuals in the camps alienated their fellow prisoners because of the predatory nature of their sexual drive. Polish sociologist, Anna Pawelczynska, in Values and Violence in Auschwitz, describes this situation:

Sometimes a confirmed homosexual would lead a prisoner of normal inclinations into homosexual practices. Such relationships were usually deeply immoral or deeply demoralizing. A prisoner-functionary's [*Kapo's*] desire to satisfy his or her pederastic sexual needs could also manifest itself in various brutal forms of terror and blackmail used to bring the partner into compliance (Pawelczynska:98).

Pawelcznska's record also refutes Plant's suggestion that homosexual prisoners were "utterly disunited" and therefore powerless. She cites the use of prostitution as a form of currency among the homosexual prisoners. This was likely a common means of getting favors from the homosexual guards as well. She writes,

...paid prostitution existed in the camp and the choice of erotic partners was dictated by one's ability to pay — either in the form of help in gaining a better place in the camp structure or, at each visit, in the form of food or better clothes. Homosexual erotic availability became a coin of incommensurate worth, in return for which the chance of biological survival could be won, depending on the client's possibilities (ibid.:99).

In Buchenwald, however, we are told that "[a]ssisted by isolation from the other camp and more supported than supervised by the SS, a number of bandits were completely terrorizing the workforce, stealing the packets they were supposed to receive since winter 1941, and holding real orgies of brutality and the most shameless sadism. Sexual abuse and the foulest murder were the order of the day" (Grau:268).

There is one other distinction between homosexual and other prisoners. Toward the end of World War II, many homosexuals were released from the concentration camps and drafted into the *Wehrmacht* (Shaul:688). A leading his-

The Massachusetts News

Holocaust Survivor: Molested by Homosexual Guards

Founder of Boston Holocaust Museum spent five years in Nazi camps

Massachusetts News

It's commonly accepted that Hitler targeted homosexuals for extermination – just as he did the Jews.

"Not so," says Stephan Ross, the Newton resident who is the founder of the Holocaust Museum in Boston.

And he should know. Ross was there. He lived, and almost died, in Nazi prison camps from the age of 9 to 14.

And while the abuse of the Nazis took many forms, he says he was sexually molested more than once by homosexual Nazi prison guards. He knew it was also going on with other prisoners, "although I didn't go looking for it."

Founder of New England Holocaust Memorial tells of his abuse by homosexual guards in a concentration camp.

torian of the period, Steven Katz cites records that "indicate that 13% of all homosexual camp inmates were reprieved and released" (S. Katz:146). This, of course, happened as the Nazis frantically increased their "production" in the death camps, trying to exterminate every last Jew in Europe before the Allies could liberate the camps.

Were these homosexual volunteers mere cannon fodder in the Nazi military? Not for those with the right sadistic temperament. Many homosexual men chose to "transfer to a delinquent battalion like the vicious 'Strafbataillon Dirlewanger'(*IGLA Euroletter* 52, August, 1977).

Oskar Dirlewanger, a former Freikorps commander in the 1920s, was the creator of this extremely barbarous unit, also known as the *Sonderkommando Dirlewanger*, "the most notorious of Waffen-SS units under perhaps the most sadistic of commanders" ("36th WaffenGrenadier-Division der SS," www.wssob.com). Dirlewanger put together this unit from concentration camp inmates after he himself was released from a camp after serving a sentence for sexual assault of a female child under fourteen "and other sex crimes

of a vile nature" (www.eliteforcesofthethirdreich.com).

Survivor Stephan Ross says that many homosexuals were released without any requirement of military service:

> All they [those accused of homosexuality] had to do to get out [of the camp] was to sign a paper to say that they had been rehabilitated and wouldn't do it [engage in homosexual behavior] anymore...They were not targeted to die. Not like we were. (*The Massachusetts News*, April 5, 2000).

Before we leave this subject we should mention the fact that many of the non-effeminate homosexuals interned in Nazi work camps were former Storm Troopers whose allegiance had been to Ernst Roehm and not to Hitler. When "Roehm's Avengers" began killing SS leaders in retaliation for Hitler's assassination (Snyder:298), Himmler cracked down on these homosexual former SA soldiers and many were sent to the camps. (This would account for many of the incidents of sadism and brutality.) Holocaust survivor Eugen Zuckerman wrote the following in a letter

to the *New York Post*, protesting the portrayal of homosexuals as Nazi victims in the New York Holocaust
museum.

> As a Jewish ex-inmate of several concentration camps, in-
> cluding Mauthausen, and as one who grew up in Berlin
> from the late 1920s until October 1939 and knows the
> history that led to the internment of gay men in concentra-
> tion camps, I am opposed to a memorial to homosexu-
> als...The first thousands of homosexuals interned were all
> members of the Sturm Abteilung (SA), the Nazi Storm
> Troopers (*New York Post*, February 16, 1997).

(For the reasons he cited above, Raul Hilberg also believes that the inclusion of homosexuals in any memoriali-
zation of Holocaust victims "would be a travesty" --
Hilberg in Rector:139).

Thus, if we add up the numbers, it appears that very few
of the millions of European homosexuals were ever sent to
concentration camps and of those who were, only a fraction
were interned for purely sexual reasons. If, of the
5,000-15,000 homosexuals interned, the "first thousands"
were SA Brownshirts and many others were non-
homosexuals falsely charged with homosexuality, it is
possible that mere dozens or hundreds were actually sent to
camps for homosexuality over the twelve years of Nazi
rule.

DEBUNKING THE "GAY" HOLOCAUST MYTH BY COMPARING "GAYS" TO JEWS

Variables	Jews	Homosexuals
1.Number of victims	As many as six million.	5,000-15,000 of which an undetermined number were political prisoners falsely accused of homosexuality.
2. The % of population sent to concentration camps	Up to 85% of all Jews in Germany and German-occupied countries.	Less than 1% of European homosexuals were interned.
3. The % sent to camps of those who were arrested	Virtually all Jews arrested were sent to extermination camps.	Of all homosexual arrests, criminal and political, 10-15% were sent to work camps.
4. Destination upon arrest	Directly or indirectly to one of six death camps: Auschwitz-Birkenau, Sobidor, Chelmno, Belzec, Maidenek or Treblinka	Homosexuals were sent to several of the 10,000+ work camps.
5. Reason for arrest	Genocide. Jews were targeted for extermination. Compare to Gypsies, Slavs and other ethnic groups.	Criminal acts. Homosexuals were arrested for violating laws against sodomy and child molestation which predated the Nazi regime. Compare to thieves, blackmailers and other behavior-based groups.
6. Number that died in the camps	As many as six million.	Probably less than 6,000
7. Primary cause of death	Mass execution by firing squad, gas chamber, etc.	Starvation, disease, mistreatment by guards. Homosexuals as a class were not targeted for extermination
8. Chance of release	Jews had almost no chance of release.	Homosexuals were routinely released if they convincingly renounced homosexuality or joined the military.

Variables	Jews	Homosexuals
9. Use in medical experiments	Jews were used as guinea pigs in horrific experiments which usually resulted in mutilation or death.	To increase the breeding population, some homosexuals received surgical implants to raise testosterone levels or were forced to have sex with female prostitutes. Some were castrated. Death was rare and unintended.
10. Punishment for harboring	Punishment for hiding Jews was death.	There was no punishment for harboring homosexuals. Many were protected by Nazi leaders.
11. Representation among camp guards	There were no known Jewish guards in the concentration camps.	By some estimates, up to 20% of camp guards were homosexuals.
12. Responsibility for the Holocaust	The Jews were not in any way responsible for the Holocaust.	A high percentage of Hitler's cronies associated with Nazi atrocities were homosexuals.
13. Use of Holocaust "victim status" as a political tool	Jewish groups do not flaunt the yellow star or exploit the Holocaust for political gain.	"Gay" activists use the pink triangle as their movement's symbol and routinely invoke the "Gay Holocaust" myth for political advantage.
14. Relationship of Holocaust memorial sponsors and benefactors to victims	Jewish sponsors and benefactors of Holocaust memorials are often family members of victims. Non-relatives still share a 6,000 year ethnic and cultural heritage.	The only bond that links homosexuals in today's movement with those interred in Nazi work camps is the common practice of sodomy and a shared sense of social ostracism because of it.

Chapter Seven

THE NAZI HATRED OF JUDEO-CHRISTIAN MORALITY

A common misperception held by present day Americans is that the Nazi campaign against the Jews was driven solely by racism. However, the Nazis were equally motivated by a vicious hatred of Biblical morality. In fact, the two were inseparable. Samuel Igra addressed this question in *Germany's National Vice*

> Why should it be the Jews particularly that the German forces arrayed under Hitler want to exterminate?...What does this small people stand for which was accounted hateful and obnoxious to the Nazi rulers of Germany? Or, to put the question in another way, what is there in the Jewish traditional code of morals which induced Hitler to come forward as the protagonist of the German people against the Jews?....He was....the *condottiere* of a band of evil men who were united together by a common vice [homosexuality, whereas] Jewish national tradition for thousands of years has been actively opposed to this particular evil; because it is germinal vice, a virus that poisons the whole life-blood of human existence (Igra in Lively, *The Poisoned Stream*, p.13f) .

Race Defilement by Dietrich Hutton, published by "Deutsche Revolution" of Duesseldorf, was widely distributed in Germany.

A widely circulated German publication by racial theorist Dietrich Hutton, titled <u>Defilement of Race</u>, helps to illuminate this point. It preached that Germany could only achieve its racial goals (and its destiny) by destroying Judeo-Christian morality.

> Through the German soul and through unadulterated German blood, the world will be able to return to a state of health, but only after it has been freed from the curse of Judaism and of Christianity....The mission of German nationality in the world is to free this world of Jews and Christians....It is the very essence of Christianity...for all people to become "united in brotherhood." To achieve this, all barriers of race must fall. The maintenance of such barriers means the preservation of national individuality, which is essentially irreconcilable with the Christian aim of universal brotherhood....Because this disintegration of racial culture has been consciously and systematically pursued by Christianity, and is still being pursued today, it is race defilement. (Hutton:3ff).

The Nazi regime viewed Judaism as the *source* of the problem but identified Christianity as the essential and willing tool by which the Jews sought to gain world domination. Hutton writes,

> The way in which Christianity is directed in the interests of world Jewry and its attitude toward Judaism is traceable to the undeniable fact that the founders and proclaimers of the teachings of Jesus of Nazareth were full-blooded Jews....It cannot therefore be coincidence, or negligence or ignorance that consciously makes Christians...deviate from the fundamental tenets of conserving nationality and cultivating race. The reason for this is to defile non-Jewish races, weaken and destroy them so that Judaism, as the "chosen people," can...[erect] a world

"The Flight of Lot," by Gustave Dore depicts God's destruction of Sodom by fire and brimstone because of homosexuality.

sovereignty on the ruins of the non-Jewish races which Christianity has destroyed. (ibid:19).

Significantly, Hutton's argument is not fundamentally an attack upon race, but upon theology. Both Jews and Christians are evil because of what they *believe* and how they thus organize their societies.

Why then did the Nazis maintained a murder campaign against all Jews but only against certain Christians? One factor was obviously political pragmatism since a sizable number of Germans identified themselves as Christians. But another factor was that, distinct from Christianity, the Jewish identity is ethnic as well as religious. The simple solution to the "Jewish problem," therefore, was to scapegoat and kill all ethnic Jews (even those who had abandoned Biblical morality).

In contrast, Christianity was perceived by the Nazis as

merely the theological puppet of Judaism; a tool to enslave the minds of otherwise rational people of every race. Thus, the Nazi approach to Christianity was a campaign of "reeducation" by advancing Nazi ideology through relentless propaganda, while simultaneously suppressing the opposing Christian view.

If we wish to create something new [writes Hutton] we cannot permit the existence and operation of disorganizing factors such as Christianity...we must overthrow and shatter all opposing and destructive forces -- unsparingly and without compromise. Germanic blood and Christian baptismal water can never mix " (ibid:15).

The Biblical Condemnation of Homosexuality

A brief review of the Judeo-Christian perspective of homosexuality is appropriate here to show *why* Nazi homosexuals reacted so harshly to it. We will see that homosexuality is condemned in every place in which it is mentioned; that all forms of homosexuality are equally condemned; and that homosexuality is always linked to personal and/or social destruction   The primary passages addressing homosexuality in the Torah (1-3, 7a) and the Christian Bible (1-7) read as follows:

1) **Sodom & Gomorrah, Genesis 19:19.** [T]he men of Sodom...surrounded the house. And they called to Lot and said to him, 'Where are the men who came to you tonight? Bring them out to us that we may know them carnally.'...Then the angels said to Lot... 'We will destroy this place, because the outcry against them has grown great...and the LORD has sent us to destroy it.'

2) **The Curse on Sexual Perversion, Leviticus 18:22-30** You shall not lie with a male as with a woman. It is an abomination. Nor shall you mate with any animal,

to defile yourself with it...It is perversion...[F]or by all these the nations are defiled...therefore I visit the punishment of its iniquity upon it, and the land vomits out its inhabitants. You shall therefore keep My statutes and My judgments and shall not commit any of these abominations...I am the Lord your God.

3) The Benjamite Wars, Judges 19-21 [S]uddenly certain men of the city, perverted men, surrounded the house and beat on the door...saying, 'Bring out the man who came to your house, that we may know him carnally!'...Then the tribes of Israel...[said] 'What is this wickedness that has occurred among you? 'Now therefore, deliver up...the perverted men who are in Gibeah...But the children of Benjamin would not listen to the voice of their brethren...Instead...[they] gathered together...to go to battle against the children of Israel.'

4) The Reprobate Mind, Romans 1:18-32 Therefore God also gave them up to uncleanness, in the lusts of their hearts, to dishonor their bodies among themselves, who exchanged the truth of God for the lie, and worshiped and served the creature rather than the Creator, who is blessed forever. Amen. For this reason God gave them up to vile passions. For even their women exchanged the natural use for what is against nature. Likewise also the men, leaving the natural use of the woman, burned in their lust for one another, men with men committing what is shameful, and receiving in themselves the penalty of their error which was due.

5) Homosexuals Must Repent To Go To Heaven, 1 Corinthians 6:9-11 Do you not know that the unrighteous will not inherit the kingdom of God? Do not be deceived. Neither fornicators, nor idolaters, nor adulterers, nor homosexuals, nor sodomites, nor thieves, nor covetous, nor drunkards, nor revilers, nor extortioners will inherit the kingdom of God. And such were some of you. But you were washed, but you were sanctified, in the name of the Lord Jesus Christ and by the Spirit of our God.

6) The Reason God Destroyed Sodom, Jude 1:7 Sodom and Gomorrah...having given themselves over to sexual immorality and gone after strange flesh, are set forth as an example, suffering the vengeance of eternal fire.

7) Regarding Homosexuality Generally, see also (a) Gen 2:24, 9:22, Deut 23:1, 1 Kings 14:24, 15:9-12, 22:46, 2 Kings 23:7, Job 36:14, (b) 1 Tim 1:9-10, Rev 22:15.

While today certain "gay theologians" misinterpret these passages to try and strip them of their proscriptive authority, these arguments were unknown to the Germans in the Nazi era. What was known, especially in faithful Jewish circles, was that the Torah (Old Testament) designates homosexuality as *toeva*, or abomination. This Hebrew word is in fact the severest term of opprobrium in the Bible. Used particularly in connection with homosexuality, *toeva* connotes a degree of moral perversion so heinous that (as cited above) the land will literally "vomit out" the nation which practices it (Rabbi Samuel Dresner: Private letter).

In light of this, Nazi hostility to Jews and Christians (especially those who remained true to their faith) is thus easier to understand. Yet even this insight does not fully explain the depth of Nazi hatred.

Towards the Final Solution

There is perhaps no more terrible expression in human speech than the "Final Solution." In it is contained an evil so profound as not to be easily assimilated by the human mind. How could people be so filled with malice, we wonder, that they would seek to exterminate whole races of fellow human beings from the face of the earth? Only in a spiritual context can we truly understand the meaning of the "Final Solution," the Holocaust of the Jews.

It is not surprising, then, that the roots of the Nazi evil are found in the neo-pagan revival of the late 1800s, which manifested itself in the glorification of occultism and the subversion of the Judeo-Christian foundations of German culture.

We have addressed many elements of the neo-pagan revival in previous chapters, but to find the specific roots of the Holocaust we must revisit the occult ideologue, Jorg Lanz von Liebenfels. Remember that Lanz, the homosexual male supremacist, was called "the man who gave Hitler his ideas," by Austrian psychologist Wilhelm Daim. Anti-Semitic pamphlets by Lanz and Guido von List shaped Hitler's early hatred of the Jews. It was Lanz who originated the concept of Himmler's *Lebensborn*, the Aryan breeding colony. And it was Lanz, again, who can be seen behind Hitler's answers to "the Jewish question."

Jorg Lanz von Liebenfels

Goodrick-Clarke writes,

The similarity between Lanz's proposals...and the Nazi plans for the disposal of the Jews and the treatment of the enslaved Slav populations in the East [is unmistakable]. Lanz's specific recommendations for the disposal of racial inferiors were various and included: deportation to Madagascar; enslavement; incineration as a sacrifice to God; and use as beasts of burden. Both the psychopathology of the Nazi Holocaust and the subjugation of non-Aryans in the East were presaged by Lanz's grim speculations (Goodrick-Clarke:97).

We are all too familiar with the Nazi enslavement of "non-Aryans" and with their incineration of the Jews in the death camps, but these atrocities, though they agree perfectly with his ideas, do not by themselves prove any special influence by Lanz. In the Nazis' "Madagascar Plan" (which was nothing more than a proposal to put all the Jews on the island of Madagascar), however, we find an indisputable connection to Lanz. In Harvest of Hate: The Nazi Program for the Destruction of the Jews of Europe, historian Leon Poliakov writes about the "Madagascar Plan," but reveals that he was unaware of Lanz's influence:

> Goering had mentioned the "Madagascar Question" during the...meeting of November 12, 1938. Himmler had been dreaming of it since 1934, as one witness testified. Putting all the Jews on a large island — moreover, a French island — would satisfy the Nazi love of symbolism. At any rate, the idea was put forth by the Minister of Foreign Affairs...[and] was accepted by Himmler as well as by the Fuehrer himself. Great inventions always have several originators; other more or less famous dignitaries can claim the honor of fathering this "philanthropic solution." For example, Philip Bouhler, Chief of the Fuehrer's personal chancellery...hoped to become the governor of the island (Poliakov:43).

Guido von List directed *his* hatred more specifically against Christians, and developed an elaborate mythology to justify attacks against Christianity. Goodrick-Clarke explains List's ideas:

> [List developed] a conspiracy theory that identified Christianity as the negative and destructive principle in

the history of the Ario-Germanic race. If it could be shown that Christian missionaries had been intent upon the destruction of Armanist culture, its actual non-existence in the present could be related to empirical events...List's account of Christianization in the historic German lands reiterated the debilitation of Teutonic vigour and morale and the destruction of German national consciousness. He claimed that the Church's gospel of love and charity had encouraged a deviation from the strict eugenics of 'the old Aryan sexual morality'...it was he who had demonized the Church as the sole source of evil in the pan-German scheme of belief (Goodrick-Clarke:68f).

Unfortunately, the occult dimension of Nazi history is overlooked by many historians who must attempt, therefore, to find materialist answers to ideological questions. And if the occult dimension has been ignored, this is doubly true of the homosexual dimension. As Duberman, Vicinus and Chauncey have stated in the title to their "gay studies" text, the role of homosexuals and pederasts has been Hidden from History. They, of course, imagine the influence of homosexuality to be positive. Yet the rise of homosexuality in a Judeo-Christian-based culture necessarily represents the diminution of Biblical morality as a restraint on human passions. Consequently, where Judeo-Christian ideals decrease, violence and depravity increase.

It was the pederasts of the Community of the Elite who, in large part, sponsored the revival of Hellenic pagan ideals in German society. These men were fanatically anti-Jew and anti-Christian because of the injunctions against homosexuality implicit in the Judeo-Christian sexual ethic. Johansson notes that Hans Blueher, one of the leading theoreticians of the Community of the Elite, "maintained that Judaism had suppressed the homosexual aspect of its culture, with concomitant hypertrophy [enlargement] of the family" (Johansson:816). Benedict Friedlander, in an essay

Worship of Adolf Hitler was promoted as an alternative to Christianity.

for *Der Eigene* titled "Seven Propositions," chose as his first proposition an attack on Christianity. "The white race is becoming ever sicker under the curse of Christianity, which is foreign to it and mostly harmful," writes Friedlander. "That is the genuinely bad 'Jewish influence,' an opinion that has proven true, especially through the conditions in North America" (Friedlander in Oosterhuis and Kennedy:219).

For his part, Adolf Brand called Christianity "barbarism" and "expressed his desire to fight 'beyond good and evil,' not for the sake of the masses, since the happiness of 'the weak' would result in a 'slave mentality,' but for the human being who proclaimed himself a god and was not to be subdued by human laws and ethics" (Oosterhuis and Kennedy:183). We should not forget Nietzsche, who called Christianity "the lie of millennia" (Macintyre:188).

Much has been made of the reported silence, and in some cases complicity, of the supposed Christian churches during the Third Reich. But few have noted the long period of "Biblical deconstruction" that preceded the rise of Nazism, and fewer still have chronicled the systematic perversion of German religious culture by the Nazis themselves. While the neo-pagans were busy attacking from without, liberal theologians undermined Biblical authority from within the Christian church. The school of so-called "higher criticism," which began in Germany in the late 1800s, portrayed the miracles of God as myths; by implication making true believers (Jew and Christian alike) into fools. And since the Bible was no longer accepted as God's divine and inerrant guide, it could be ignored or reinterpreted. By the time the Nazis came to power, "Bible-believing" Christians, (the Confessing Church of Barth and Bonhoeffer) were a small minority. Francis Schaeffer writes of this phenomenon in The Great Evangelical Disaster:

> In the late nineteenth century it was these ideas [the all-sufficiency of human reason and the falsehood of supernatural religion] which began to radically transform Christianity...This started especially with the acceptance of the "higher critical" methods that had been developed in Germany. Using these methods, the new liberal theologians completely undercut the authority of Scripture...in spite of the efforts of...[theologians Hodges, Warfield and later Machen], the destructive methods of biblical criticism came into power and control in the denominations. By the 1930s liberalism had swept through most of the denominations and the battle was all but lost (Schaeffer:34).

The replacement for Biblical Christianity in Germany was a pseudo-Christian "pietism" that grew increasingly more bizarre as devotion to the social ideals of traditional Christianity was divorced from its source. In The Twelve Year Reich, social historian Richard Grunberger writes of Nazi-sponsored "charity" drives, for example, in which collectors of surplus goods for the poor became irrational fanatics:

[Collectors] indefatigably pounded the staircases of apartment houses in the large towns, rooting out the last possible donor...Small rural communities erected what were known as Boards of Shame, listing those who, 'despite financial ability, refuse to make donations.' Not infrequently, 'selfish elements' were victims of organized physical violence: 'Widow B. of Volksdorf, who had only contributed riding boots to a Winter Relief collection of clothing, had to ask the police to take her into protective custody after a threatening crowd gathered outside her house and started to smash her greenhouses.' Hereditary farmer, Bernard Sommer Kempdorf, who had told the collectors that if they wanted any fruit from him they were at liberty to pick it off the trees themselves, had to be taken into protective custody when a crowd of hundreds gathered around his farm chanting demands for his imprisonment. (Grunberger:88).

The Germans under Hitler developed a "purely German i.e. de-Romanized and de-Judaicized form of Christianity," writes Grunberger, while the growing "New Heathenism" rejected Jesus entirely and substituted "either Wotan worship or a cult of nature centered on the Sun" (ibid.:482). Soon, this neo-paganism had entered the weakened churches. "German Christianity [began to focus] on the Aryan savior Jesus...[and theological studies appeared] under such titles as 'Wotan and Jesus,' 'Baldur and the Bible,' and 'The German Savior'" (ibid.:482).

Despite all this, however, it would be a mistake to believe that the German church, as liberal and/or heretical as it had become, would have supported Hitler's total agenda on its own. On the contrary, Hitler and the Nazi elite were forced to conduct a slow and methodical takeover of the German churches to silence their dissent.

In September of 1933, a pro-Nazi cleric named Ludwig Muller was appointed by Hitler to bring all evangelical congregations into one State Evangelical Church. Heiden

This World War II U.S. propaganda poster, displayed in the National Archives, reveals that Americans knew what was truly at stake in the battle with Nazism.

writes that "The Reich Bishop [Muller] was not formally inducted into his office before the year had expired and the last independent Churches in Bavaria and Wurttemberg had been suppressed" (Heiden, 1935:405). Justice Robert Jackson, prosecutor of the Nazi war criminals at Nurnberg many years later noted that "the policy toward the Evangelical Churches...was to use their influence for the Nazis own purposes" (Jackson:51). This was perhaps best evidenced by Muller's decision in December, 1933 to transfer the Evangelical youth organization into the Hitler Youth which caused a complete break with the so-called Confessing Church of anti-Nazi congregations (Zentner and Bedurftig:608). Pastor Niemoller, leader of the Confessing Church, was later sent to a concentration camp (Jackson:51).

In March of 1935 seven hundred Protestant priests were arrested by the Gestapo in Prussia "for issuing condemnations of neo-paganism from the pulpit," and later a similar number of clergy in Wuerttemberg had their teaching credentials stripped for "'violating the moral instincts of the German race' by references to Abraham, Joseph and David in the course of their teaching" (ibid.:494). The Nazis confiscated Protestant seminaries in Wuerttemberg and Catholic convents and monasteries in the Rhineland (ibid.:500). In May of 1941, a Nazi decree banned all Catholic periodicals and newspapers (*Fact on File Yearbook*, 1941:240).

As Grunberger asserts, Nazism itself was a "pseudo-religion" (Grunberger:79) that competed, covertly, with Christianity and Judaism. The Nazi regime, attempting to usurp the role of the church and eliminate its influence on German culture, "spawned an unending series of relatively minor, but cumulatively effective, anti-Church measures" (ibid.:500). The Nazi Party's spiritual adjunct, the German Faith Movement (*Deutsche Glaubensbewegung*), represented one of several fronts in this war on the church. Its most profound attack upon Christianity, expressed by a Faith Movement leader, was the doctrine that "God has manifested himself not in Jesus Christ, but in Adolf Hitler" (Snyder:104). Grunberger writes,

The movement...could best be defined by its negative articles of faith of which the chief was enmity to Christianity and the established churches. Planning to use neo-pagan "conversion" to complement its own more general anti-Church measures (such as hamstringing communal and youth organizations, or attenuating religious instruction in schools), the Party therefore launched a drive to make individual parishioners withdraw from Church membership. The "Church Secessionist Campaign" was particularly effective among professionals materially dependent on the regime: civil servants, municipal employees, teachers, [and] full-time party workers (Grunberger:491).

As soon as the Nazis came to power they replaced many Christian holidays with pagan celebrations: "The Day of the Summer Solstice," "The Day of the Winter Solstice," and "Mothering Sunday" (which featured the so-called "Rune of Life" as a symbol to honor births) (ibid.:80f.). Marriage ceremonies increasingly invoked "Mother Earth" and "Father Sky" as the deities by whom the covenant was blessed (ibid.:492). Birth and death announcements began to feature the life and death runes, respectively, as part of a campaign to eliminate the star and the cross from public life, and crucifixes were gradually removed from hospitals and schools (ibid.:494). The Nazis made all religious activities which were not centered in the churches dependent on official permission and confiscated lists of churchgoers who were on active duty in the military (ibid.:500).

The schools were heavily targeted in the strategy to deChristianize the young. Mandatory prayer in schools was stopped in 1935, and from 1941 onward, religious instruction was completely eliminated for all students over fourteen years old (ibid.:494f). The Nazi Teachers Association actively discouraged its members from taking religious instruction, while at the same time many teachers of religious studies (who were all required to be licensed by

This poster from the National Archives contrasts Nazism with Christianity as opposing and incompatible views.

the state) "inculcated neo-paganism into their pupils during periods of religious instruction." Later, teachers were outright prohibited from attending voluntary religion classes organized by the Catholic church (ibid.:495).

In an obscene twist, the Nazis used former Christian religious facilities, seized by the government, to establish schools in which students were trained in male supremacist ideology, using teachings from the works of homosexual theorists such as Otto Weininger (Rosenthal:69). Igra writes,

> [Weininger's Sex and Character] was revived as a kind of text book in the Nazi Ordensburgen, those schools for the training of future German leaders which have been set up in the confiscated monasteries and convents. There they learn the doctrine that 'the lowest type of male is infinitely higher than the noblest woman,' and that 'by her

very nature, woman is deceitful, mentally inferior to man and unmoral' (Igra:99).

The de-Christianization of German society was carried out in the Nazis' characteristically duplicitous style. Ever masters of the euphemism and of political sleight-of-hand, they kept the general population confused about their true motives. When Hitler needed the support of the churches in the early days of the regime, for example, the SA attended Sunday services *en masse*, creating "veritable SA church parades" (Grunberger:485). But just months later these same troops marched in the Nuremberg Party Rally alongside the Hitler Youth as they sang anti-Christian songs. "No evil priest can prevent us from feeling that we are the children of Hitler," the children sang. "We follow not Christ, but Horst Wessel. Away with incense and holy water...The swastika brings salvation on earth" (ibid.:489). For their part, the SA sang, "Storm Trooper Comrades, hang the Jews and put the priests against the wall" as the refrain to one of their favorite tunes.

Horst Wessel was declared a martyr by Hitler after being killed in the "Beer Hall *Putsch*" in 1923. As an early SA member, he was probably "gay."

In <u>Hitler and I</u>, Strasser records a conversation he had with Hitler, in which Strasser criticized Nazi propagandist Alfred Rosenberg for his pagan ideals. "Hitler stopped and looked me in the eyes," writes Strasser, "'Christianity is, for the moment, one of the points in the programme I have laid down. But we must look ahead.

Rosenberg is a fore-runner, a prophet. His theories are the expression of the German soul'" (Strasser, 1940:96). Much later, as Hitler's religion of hate appeared to have completely overwhelmed the German culture, Hitler proclaimed, "Do you really believe the masses will ever be Christian again? Nonsense, that tale is finished" (Newton:16).

Martin Bormann authored a vicious anti-Christian directive that called for regional Nazi leaders to eliminate the Christian faith in Germany.

From the early years, leading Nazis openly attacked Christianity. Joseph Goebbels declared that "Christianity has infused our erotic attitudes with dishonesty" (Taylor:20). Himmler is reported to have considered Christianity "the greatest plague delivered by history, and demanded that it be dealt with accordingly" (Ziegler:85).

Martin Bormann, who replaced Hess as Deputy *Fuehrer*, issued a decree to the Party *Gauleiters* titled, "The Relations Between National Socialism and Christianity" in which he said "National Socialist and Christian conceptions are incompatible. The Christian churches build upon men's ignorance...The people must be increasingly wrested from the churches...Never again must the churches be allowed any influence over the leadership of the people. This must be broken totally and forever" (Fest, 1970:132f). The Nazis ultimate goal was the elimination of all the Christian churches. Grunberger points out that "[j]ust as the genocide programme provided for certain areas to be made 'free of Jews' before others, so the Warthegau [the Posen-Lodz civil defense region] was envisioned as the first region to be 'free of churches' in the Reich" (Grunberger:498).

It is in the Nazi campaign against Judeo-Christian morality that we find one of the reasons for the German people's acceptance of Nazism's most extreme atrocities. Their religious foundations had been systematically eroded over a period of decades by powerful social forces. By the time the Nazis came to power, German culture was spiritually bankrupt. Historians have largely ignored the spiritual element of Nazi history, but if we look closely at Hitler's campaign of extermination of the Jews, it becomes clear that his ostensible racial motive obscures a deeper and more primal hatred of the Jews as the "People of God."

The probable reason for Hitler's attack on Christianity was his perception that it alone had the moral authority to stop the Nazi movement. As late as March 19, 1942, Julius Streicher, in an article appearing in his publication *Der Sturmer* complained that Christian teachings stood in the way of a "radical solution the Jewish question in Europe" (Jackson:54). But Christians stumbled before the flood of evil. As Poliakov notes, "[W]hen moral barriers collapsed under the impact of Nazi preaching...the same anti-Semitic movement that led to the slaughter of the Jews gave scope and license to an obscene revolt against God and the moral law. An open and implacable war was declared on the Christian tradition...[which unleashed] a frenzied and un-avowed hatred of Christ and the Ten Commandments" (Poliakov:300).

As we examine the issue of Nazi hatred for Christianity we are reminded of the common moral standard shared by believing Christians and Jews. It is a standard which un-equivocally condemns homosexuality. This fact assumes enormous significance in the context of this book and causes us to question the common wisdom, which explains the Holocaust in purely racial terms.

We have shown how homosexuality figures prominently in the history of the Holocaust. The ideas for disposing of the Jews originated with Lanz. The first acts of terrorism against the Jews were carried out by the homosexuals of the SA. The first *pogrom, Kristallnacht,* was orchestrated in 1938 by the homosexual Reinhard Heydrich. And it was the sometime transvestite Goering who started the "evolution of the Final Solution...[with an] order to Heydrich (Jan. 24, 1939) concerning the solution of the Jewish question by 'emigration' and 'evacuation'" (Robinson:25).

Homosexuality and Islamist Terrorism

We turn next to the relationship between the Nazi regime and the Islamist terror groups which share its militarism and its anti-Semitism. We distinguish the Islamist terrorists from the specifically fascist and "neo-Nazi" successors to the Third Reich which will be addressed in the next chapter. Interestingly, while Hitler ranted against Judaism and Christianity, he contrasted the "[Judeo-Christian] theological doctrines devoid of any depth" with "those of...Mohamed [which provided spiritual] sustenance of a much different value" (Angebert:246).

Islamist terrorism has become an issue of great interest since the attacks of September 11th, 2001, against the United States. Interestingly, the leaders of the nineteen terrorists, including ringleader Mohamed Atta, have been reported to be homosexuals. "Gay" journalist Rex Wockner, quoting what he described as "the sensationalistic-yet-often-accurate *National Enquirer*" reported that "'Atta's gay lover for the past two years was his right-hand man, Abdulaziz Alomari, who was with Atta when he crashed the plane into the North Tower'....Atta and other terrorists believed that 'women are for procreation only and men are for recreation'" (Wockner Wire, www.PlanetOut.com, November 9, 2001). Uncharacteristically, the left-leaning *Newsweek* magazine "scooped" the *Enquirer* with a piece about the *Enquirer* story before it was released: "gay" strategist Michelangelo Signorile produced an editorial which, while not denying the truth of the *Enquirer* claims, dismissed them as irrelevant to the evil behavior of the terrorists.

Few are aware that some of the earliest terrorism of the modern era sprang from a Nazi/Arab collaboration. According to Icelandic historian, S. G. Bergsson, in <u>Muftism and Nazism</u>, the leading figure in this collaboration was Haj Amin Husseini, the Mufti (supreme religious leader) of Jerusalem. One of the leaders of the massacre of Jews in the 1920 Arab riots in Palestine, he became Mufti in 1921 and celebrated by organizing a Jewish *pogrom* that year.

Husseini first made contact with the Nazi regime in 1933, and by 1936 was carrying out anti-Jewish riots "with funds supplied by the Nazis" (Bergsson:chapter 3, p.2f.). In 1937, "during the celebration of Mohammed's birth, the German swastika flag was flying high as well as pictures of Hitler" (Ibid.). When the British stopped secret arms shipments to the Mufti in 1938, he declared *jihad* against them, was quickly defeated and fled to Germany. From then on he coordinated a large and active worldwide network of pro-Nazi Moslems from Berlin and agitated for the extermination of all Jews. Hitler was friendly with Husseini, giving him the honorary rank of SS Major (Ibid.).

The Sowetan newspaper of Johannesburg published this editorial by South African legislator Jack Bloom:

> Ambiguous Arab-Muslim attitudes to Hitler can be traced to his popularity in much of the Arab world both before and during the Second World War. Political parties that imitated the Nazis were founded, such as the Syrian Social Nationalist Party and Young Eqypt, replete with storm

troopers, torch processions and Nazi slogans. The most significant collaborator with Hitler was...Haj Amin el-Husseini....His energetic pro-Nazi efforts included a Muslim SS unit in Bosnia... General Abdul Nasser was a member of Young Egypt and made no secret of his earlier Nazi sympathies when he became president of Egypt. Former Nazis served in his army and secret police, and his personal bodyguard was SS General Oskar Dirlewanger (*The Sowetan*, October 2, 2001).

One of the reasons for Nazi popularity in Egypt is that Nasser's brother Nassiri published and distributed an Arab edition of *Mein Kampf* in 1939 (Mac Mathuna, *Flame Magazine*, 1999).

Oskar Dirlewanger (see Chapter Six), was the creator of the dreaded *SS Sonderkommando Dirlewanger* which some homosexual inmates joined to gain release from Nazi concentration camps. Dirlewanger, was assisted by former Hitler buddies, Otto Skorzeny and Eugen Dollman, who recruited "'large numbers' of former Nazi fugitives from Argentina for key posts in the new republican regime in Egypt" (ibid.). Dollman was well known as a homosexual; less is known about Skorzeny, although he had been Hitler's bodyguard in 1939, and is thus likely to have been "gay."

We have not found evidence that Husseini was homosexual.   However, historian Jamie Glazov explains the phenomenon of Islamist terrorism itself as the consequence of rampant

Otto Skorzeny

pederasty in parts of the Arab world. He writes,

> Socially segregated from women, Arab men succumb to homosexual behavior. But, interestingly enough, there is no word for "homosexual" in their culture in the modern Western sense. That is because having sex with boys, or with effeminate men, is seen as a social norm. Males serve as available substitutes for unavailable women. The man who does the penetrating, meanwhile, is not emasculated...The man who is penetrated *is* emasculated. The boy, however, is not, since it is rationalized that he is not yet a man.
>
> In this culture, males sexually penetrating males becomes a manifestation of male power, conferring a status of hyper-masculinity....In all of these circumstances, the idea of love is removed from men's understanding of sexuality. Like the essence of Arab masculinity, it is reduced to hurting others by violence....It is excruciating to imagine the sexual confusion, humiliation, and repression that evolve in the mindsets of males in this culture. But it is no surprise that many of these males find their only avenue for gratification in the act of humiliating a foreign "enemy," whose masculinity must be violated at all costs -- as theirs once was (Glazov, "The Sexual Rage Behind Islamic Terror," FrontPage magazine, 10-4-01). [For a comparison with the Spartan military camps, see pp. 54-61.]

Scholar Bruce Dunne of Georgetown University portrays the sexual world of some Arab males as a realm of unspoken and unequal "Butch/Fem" bisexuality. In this world, as with the pre-Nazi "gay" factions in Weimar Germany, "Butches" are "not [even] considered homosexual" while "Fems" are considered to be suffering from an "inexplicable...pathology" (Dunne, "Power and Sexuality in the Middle East," *Middle East Report*, Spring, 1998). (This attitude is not found in all Islamic societies, only those which combine hyper-masculine militarism with misogyny.)

Another parallel is the case of terrorist leader Yasir

Arafat. According to Dr. Asher Eder, Jewish Co-Chairman of the Islam-Israel Fellowship organization, the name "Yassir Arafat" is an alias. Arafat changed his real name, Abdul Rauf el-Codbi el-Husseini, to hide his relationship to Mufti Haj Amin Husseini, his uncle (Eder, "How to Disarm the Terrible Jihad Psychosis Against Jews and Israel that Afflicts the Muslim World Today," www.rb.org, February 24, 2000).

Yasir Arafat

Arafat's homosexuality has been widely acknowledged since at least 1976, when the testimony of a former associate (also homosexual) was published in a Canadian biography, <u>Arafat, the Man and the Myth</u> by Thomas Kiernan. Kiernan quotes this man at length:

> We went one night on a training exercise, about twenty of us. We were camped in a citrus grove near Gaza in tents. There was an emergency of some kind...Several of us ran to Abu Khalid's tent to find out what we should do. There we discovered Abu Khalid and Yasir giving themselves pleasure -- or should I say Yasir was giving Abu Khalid pleasure? After that, Abu Khalid was quite open about what he did with Yasir. In fact, he encouraged all of us to participate in such activities. He said it should be a part of the guerrilla way of life....It created a closer bond among us. Most of us sooner or later were doing it as a regular way of life. Some of us even gave pleasure to Abu Khalid, and him to us. But he would never let us touch Yasir. Yasir was his special province (Kiernan:108).

Arafat is more often identified by his critics as a pederast than simply a homosexual, but we did not find documentation of his alleged abuse of boys. Recent events show that common cause still exists between Islamic radicals and Nazis: both celebrated the terror attacks of September 11th. Arafat's Palestinian supporters, including police officers, were caught on camera celebrating wildly in the streets upon hearing the news. Meanwhile, German neo-Nazi Horst Mahler used his website to thank the terrorists for "knocking out" the "common enemy," while another Nazi group, the National Resistance (NW) said September 11th was a day for celebration (*The Observer*, UK, 10-7-01). Hans-Joachim Kunz, of the Bavarian section of the German Office for the Protection of the Constitution, explained that "neo-Nazis and Islamic fundamentalists have a common ideology and that is they both see the USA as their enemy" (ibid.).

We have shown that a hidden motive for Nazi anti-Semitism was a deep hatred of Biblical morality. This conclusion, supported by the comments of key Nazi thinkers, provides a more satisfying explanation for Nazi policies than does racism alone. For while widely-promoted racial theories *seem* sufficient to explain the persecution of the Jews, they do not explain the Nazi's equal hatred of Bible-believing Christians. The Nazis were apparently not hostile to Moslems, even though Islam ostensibly draws its authority from the same Bible. This was not merely the pragmatic tolerance of a military ally. It seems likely that the Nazis were genuinely drawn to their hyper-masculine brothers-in-arms because they shared a common homoerotic spirit.

We will find that this thread of homoeroticism is woven throughout the history of post-Hitler fascism as well.

Chapter Eight

HOMO-FASCISM AFTER HITLER

History never repeats itself, man always does.
Voltaire (In Cecil Genese, The Holocaust: Who Are The Guilty?)

One of the symbols with which homosexuals in the United States have chosen to represent their movement is the phoenix, a mythical bird that was said to burn itself on a funeral pyre every five hundred years and then rise from the ashes more majestic than before (Alyson Almanac:56). A more apt symbol for the historic cycle of homo-fascism and resulting social chaos would be hard to find. From the ashes of Nazi Germany, the homo-fascist phoenix has arisen again — this time in the United States.

The Fascist Roots of the American "Gay" Movement

The first "gay rights" organization in the United States was an American chapter of the German-based Society for Human Rights (SHR). The German SHR, formed in 1919 by Thule Society member Hans Kahnert, was a militant organization led by "Butch" homosexuals. Many of the early Nazis, including SA leader Ernst Roehm, were also SHR members.

The American SHR was formed on December 10, 1924, in Chicago, by a German-American named Henry Gerber

(J. Katz:388). Gerber had served with the U.S. occupation forces in Germany from 1920 to 1923 and had been involved with the German organization. Together with a small group of fellow "revolutionaries," Gerber legally chartered the group without revealing its purpose and began publishing a pro-homosexual journal called *Friendship and Freedom* (ibid.:389), patterned after the German chapter's publication of the same name (ibid.:632n.).

In 1925, however, the organization collapsed when Gerber, Vice President Al Menninger and another member were arrested on charges of sexual abuse of a boy, all three having been turned in by Menninger's wife. The Chicago *Examiner* ran a story titled "Strange Sex Cult Exposed," and spoke of "strange doings" in Menninger's apartment. Menninger confessed, but Gerber claimed the incident was a set-up, saying that their arrests were "shades of the Holy Inquisition." Rather than take his chances in court, however, Gerber hired a lawyer who "knew how to fix the State Attorney and judges" and the case was dismissed (ibid.:392). After going underground for a time, writing under the pen-name "Parisex," Gerber reemerged in 1934 on the staff of a pro-homosexual literary magazine called *Chanticleer* (ibid.:394). He also retained his ties to the German SHR and published several articles in their publications (ibid.:633n.).

In *Chanticleer*, Gerber revealed himself as a militant socialist who regarded capitalism and Christianity as the twin pillars of ignorance and repression of "sexual freedom" (ibid.:394). In response to the news of the Roehm Purge in the American press, he admitted that the Nazis were led by homosexuals and praised "Roehm and his valiant men" (ibid.:396). Gerber is quoted at length in Katz's Gay American History regarding the Nazi regime. He writes,

A short time ago an American journalist pointed out in the liberal "Nation" that the whole Hitler movement was based on the homosexual Greek attachments of men for each other, and the same Jewish author stated that it was another of the Hitler contradictions that the "Leader" should have acquiesced in the burning of the books of Dr. Magnus Hirschfeld...Thus we get a glimpse of the insanity of the whole movement: A Jewish doctor working for the interests of homosexuals is persecuted by a heterosexual mob, led by homosexuals (Gerber in J. Katz:395).

It is interesting to note that the homosexual inclinations of the Nazis were a matter of at least limited public knowledge in the United States at this time, as well as their Greek origins. We can also infer from this passage that Gerber himself was not an overt fascist, though he clearly identified with the Brownshirts in Germany. Open fascism in the homosexual movement would come later, but Gerber and his pederastic friends had established its foundation. By 1972, when he died at the age of 80, Gerber had witnessed the emergence of homo-fascism as a permanent theme in the movement.

American Nazis

Like it's German counterpart, the American Nazi movement presents a decidedly anti-homosexual face to the world, while hiding widespread homosexuality among its leaders.

George Lincoln Rockwell formed the American Nazi Party in 1959. Rockwell exemplified the narcissistic personality type so typical of male homosexuals, but we have no solid information that he was "gay." However, one researcher noted that Rockwell's small group was riddled with homosexuals. "Jeffrey Kaplan, a well-known scholar of extremism...writes, gays made up a 'significant' — if carefully hidden — part of George Lincoln Rockwell's

American Nazi Party in the 1960s." The same source reports that "in America homosexuality continues to be a 'secret of postwar American National Social-ism'"(Southern Poverty Law Center Intelligence Report, "Fringe of the Fringe," Issue No. 100, Fall 2000.

Frederick J. Simonelli addressed the issue of homosexuality in the American Nazi Party in his 1999 biography of Rockwell, <u>American Fuehrer</u>. He reports that Rockwell's rhetoric, like Hitler's, was viciously anti-homosexual, but that questions about his private life and those of his staff persisted

> Homosexuality within the ranks of the ANP was a constant concern to Rockwell and a constant source of speculation among his enemies. "There is a tendency for queers to come here," Rockwell admitted to a hostile interviewer at the ANP's Arlington Barracks; then he quickly distanced himself homosexuals by adding, "because to a queer, this place is as tempting as a girls school would be to me." According to FBI surveilance, Rockwell's fear of gay storm troopers was well founded. The ANP's Western Division, particularly, was shaken by the revelation that the unit's chief, Leonard Holstein -- who was also half-Jewish -- was gay.
>
> Persistent rumors of gays within the ANP's top echelon -- primarily centering on Rockwell's chief of staff, Matt Koehl -- damaged the party....[while] throughout

Rockwell's career...[speculation persisted] about his own
sexual orientation....Without digressing into a psychological analysis, suffice it to say that Rockwell's em-
phatic and frequent affirmations of his own masculinity
raise questions about his subconscious (Simonelli:77ff).

Another branch of the American Nazi movement, the
National Socialist League, was openly homosexual:

Founded in 1974 by de-
fecting members of the
National Socialist White
People's Party, this San
Diego-based NSL is
unique in restricting its
members to homosexual
Nazis. Led by veteran
anti-Semite Russell Veh,
the group distributes
membership applications
declaring NSL's "determi-
nation to seek sexual, social and political freedom"
(Newton:46).

While normally low-profile, the NSL stirred a controversy in 1983 when it attempted to market an infamous
1930's Nazi hate film that had been pirated by the group.
An article in the Los Angeles-based *Heritage and S.W.
Jewish Press*, titled "'Gay nazis' peddling vile 'Jud Suss'
film," named Veh and the National Socialist League. "We
are most familiar with Mr. Veh (which is an alias, incidentally) and his notorious operations," said legitimate film
distributor, David Calbert Smith III (*Heritage and S.W.
Jewish Press*, September 16, 1983). Veh solicited members for his group through a publication called "The N.S.
Mobilizer" and through personal ads in homosexual publications, including the leading national "gay" magazine, *The*

American Nazi Party leader Frank Collin (pointing) leads Nazi march in Chicago. Collin was a homosexual who later served time for sexual abuse of teenage boys.

UPI/Bettman

Advocate (Reisman, 1994:57).

Before disappearing in the 1980s, the National Socialist League put out a journal — NS Kampfruf. (*Southern Poverty Law Center Intelligence Report*, Fall 2000).

The most famous incident in the history of the modern American Nazi Party (a decade after Rockwell's assassination in 1967) resulted from its 1977 demand to stage a march through the largely Jewish neighborhood of Skokie, Illinois, a Chicago suburb and the home of many Holocaust survivors. This plan was devised by Frank Collin, who often appeared with his followers "in full Nazi regalia: brown shirts, black boots, and armbands with swastikas" and who "advocated that all African-Americans, Jews and Latinos be forcibly deported" (Johansson:129). Civil authorities effectively blocked the march at first, but the American Civil Liberties Union (ACLU) rose to Collin's aid. The Nazis won the right to march but a settlement was reached in which the City of Chicago and not Skokie became the site. The subsequent event drew international media attention. Homosexualists Johansson and Percy, in <u>Outing: Shattering the Conspiracy of Silence</u>, have finally revealed, more than fifteen years later, that Collin was a homosexual pederast. In 1979 Collin was arrested "for taking indecent liberties with boys between ages 10 and 14" and was sentenced to seven years in prison (Johansson and Percy:130).

"Gay" Nazi Skinheads

Today, Nazism survives primarily in a broad international skinhead movement made up of disaffected white male youths. Not surprisingly, homosexuals are among the most influential leaders of Nazi skinhead culture. For example, in England, birthplace of the movement, the notorious National Front (NF) was headed by "gay" skinhead Nicky Crane. As reported by Murray Healy in *Gay Skins,* "Crane [was] by his own admission a devout Nazi who idolized Hitler" (Healy:134). Crane actively sought to re-

vive the street-terrorism of the Nazi Brownshirts in the British urban centers "'[trying] to create a street fighting force...for street destabilization, fighting at sports events and keeping up racial attacks'...[S]kinheads 'giving Nazi salutes and chanting racialist slogans' [became] a common sight " (ibid:124).

Searchlight magazine reported that

At over six foot tall and extremely violent, Crane was the archetypical nazi skinhead, so much so that it was his picture that adorned the cover of "Strength Through Oi," a seminal "Oi" album [music of the skinhead movement]. As a nazi Crane was involved in much violence, including gay bashing. Yet at the same time, presumably unbeknownst to those close to him in the nazi scene, he was a hardcore gay porn star...[In 1993] he died of AIDS (*Searchlight*:September, 1999).

In the 1970s, the best known "gay" nazi was the National Front's national organizer, Martin Webster (ibid). Another homosexual nazi, Peter Marriner, was a leader in both the National Front and another fascist group, the British Movement (*Searchlight*:August, 2000).

The Nazi skinhead movement has now spread far beyond England. Healy writes that "the same alignment of 'skinhead' and 'fascist' is also occurring globally...as far-right groups in Europe, Australia and parts of the United

States have imported skinhead imagery as the uniform for its urban terrorists" (ibid:205).

In France, the neo-Nazi movement is closely and openly tied to the "gay" community. One of the founders of the fascist group *Franciose Nacionale* is also the editor of the homosexual publication *Gaie France* (Andriette, Bill, "Is Gaie France Fascist?" NAMBLA Bulletin, September, 1992). Meanwhile, back in Germany, the alarming increase of neo-Nazi skinheads is also linked to homosexuality. Elmay Kraushaar, a journalist for *Der Spiegel*, the German equivalent to *Time Magazine*, is quoted in *The Advocate*:

There is a gay skinhead movement in Berlin. They go to cruising areas with leaflets that say, "We don't want foreigners." A major leader of the neo-Nazis in Germany, Michael Kuhnen, was an openly gay man who died of AIDS two years ago. He wrote a paper on the links between homosexuality and fascism, saying fascism is based on the

Emblem of the "Queer Skinhead Brotherhood."

love of comrades, that having sex with your comrades strengthens this bond (Anderson:54).

In The Beast Reawakens, author Martin Lee described Kuhnen as the most important neo-Nazi of the 1980s, calling him the "fuehrer" of the Action Front of National Socialists, whose open homosexuality did not diminish his stature in the fascist community (Lee:195). Kuhnen's "comrade" and successor, Christian Worch, was jailed in 1994 in connection with crimes of violence and racial hatred (*Neighborhood Queen* Internet Posting, Dec. 1, 1994). Another prominent German neo-Nazi leader, who is also

NEWS 26

ARRESTED IN GERMANY: Right-wing extremists are pictured after being arrested in Worms, Germany, on Saturday. They marched to commemorate the death of Hitler deputy Rudolph Hess.

The Associated Press

Neo-Nazis march in Germany, clash with leftists in Sweden

SOCIAL ISSUES: The ultra-rightists marked the ninth anniversary of the death of Hitler deputy Rudolph Hess.

By MICHAEL SHIELDS
Reuters

BONN, Germany — Neo-Nazi demonstrators marched in Germany and clashed with leftist groups in Sweden on Saturday as they marked the ninth anniversary of the death of Rudolf Hess, Adolf Hitler's former deputy.

Police took 146 radical-right activists into custody after breaking up a march by 200 people in the southwestern German city of Worms.

The Point

Out & About

Neo-Nazis commemorate the anniversary of Rudolf Hess' death with marches. Hess is well known in "gay" cricles as a homosexual as indicated by this caricture of him in a prominent newspaper of the "gay" movement (insert).

homosexual, is Bela Ewald Althans (*Searchlight*: September, 1999). The subject of two neo-Nazi recruiting videos, Althans was jailed in 1995 for "inciting racial hatred." We must emphasize that not all skinheads are Nazis, and fewer still are open homosexuals. As Healy notes "A skinhead does not signify fascism as unequivocally as the swastika" (Healy:142). Nevertheless, the movement has become virtually synonymous with "gay" fascism in certain circles. "Skinhead identities" writes Healy, "have become increasingly popular among gay men since the mid-1980s....So widespread are these elements [of skinhead styles] in British urban gay networks that they have ceased to signify skinhead, sending out the message 'I'm gay' instead. (Healy:2f).

The connections between skinheads and homo-fascism are not as well known in the United States, even though this country hosts numerous "gay Nazi" organizations. One such group is the American Resistance Corps (ARC), which offers the following history on its website:

> ARC was founded by an American skinhead with the help of a Canadian skin who were dissatisfied with the state of the skinhead nation (so to speak). These two skins were both firm believers in white racialism. They also happened to be gay. The founding of ARC was a response to the two extreme ends of the skinhead scene. On the one hand were gay skinheads who denied racialism and on the other hand were non-gay racialists who advocate group hatred for gays....ARC skinheads have the pleasure of being both traditional fascists and progressive activists (ARC website, www.geocities.com/ARCOrg /Historical.htm).

The skinhead movement is not the exclusive home of "gay" Nazis in America today. Less youthful homo-fascists can be found in other Nazi and white supremacist groups. For example, The *Arizona Republic* ran a headline story on

April 12, 1996 about a sting operation that netted 30 Aryan Brotherhood members who had allegedly smuggled guns and drugs into prisons. One of us (Lively) spoke to a detective with firsthand knowledge of the case. The detective, speaking on condition of anonymity, confirmed that he had observed a high incidence of homosexuality in this white supremacist organization. Lee reports that neo-Nazis David McCalden and Keith Stimely, both associated with the California-based Institute for Historical Review, died of AIDS in 1991 (Lee:226). It is presumed that they acquired the disease through homosexual encounters. Another interesting news item is the case of Louisiana Ku Klux Klan organizer Gregg David, charged with raping a black man in 1997 (Reuters, undated).

A final revelation about post-Hitler homo-fascism comes to us from Hitler's homeland of Austria. There, powerful pro-Nazi politician Jorg Haider, head of the Freedom Party, stepped down in the Spring of 2000 amid rumors that he is homosexual. While there is no direct evidence of his alleged homosexuality, the British newspaper, The Mail, reports

> There are unsubstantiated claims that he has been spotted in gay bars in Vienna; what is beyond dispute is the fact that the charismatic leader has surrounded himself with fanatical young men, some of whom have confirmed their homosexuality...This is the man who has appeared to justify Hitler's death camps as 'punishment centers', and who has proudly declared that his parents were Nazis...The Freedom Party is referred to as the 'Buberlpartie' - the young boy's party -- and the Press talks about Haider surrounding himself with 'young functionaries faithful to him'...[including] its general manager Gerald Mikscha...named in the German Press as Haider's gay lover ("The Gay Acolytes haunting Haider," *The Mail on Sunday* (UK), April 30, 2000.

Nazi Themes in "Gay" Culture

Glorification of Nazi styles and symbolism would be virtually unthinkable in mainstream society, but the homosexual community flatly rejects such limitations. Within just a few short years after the hard won Allied victory over the Nazi regime, American "gay" style setters were already adopting Nazism imagery as their own. Healy writes

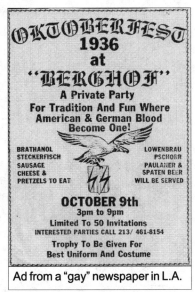

OKTOBERFEST
1936
at
"BERGHOF"
A Private Party
For Tradition And Fun Where
American & German Blood
Become One!

BRATHANOL
STECKERFISCH
SAUSAGE
CHEESE &
PRETZELS TO EAT

LOWENBRAU
PSCHORR
PAULANER &
SPATEN BEER
WILL BE SERVED

OCTOBER 9th
3pm to 9pm
Limited To 50 Invitations
INTERESTED PARTIES CALL 213/ 461-8154
Trophy To Be Given For
Best Uniform And Costume

Ad from a "gay" newspaper in L.A.

As Kenneth Anger's films (most notably *Scorpio Rising*) attest, flirtation with Nazi fantasies and the use of fascist iconography were not uncommon on the urban American homosexual underground leather scene of the 1950s (Healy:115).

Today, a simple perusal of the premier magazine of the homosexual movement, *The Advocate,* reveals that Nazi themes are common in the "gay" community. Reisman, who studied personal advertisements in *The Advocate* in issues from 1972 to 1991 found that the content of the ads reflected a fascist mentality. She writes,

Overall, 72% of THE ADVOCATE data socialized a set of core values—glorified nazi dress, language and "blonde" Aryan male beauty and brutality; contempt for "fems, fats," and blacks; threats toward "politically incorrect" homosexuals, churches and others — Romanticizing "fascist" culture to a "younger generation." Nazi costumes/fascist concepts are a common component of THE ADVOCATE and thus largely condoned by prevailing "gay" cultural values (Reisman:1992, 57).

Other elements of "gay" culture demonstrate a similar pro-Nazi ideal. One popular film, by Finnish "gay rights" advocate Iippio Pohjala, is titled Daddy and the Muscle

Pro-Nazi "Tom of Finland" is the epitome of the modern "Butch" homosexual.

Academy (1992). Tom, the hero in the film, is a homosexual fascist and a pornographer. The film, combining themes of pederasty and Nazi glorification, was shown in San Francisco on June 26, 1992, at the Castro Theatre. It was part of the 16th Annual Gay and Lesbian Film Festival. A reviewer for the *San Francisco Examiner* provided the following description of the film:

Daddy and the Muscle Academy candidly acknowledges Tom's infatuation with body types encouraged by the National Socialists. His fantasies...[involve] sex between clean-cut Finnish boys and storm troopers, the swastika flying behind them (Bonetti: *San Francisco Examiner*, June 26, 1992).

A review of a stage production of "Cabaret" in *The Washington Blade* (September 1, 1996) reveals a similar infatuation with Nazism.

[The director]...obviously aims to disquiet...the Emcee... sings the final line — in a tight spotlight — of the anthem to the Fatherland, "Tomorrow Belongs to Me"; and in a shocking move during the finale, he visually allies himself with Nazism. Clearly, the Emcee connects decadence, queerness, and Nazism...He raises frightening questions of queerness, fascism and doom in two periods: World War II and the end of the twentieth century.

The attraction of American "gays" to Nazism is not the exclusive domain of male homosexuals, however. Gertrude Stein, who, because of her relationship with Alice B. Toklas, is described by The Alyson Almanac as half of "history's best known lesbian couple" (149), was a great fan of Adolf Hitler. Toland reports in Adolf Hitler that in 1937 "Gertrude Stein thought Hitler should get the Nobel Peace Prize" (Toland:409). (The same source states that George Bernard Shaw, a Fabian socialist and outspoken defender of homosexuality, also "defended Hitler...in magazine and newspaper articles" -- ibid.:409. Interestingly, Shaw is accused by Samuel Igra of being the true author of The Protocols of the Learned Elders of Zion a purportedly Jewish "secret plan"for global conquest, which has ever since been used by anti-Semites as proof of a Jewish world conspiracy -- Igra:1960.)

Where homosexuals live in the highest concentrations, some seem to feel more comfortable acting out Nazi fantasies. In Against Sadomasochism: A Radical Feminist Analysis, Susan Leigh Star, a Jewish sociologist, describes her experience in San Francisco:

Gay Nazi Sex Ads

Page from a homosexual "dating" website.

For four years I have lived in the Castro section of San Francisco, the gay (predominantly male) district. When I walk down the street in my neighborhood, I often see people dressed in black leather, wearing chains and sometimes carrying whips. In the magazine stores there are many sadomasochist publications. Often these include pictures of people wearing replicas of Nazi Germany uniforms. Iron crosses, storm trooper outfits, military boots. And swastikas. Once and a while someone on the street is dressed in full Nazi regalia (Star:132).

Nazi Tactics in "Gay" Politics

"I shall torture you during the daytime, and will keep you from a peaceful sleep at night."

Larry Kramer, Founder of ACT-UP (Leo:18).

The "gay" movement has done more than simply adopt Nazi styles and symbolism. Homosexual strategists have also embraced the terroristic tactics of the Nazi Brownshirts to advance their political agenda.

One of the most notorious groups to employ Nazi thuggery is the AIDS Coalition to Unleash Power (ACT-UP) which was founded in New York by Larry Kramer and approximately 300 other activists in March, 1987. (Alyson Almanac:42). Within a few months its members had gained national attention for their aggressive actions against those whom they considered enemies. ACT-UP groups invaded Catholic churches in New York during religious services, screaming obscenities and "stomping on communion wafers" (Miller:460). Catholic churches were also targeted in Washington, Los Angeles and Puerto Rico. Newspaper boxes were smashed in Sacramento to punish an editor for his views (Grant, 1993:104). One militant who later regretted his involvement was Washington, D.C. ACT-UP founder, Eric Pollard. The following is an excerpt from his 1992 letter to the *Washington Blade* titled, "Time to give up fascist tactics":

This is very hard for me to write. It forces me to squarely confront my past actions and to accept responsibility for the damage I have had a part in causing. I sincerely apologize for my involvement in and my founding of the AIDS activist organization, ACT-UP D.C.. I have helped to create a truly fascist organization...The average Gay man or woman could not immediately relate to our subversive tactics, drawn largely from the voluminous *Mein Kampf*, which some of us studied as a working model (*Washington Blade*, January, 1992).

In his 1998 <u>War on Heterosexuality</u>, author Michael P. Wright, quotes AIDS "dissenter" Alex Russell on the fascist character of contemporary "gay" activism.

Many attributes of the HIV Homofascist Movement (or HIVism) resemble those of Fascism and the psychology of Freikorpsmen: an authoritarian personality; extreme emphasis on the masculine principle, male dominance and blood brotherhood; exclusive membership in an elite in-group; and the fetishization and aestheticization of suffering, self-sacrifice and death.

Freikorpsmen made war a way of life....Many HIV Blood Brothers see the war on AIDS as a way of death where the Freudian pleasure principle and the death drive become indistinguishable. The Swastika armband has now been replaced by the HIV positive tattoo and the red ribbon (Russell in Wright:Chapter 5).

Within a few years of its founding, ACT-UP spawned
the more radical Queer Nation. Miller writes that Queer Nation's "in your face" tactics antagonized some in the "gay"
community. Randy Shilts [a prominent homosexual writer]
called Queer Nationals "brownshirts" and "lavender fascists" (Miller:460). Queer Nation adopted highly militant
rhetoric and openly threatened violence. Grant describes
their tactics during an Oregon election campaign (see Introduction) in which voters considered a law to ban minority
status based on homosexuality:

> ...flyers appeared on telephone poles warning people to
> vote against it. One showed the Christian ichthus fish be-
> ing roasted on a stick over a fire. It read, YOU BURN US,
> WE BURN YOU...another said CIVIL RIGHTS or CIVIL
> WAR. Your choice for a limited time only...It also clari-
> fied what it meant by "civil war" by listing "QUEER
> KNIVES, QUEER GUNS, QUEER BULLETS, QUEER
> MISSLES, QUEER TANKS, QUEER TRENCHES,
> QUEER FIRE, QUEER WARFARE, QUEER
> PATRIOTS (Grant, 1993:104f).

One of us (Lively) was active in that campaign and personally witnessed stencils painted on sidewalks in the City
of Portland which
threatened "Queers
Bash Back." In the
City of Eugene busi-
nesses that had sup-
ported the Oregon
Citizens Alliance
(which had sponsored
the ballot initiative)
had bricks, wrapped in
swastika-embellished
flyers, thrown through
their windows. A

Ad for a "gay" militancy website.

Queer Nation spokesman in Eugene denied responsibility but defended the violence as justified. A separate organization which called itself "Bigot Busters" specialized in harassing and threatening petitioners seeking signatures to put the measure on the ballot. Petitions were ripped from circulators hands or doused with paint, activists blockaded petition tables, and several circulators were physically assaulted. Hundreds of false signatures were put on petitions in an effort to invalidate them. In every case "Bigot Busters" denied responsibility.

In classic Nazi style, the Oregon homosexual activists cast themselves as victims during this campaign of violence. A series of phony late-night cross-burnings were staged in the front yard of Azalea Cooley, a black, apparently wheelchair-bound lesbian in Portland. This highly publicized charade continued for six months and was blamed on a "climate of hate" created by OCA. On the eve of the election, however, police caught Cooley herself on video *walking* out of her own front door with a wooden cross and materials to burn it. She later confessed to all of the crimes (*Oregonian,* December 10, 1992).

As we have seen with Roehm's Brownshirts, the wrath of militant homosexuals can be fierce. On September 29, 1991, following Governor Pete Wilson's veto of Assembly Bill 101 (which would have extended minority status to homosexuals)

Radical "gays" use ear-splitting whistles to harass police (above) and later set fire to a govt. building.

thousands of homosexuals rioted in San Francisco, setting fire to a government building and clashing with police. This fury is often turned against individuals and families as well. Chuck and Donna McIlhenny experienced it after the San Francisco Presbyterian church (where Chuck is the pastor) fired a homosexual organist, sparking a wave of terrorism against their family and their church. They describe the campaign of hatred that was waged against them in *When the Wicked Seize a City*:

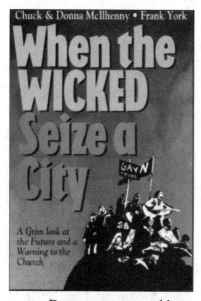

The harassment started. Rocks, beer bottles, beer cans were thrown through the church windows on many occasions. Swastikas were carved in the church doors and drawn on our house. A window in our car was smashed out. Graffiti was spray-painted all over the church, house, and sidewalk. Anti-Christian, pro-homosexual leaflets were scattered around the neighborhood calling us Nazis, bigots, anti-gay, etc. Demonstrators would come into our Sunday services and disrupt the worship...One time a man came pounding and spitting on our front door in the middle of the night, screaming, "We're going to get you McIlhenny—we're going to kill you politically!" We were verbally threatened outside the house on the way to the car. There were daily — 24-hours-per-day — telephone calls. They began with screaming and obscenities. They graduated into phone calls describing our children—by name, appearance, where they attended school, when they got out of school, and what sexually deviant behavior was to be practiced on the children before killing them...Then on 31 May 1983 at 12:30 a.m., someone actually attempted to follow through with their threats to kill us [by firebombing the house while the children were asleep inside] (McIlhenny and York:109f). [Author's note:The McIlhenny" survived these and other efforts against them and continue to serve the membership of their church in San Francisco].

On April 12, 1996, a near-riot by 400 homosexual militants in Madison, Wisconsin delayed a scheduled speech on The Pink Swastika by one author (Lively). Shouting obscenities and slogans, activists invaded and occupied the tiny Trinity Evangelical Fellowship church for nearly an hour while hundreds of others banged on the outer walls and windows with rocks and trash-can lids. Chants of "Crush the Christians!" and "Bring back the lions!" could be heard through the windows. Police refused to clear the church but later agreed to remove individual protestors who refused to be civil. Eventually, the meeting was allowed to continue, though not before some of the protesters went into the church basement and urinated and defecated on the floor.

Meetings in Janesville and Stevens Point, Wisconsin were similarly disrupted. For those who attended, however, the homo-fascism of the Wisconsin "gay" community provided a living testimony to the validity of claims of this study.

Attacks like these are not isolated incidents, but part of the strategy for increasing the political power of homosexuals in American society. Dr. Brian Clowes, in *Debating the Gay Rights Issue*, has compiled the following advocacy of the use of terrorism and violence by "gay" fascists:

> If [AIDS] research money is not forthcoming at a certain level by a certain date, all gay males should give blood. Whatever action is required to get national attention is valid. If that includes blood terrorism, so be it. (Robert

Schwab in Kirk Kidwell, "Homosexuals Flex Muscles in Washington." *American Family Association Journal*, January, 1988, pages 6 - 8).

We should have shut down the subway and burned down city hall. I think rioting is a valid tactic and should be tried...If someone took out [killed] Jesse Helms or William Dannemeyer of California, I would be the first to stand up and applaud. (ACT-UP member Michael Petrelis, quoted in Michael Wilrich. "Uncivil Disobedience." *Mother Jones*. December, 1990, page 16).

It's hard to refrain from taking this man [Pat Buchanan] by the throat and squeezing as hard as you can while you look at his ugly, disgusting face and watch the eyeballs burst and pop out of their sockets. Or maybe you feel like stepping on his face and squishing his demented brain until the rot oozes out of it and onto the pavement. I have no problem imagining violence against this wacko... (Michelangelo Signorile, editor-at-large of the homosexual magazine *Outweek*, quoted in *National Review*, June 24, 1991. (Clowes:78f)

In recent years, the "gay" movement has drastically reduced its use of overtly terroristic tactics, probably because it made huge political gains during the eight years of the Clinton administration. Increasingly, the "gay" movement is being viewed more as a part of mainstream culture and less as an alien and destructive sub-culture. In most cases, homosexual activists no longer need to go to the streets to harass and intimidate their opponents. They now can use their enormous power in media, academia and government to marginalize and punish them. One example of this phenomenon is the rise of so-called "hate crimes" legislation. Ostensibly, "hate crimes" statutes are designed to deter violent criminal acts motivated by prejudice against the victim. However, the authors perceive the enactment of these laws (which are primarily sponsored by the "gay" movement), as

Adolf Hitler would have felt very much at home in the American "gay" movement as represented by ACTUP and Queer Nation. Yad Vashem

the first phase of a process to criminalize speech that is hostile to the legitimization of homosexuality.

As it is currently envisioned, only speech that occurs during the commission of a violent crime will be deemed criminal under "hate crimes" statutes. Eventually, however, it is highly probable that speech standing alone will be prohibited. This evolution has partially occurred in California where the "gay" lobby pushed through a bill in 2000 which created a new category of "hate crime" called a "hate motivated incident." Assembly Bill 1785, signed into law by Governor Gray Davis, defines a "hate motivated incident" as "an act or attempted act which constitutes an expression of hostility" toward homosexuals or other protected groups.

As we can see, then, homo-fascism did not die with Adolf Hitler. It lives on in the neo-Nazi movement and in "gay" culture itself. Clearly, actual Nazis exist today as a radical fringe of society with no real power to threaten civilization. This would be a comforting realization if we presumed that Nazism was itself the source of the evil that threatened to engulf the world and was not merely the product of a deeper and still-enduring social problem. Our thesis, however, is that Nazism was the consequence of Germany's abandonment of Judeo-Christian morality and that the primary sponsors of its transformation were homosexuals. If this thesis is true, we would expect to find many parallels to the German experience in America, as indeed we do.

Chapter Nine

THE HOMOSEXUALIZATION
OF AMERICA

If the rise of Nazism in Germany was made possible, at
least in part, by the homosexualization of German society,
what does this bode for America as we watch the steady advance of the "gay" agenda in this culture? Should we expect to witness something like the rise of a Third Reich on
American soil? Or would the effect on American society be
of an entirely different character? Is the "gay" movement
in the United States sufficiently similar to its German counterpart as even to warrant concern? (Certainly the German
"gay" culture was far more militaristic than the homosexual
movement here, for example). Or is this the wrong question? Is there something about homosexuality (or the
broader problem of sexual libertinism) that inevitably destroys the society that embraces it?

In many ways these are questions beyond the scope of
this book, yet the implications of the material we have presented compel us to address them. Perhaps the most helpful
approach is to search the history of homosexual activism in
America for parallels with the German experience.

As we noted in the previous chapter, the first openly homosexual organization in the United States was the Ameri-

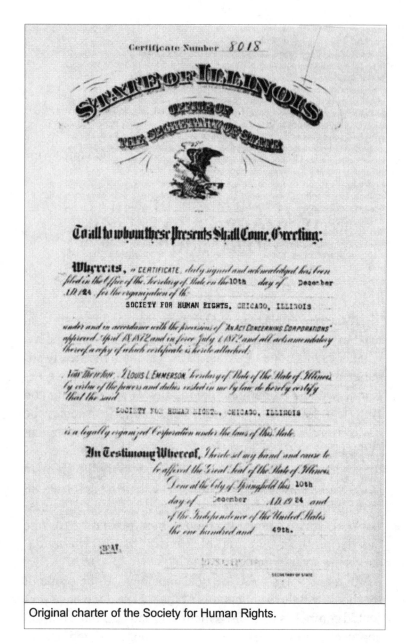

Original charter of the Society for Human Rights.

can chapter of the German Society for Human Rights, started in 1924. The SHR was an aberration, however. The American homosexual movement really only began in the

1940s after the Allied defeat of the Nazis. We must begin our time line, then, with the observation that the center of international "gay" power in the world did in fact shift from Germany to the United States after the demise of the Third Reich. This represented a huge setback for the "gay" movement, requiring it to begin "from scratch" as it were, since America in the 1940s was at least as family-centered as Germany had been in the 1860s.

We know that the implicit goal of homosexual political activism is to legitimize homosexual conduct and relationships in a society. This necessarily requires a society to abandon its commitment to marriage as the exclusive domain of acceptable sexual conduct. The abandonment of this standard logically opens the door to every other form of sexual promiscuity. Clearly, such a transformation of attitude is now occurring in America. What we will find is that this transformation is not the result of random social forces, but of deliberate and systematic political activism by the "gay" movement.

Harry Hay and the Mattachine Society

In the words of Jonathan Katz, "a link of a kind peculiar to Gay male history connects the abortive Chicago Society for Human Rights (1924-25) and Henry Hay, the founder of the Mattachine Society" (J. Katz:407). This "peculiar link" is the fact that the man who recruited Hay into homosexuality (at age seventeen), Champ Simmons, was himself seduced by a former member of the SHR. In a perverse sort of way, then, it seems appropriate that Hay would become known as the "founder of the modern gay movement" (Timmons:cover). (In another account, Hay claims his earliest homosexual experience was a molestation at age fourteen by a twenty-five-year-old man) (ibid.:36).

On August 10, 1948, at the tail end of an eighteen-year stint as a Communist Party leader, Hay began to organize a

group that would become the Mattachine Society (ibid:132). Not until the spring of 1951 did it receive its name, but from the beginning it was seen as a vehicle to destroy social restraints against homosexuality in American culture (J. Katz:412f). The name Mattachine was taken from "medieval Renaissance French...secret fraternities of unmarried townsmen" (ibid.:412). The organization's stated agenda was to preserve the "right to privacy." Like the SHR, the Mattachine Society became controversial upon the arrest of a prominent member. Dale Jennings, one of the founders of the organization, was arrested for soliciting an undercover police officer to commit a homosexual act in a public restroom (ibid.:414).

Hay was not a fascist, but he was a neo-pagan. He participated in occultic rituals at "the Los Angeles lodge of the Order of the Eastern Temple, O.T.O., Aleister Crowley's notorious anti-Christian spiritual group" (Timmons:76). Hay provided musical accompaniment to ceremonies performed by the lesbian "high priestess." Later in life he founded a New Age group called Radical Faeries, which met in an *asram* in the high desert of Arizona to offer invocations to pagan spirits (ibid.:265).

In some ways, Hay can be compared to Karl Heinrich Ulrichs, the "grandfather" of the gay rights movement. Hay is his American counterpart in the sense that both men launched enduring social movements in their respective cultures. The avowed purpose of each was to undermine the Judeo-Christian moral consensus in respect to homosexual relations. And both had been molested as boys (though some suggest that this is the rule rather than the exception among homosexual men). But unlike Ulrichs, Hay became increasingly militant over the course of his life until, in the 1980s, he participated in California's notoriously violent ACT-UP demonstrations (ibid.:292). ACT-UP, the AIDS Coalition to Unleash Power, was one of the earliest manifestations of homo-fascism in the "gay rights" movement. Though Hay was in his 70s, and is not directly linked to any of the property destruction associated with ACT-UP demonstrations, his presence validated the terrorist tactics of the group. Hay also openly endorsed pederasty as an essential part of the "gay rights" movement (ibid.:296).

Harry Hay and the Mattachine Society spawned large-scale political and social activism among homosexuals that soon outgrew their expectations and their control. Their highly motivated activists operated in groups designed like communist cells, each a "secret fraternity" bound by the common vice. As Hay stated in a later interview, "[we wanted to] keep them underground and separated so that no one group could ever know who all the other members were" (J. Katz:410). Slowly at first, from innumerable obscure sources, came theories, public statements and actions in support of the social acceptance of homosexuality. And as the power of the homosexualist political lobby grew, so did the ugliness of its demands and its methods.

Alfred Kinsey and the Kinsey Institute

While Harry Hay would soon take the homosexual movement public with the Mattachine Society, most homosexual activism continued to be carried out by hidden cell groups and individual "in the closet" activists. One such activist was Alfred Kinsey. No one but Kinsey's closest associates and sex partners knew that his image as a respectable family man and college professor masked his role as one of the most dedicated homosexual change-agents in America.

In 1948, sex researcher Kinsey released his cul-

ture-shattering book, Sexual Behavior in the Human Male. The first major sex study of its kind, the Kinsey Report purported to show that Americans were far more promiscuous and sexually deviant than they said they were (Reisman and Eichel, 1992:2). For over forty years, Kinsey's data went more-or-less un-challenged and the con-clusions that he drew continue to serve as the "scientific" justification for the so-called sexual revolution. His theory of sex as a mere "outlet" released human behavior from what Marcuse called "the repressive order of procreative sexuality." All forms of sexual expression were equalized in the Kinsey model.

Recently, several studies have shown that America is *not* the hotbed of promiscuity and deviancy that Kinsey's study made it appear to be, *even after forty-six years of influence by that study*, which was loudly trumpeted as "fact" by the media and much of academia. *U.S. News and World Report* reported that one such recent study, conducted by the National Opinion Research Center at the University of Chicago, that it showed that "[f]idelity reigns. Fully 83 percent of Americans had sex with one person or had no sex partners in the past year, and half of Americans have had only one partner in the past five years" (*U.S. News and World Report*, October, 1994:75).

Kinsey's study was tailor-made for the homosexual/pederast community. Indeed, just weeks after its release, Harry Hay formally launched the Mattachine Society. We have no proof that Kinsey and Hay actually coordinated their efforts, although we know that Hay and Kinsey met together more than seven years before the publication of the first Kinsey report (Timmons:111). We also know that influential Kinsey co-worker, Wardell Pomeroy, later became a member of the Mattachine Society's advisory board, perhaps indicating a deeper relationship between the Kinsey organization and the Mattachines (Marotta:80).

Kinsey's vastly inflated figure of the number of homosexuals in America is the basis of the enduring myth that at least 10% of the population is homosexual. His seven-point Kinsey Scale, "in which bisexuality occupied a middle 'balanced' position between heterosexuality (0) and homosexuality (6)" (ibid.:10), attempted to establish homosexuality as a norm by definition. He further declared adult/child sex harmless. This "finding" was based on data gathered by pedophiles from experimentation with hundreds of children as young as two months old (ibid.:36).

In Kinsey, Sex and Fraud, Reisman and Eichel state that Kinsey "purported to prove that children were sexual beings, even from infancy and that they could, and should, have pleasurable and beneficial sexual interaction with adult 'partners'" (ibid.:3). Reisman and Eichel go on to suggest that Kinsey deliberately overlooked criminal sexual child abuse and purposefully falsified data to further his personal sexual and political agenda. They cite former Kinsey coworker Gershon Legman who said that "Kinsey's not-very-secret intention was to 'respectablize' homosexuality and certain sexual perversions" (ibid.:34). They also reference sociologists Albert Hobbs and Richard Lambert who observed "that the Kinsey authors seemed purposefully to ignore the limitations of their own samples in order 'to compound any possible errors in almost any way which will increase the apparent incidence of [homosexuality]'" (ibid.:24).

Was Kinsey a homosexual, a pedophile or both? One historian proposed that Kinsey "may have discovered in himself the homosexual tendencies he would later ascribe to a large proportion of the population" (Robinson in Reisman and Eichel, 1992:204). But Reisman and Eichel suggest he manifested more of the behaviors of a pedophile. "In addition to his interest in sex experiments with children," they write, "Kinsey was an avid collector of pornography (and maker of sex films) — an elemental feature of the pedophile syndrome" (Reisman and Eichel, 1992:205). In a later work, Reisman reports more specifically that Kinsey produced and directed films of homosexual sado-masochism at Indiana University, and that his collection of pornography included films of children engaged in sexual acts (Reisman,1998:80f).

There is no question, however, that Kinsey fits the profile of a homosexual activist. Like the militant homosexuals who benefitted from his work, Kinsey was "indignant about the effect of Judeo-Christian tradition on society," write Reisman and Eichel. "It is clear that he shared [co-researcher Wardell] Pomeroy's view that Christians inherited an almost paranoid approach to sexual behavior from the Jews" (ibid.:6). Pomeroy, incidentally, is known for his support of adult/child sex. In a 1992 article on pedophilia, author Michael Ebert quotes Pomeroy as saying, "People seem to think that any [sexual] contact between children and adults has a bad effect on the child. I say this can be a loving and thoughtful, responsible sexual activity" (Ebert:6f). The Kinsey Institute should be recognized as the American counterpart and successor to the Sex Research Institute of Berlin. Indeed, E. Michael Jones, editor of *Fidelity* magazine told one of us (Lively) in conversation that he had perused some of the surviving documents of the Berlin institute in the basement of the Kinsey building. Like its German predecessor had been, the Kinsey Institute is dedicated to the legitimization of sexual perversion.

The Sexual Revolution

Within five years of the Kinsey report, Hugh Hefner launched *Playboy* magazine (and the modern pornography industry), whose initial target audience was the very generation of young men to whom Kinsey had been speaking on his college lecture circuit. More significantly, it popularized Kinsey's "gay" ethic of sexual license with the much of the rest of the male population of America. Hefner himself is quoted as saying that if Kinsey were the researcher of the sexual revolution, he (Hefner) was the pamphleteer (Reisman, 1998:108).

We are not suggesting the Hefner is homosexual, only that *Playboy* magazine serves as a tool of "gay" social engineering in that the existence of a thriving pornography industry serves the "gay" cause by morally corrupting the men who use it. It logically makes them less likely to oppose homosexuality on moral grounds and more likely to support public policies which legitimize sexual license. Exposure to pornography, especially at a young age, can also be a gateway into the "gay" lifestyle itself.

In the same manner, the "gay" cause is advanced by a

successful abortion industry (which also arose in response to the sexual revolution). The choice to kill their unborn children morally compromises both men and women (making them unwilling to criticize the choice to engage in other forms of immoral behavior), and ensures that the outcome of an unwanted child will not be a lasting deterrent to those who have chosen sexual license over family. This explains why homosexuals, who by definition cannot bear children together, are among the most militant advocates of abortion on demand.

The acceptance of sexual indulgence as an important social value inevitably initiates a downward moral spiral in a culture. In American society, the selling of the idea of recreational sex to young college-aged men in the 1950s created a "market" for immodest and sexually adventurous young women, which in turn helped to legitimize the idea of female promiscuity. In the 1960s, once immodesty and promiscuity became acceptable for some women, the pressure increased for all women, competing for the attentions of men, to adopt these behaviors. This was especially true of the youngest of marriage-age women of that generation, whose personal morals and values had been influenced by a decade of sex-saturated pop culture.

The wholesale entrance of women into the world of sexual license created a number of societal demands: for a feminist political movement to "liberate" women from social expectations about marriage and child-rearing (National Organization for Women formed 1966); for contraception on demand (Griswold v. Connecticut -- 1966); for abortion on demand (Roe. V. Wade --1973); and for "no fault" divorce (state-by-state liberalization of divorce laws began in the early 1970s). The result of these policies has been the achievement of the "gay" goal as embodied by Kinsey's teachings: the progressive denormalization of marriage and the steady normalization of sexual license. The most recent census data, published in

1998, showed a fourfold increase in divorce from 1970 to 1996, while the population of "cohabiting" couples who had never married had more than doubled.

Among the side-effects produced by these dramatic changes in the life of a people, side-effects which have increased steadily since the 1960s, are the escalation of crime (especially violent crime), the proliferation of sexually-transmitted and other diseases, and the escalation of mental illness and chronic substance abuse. These are all results which one would expect to find in a generation of citizens raised in unstable homes. Each and every one of these social problems is a direct consequence of embracing the "gay" ethic of sexual license as popularized by Kinsey. Meanwhile, as the pursuit of sexual hedonism became the personal goal of an ever larger percentage of the non-homosexual population, the "gay" movement continued its advance.

The Stonewall Riot and "Gay" Militancy

"Two, four, six, eight -- Smash the family, smash the state"
(Popular slogan of 1970s "gay" activists --Oosterhuis and Steakley:2)

By 1969, the development of a growing homosexual subculture in America had spawned an open homosexual presence in major cities. So-called "gay bars" sprang up in Los Angeles and New York, hosting a bizarre mix of "street queens," drug addicts and boy prostitutes (Marotta:71). In New York, homosexuals regularly engaged in public sex acts with anonymous partners "in the backs of trucks parked near the West Village piers" (ibid.:93) and in the public restrooms. Homosexual activity occurred so frequently in the bushes of one public park that the authorities were forced to cut down the trees to stop it (Adam:85). In response to police efforts to discourage this increasingly offensive behavior, homosexuals began to organize to de-

CARNIVAL
FRIDAY 'til MONDAY
30 June - 3 July
On Whitley, off Hollywood Bl.
50¢ at gate   KIDS under 12 FREE

GAY PRIDE '78

NO GAY HOLOCAUST IN U.S.A.

Christopher Street West

PARADE
4 PM Sunday, 2 July
Down HOLLYWOOD BL.,
Argyle to Las Palmas

"Gay Pride" Day is the anniversary of the Stonewall Riot. This "Gay Pride" flyer reveals that the "Gay Holocaust" myth was already being promoted in the 1970s.

mand the "right" to public deviancy. Emboldened by their numbers, they began picketing businesses such as Macy's Department Store, which had cracked down on homosexual behavior in their restrooms (ibid.:85).

On the evening of June 27, 1969 the "gay rights" movement officially adopted terrorism as a means to achieve power when a surly mob of "drag queens, dykes, street people, and bar boys" physically attacked police officers conducting a "raid" on the Stonewall Bar on Christopher Street in New York. Stonewall was "one of the best known of the Mafia controlled bars" (Marotta:75), and was being closed for selling alcohol without a license. It was also a haven for sexual deviants. As police began to take some bar patrons in for questioning, a mob of homosexuals gathered across the street. Homosexualist Toby Marotta's The Politics of Homosexuality includes an eyewitness report by a writer for the *Village Voice*:

> [A]lmost by signal the crowd erupted into cobblestone and bottle heaving...The trashcan I was standing on was nearly yanked out from under me as a kid tried to grab it for use in the windowsmashing melee. From nowhere came an uprooted parking meter—used as a battering ram on the Stonewall door. I heard several cries of "Let's get some gas," but the blaze of flame which soon appeared in the window of the Stonewall [where the police officers were trapped] was still a shock (ibid.:72).

By morning, the Stonewall bar was a burned-out wreck, and homosexual leaders had declared the violence a success. Interestingly, the anniversary of this event is known today as "Gay Pride Day" and features parades and other events most notable for their public sex and nudity (ibid.:158). It is ironic that the very activists who emerged from this new militant environment developed (in 1970) the strategy of claiming victim status through the use of the pink triangle and commemoration of the homosexuals who were persecuted by the Nazis (Adam:86).

The rise of homosexual militancy reflected the emergence of an aggressive "Butch" faction of the American "gay" movement, similar to that which occurred at the turn of the last century in Germany. (Ironically, while these masculine-oriented "gays" assume an attitude of superiority over "Fems," in both Germany and the United States the "gay" movement was actually launched by effeminate homosexuals and only later became dominated by "Butches"). In The Making of the Modern Homosexual, author Gregg Blachford observed that during this time "homosexuals themselves moved away from the previous stereotype of 'swish and sweaters' towards a new masculine style [that became] the dominant mode of expression in the subculture" (Blachford:187).

Following the Stonewall riot the Mattachine Action Committee of the Mattachine Society's New York chapter clamored for "organized resistance" (Adams:81), but control of the movement was taken out of their hands by a still more radical group of activists. These men quickly formed the Gay Liberation Front, so titled "because it had the same ring as National Liberation Front, the alliance formed by the Viet Cong" (ibid.:91). At the heart of this new circle of power was Herbert Marcuse (ibid.:88), a long time Socialist who had learned his politics (and perhaps homosexuality) in pre-Nazi Germany. Homosexualist historian Barry D. Adam writes,

> Herbert Marcuse, who had been a youthful participant in the 1918 German revolution and had been steeped in the thinking of the life-reform movements of the Weimar Republic, caught the attention of many gay liberationists. His Eros and Civilization, published in the ideological wasteland of 1955, bridged the prewar and postwar gay movements with its implicit vision of homosexuality as a protest "against the repressive order of procreative sexuality" (ibid.:84).

The Stonewall riot became the new symbol of the "gay rights" movement. In its wake, Gay Liberation Fronts sprang up across the country, using methods of intimidation and coercion to achieve political gains. Immediately they targeted the medical community, whose increasing effectiveness in treating homosexual disorders threatened the logical premise of the movement (Rueda:101ff). "Gay Liberation Fronts," writes Adam, "stormed San Francisco, Los Angeles and Chicago conventions of psychiatry, medicine and behavior modification," shouting down speakers and terrorizing audience members (Adam:87f). As extreme as it had itself become, the Mattachine Society predicted the GLF's "violent tactics" would fail to inspire the movement (Marotta:136), but they were wrong. Though the GLF collapsed in 1972, in part because of a conflict between "drag queens and machos" ["Fems" and "Butches"], their philosophy prevailed (Adam:90).

On December 15, 1973 the board of trustees of the American Psychiatric Association capitulated to the demands of the radicals. The homosexuals had begun to speak of unyielding psychiatrists as "war criminals" (ibid.:88), with obvious implications. Possibly in fear for their safety, and certainly wearied by constant harassment, they declared that homosexuality was no longer an illness. The resulting referendum, demanded by outraged members of the association, was conducted by mail and was partially controlled by the National Gay and Lesbian Task Force (Rueda:1982). The homosexualists won the vote and the new official definition of homosexuality as a disorder was changed to include only those who were "unhappy with their sexual orientation" (Adam:88). Historian Enrique Rueda writes,

> This vote was not the result of scientific analysis after years of painstaking research. Neither was it a purely objective choice following the accumulation of incontrovertible data. The very fact that the vote was taken reveals the nature of the process involved, since the existence of an orthodoxy in itself contradicts the essence of science (Rueda:106).

Weimar in America

How does all of this compare to the German experience? One striking parallel is the span of time over which homosexuality became culturally accepted in each country. In Germany, approximately twenty-five years passed from the formation of the Scientific Humanitarian Committee by Magnus Hirschfeld until sexual perversion was being openly practiced in Germany (roughly from 1897 to the mid-1920s). In the United States, the emergence of widespread overt homosexuality occurred in the early 1970s, a quarter-century after Harry Hay formed the Mattachine Society.

Another similarity is the extent to which perversion advanced once the moral barriers were lowered. Let us briefly compare the two societies.

Under the Weimar government, established after Kaiser Wilhelm II's abdication in 1918, many traditional attitudes were questioned, including those about sexuality. As

America does today, Weimar Germany experienced tremendous conflict as these policies clashed with traditional Judeo-Christian values.

Feelings on the 'sexual question' ran high. There were disputes about the roles of the sexes and about attitudes toward marriage, the family and child rearing, and these disputes were bound up with arguments about social policy and demographic trends (Peukert: 101).

In this climate the homosexualists made significant gains. Almost immediately, major German cities became havens for every form of sexual expression. William Manchester writes of "transvestite balls, [where] 'hundreds of men costumed as women and hundreds of women costumed as

This recently published book documents in highly pornographic detail the perverse extreme to which Germany descended during the Weimar period. The parallels to today's U.S. sexual subcultures are unmistakable.

men danced under the benevolent eye of the police," and of "mothers in their thirties, teamed with their daughters to offer *Mutter-und-Tochter* sex" (Manchester:57). Plant writes of "luxurious lesbian bars and nightclubs [that] never feared a police raid" (Plant:27).

Steakley records that "[o]fficial tolerance was manifested...in the unhindered consumption of narcotics in some homosexual bars, and transvestites were issued police certificates permitting them to cross-dress in public" (Steakley:81). And historian-biographer Charles Bracelen Flood speaks of "sad alleys patrolled by prostitutes of all ages and both sexes, including rouged little boys and girls" (Flood:196). "Berlin's specialized establishments included a bathhouse featuring black male prostitutes" that was frequented by Ernst Roehm, writes Flood, and "there was a sedate nightclub for lesbians, the Silhouette, where most of the women, sitting on hard benches along the walls, wore men's clothes with collar and tie, but the young girls with them wore dresses with accented femininity" (ibid.:197).

Germany's version of Madonna was a woman named Anita Berber, "the role model for thousands of German girls...[who] danced naked...and made love to men and women sprawled atop bars, bathed in spotlights, while voyeurs stared and fondled one another" (Manchester:57). Rector describes the Weimar scene as a "sexual Mardi Gras" (Rector:15):

> There were about as many — if not more — homosexual periodicals and gay bars in Berlin in the 1920's as there are now in New York City, and Berlin of the time was abuzz with the feasibility of forming a national homosexual political party. The sexual revolution, with its free-and-easy attitudes, including wife swapping and group sex as a moral precept, was a German "invention" of the Twenties...abortions were shrugged off and condoms were on sale in open display in grocery stores and almost every other public mart [Quoting from T.L. Jarman, Rector continues]...Freedom degenerated into license...Bars for homosexuals, cafes where men danced with men,...pornographic literature in the corner kiosks—all these things were accepted as part of the new life (ibid.:13).

Today, all of these things are manifest in American society as well. The lid to Pandora's Box that had been cracked open by Kinsey, Harry Hay and the Mattachines is now flung wide. Rueda writes,

> ...there are no fewer than 2,000 [homosexual bars in America]...They range from small "sleazy" places in dark and dangerous alleys to plush establishments...Some bars cater to a conventional-looking clientele. Others specialize in sadomasochists or transvestites. There are bars which purposefully attract young people, prostitutes

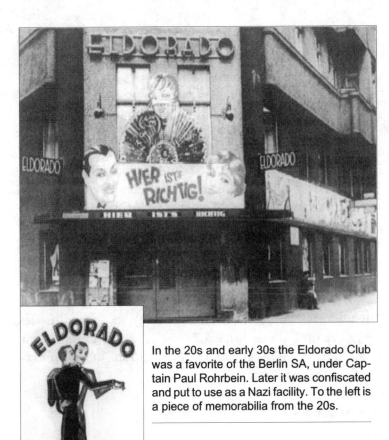

In the 20s and early 30s the Eldorado Club was a favorite of the Berlin SA, under Captain Paul Rohrbein. Later it was confiscated and put to use as a Nazi facility. To the left is a piece of memorabilia from the 20s.

who serve to attract older homosexuals who in turn purchase drinks for the youngsters while sexual deals are arranged. Printed guides for traveling homosexuals...[specify] the availability of prostitutes or "rough trade" (i.e., homosexuals who enjoy appearing violent or who actually behave violently) (Rueda:33).

American cities also host "bathhouses," which are not actual baths but meeting places for anonymous homosexual encounters. "People walk in there and have sex with multiple partners and have no idea who they're having sex with," reports former homosexual John Paulk. "I know this first hand and from the many many people I was associated with in the gay lifestyle" ("The Gay Agenda" Video). Paulk reports that these "bathhouses" remain open despite the AIDS epidemic. He also describes the activity called "cruising" in which homosexuals meet for anonymous sex in public restrooms and other public locations. While this has apparently always been common behavior in the homosexual community, Paulk implies that it is far more widespread today than ever before. This is substantiated by other observers of the "gay rights" movement (Grant, 1993:36f).

A great deal more could be written about the varieties of homosexual perversion that have proliferated in America's cities and towns today (and increasingly dominate the entertainment media). Indeed, the authors feel that the *behavior* of homosexuality needs to be exposed to a public whose attention is systematically drawn away to "cover" issues (e.g. "victim" status, "rights," etc.). But it is our intention here to focus on the social, political and spiritual ramifications of this behavior.

Consequences

Leaving religion aside, the rationale for a society to limit sex to marriage is fairly basic. Marriage "sanctifies" what is otherwise merely self-centered pleasure-seeking, while also protecting individuals and society from most of the problems associated with "unwanted" children, sexual diseases and serial relationships. (How many of our most pressing social problems today are directly or indirectly related to these factors?)

Once a society abandons marriage as the prerequisite for sexual relations, however, there remains scant logical grounds to restrict *any* form of sexual deviance or promiscuity. For example, on what grounds can a society deny homosexuals freedom of conduct if non-homosexuals have been permitted to engage in similar disease-transmitting

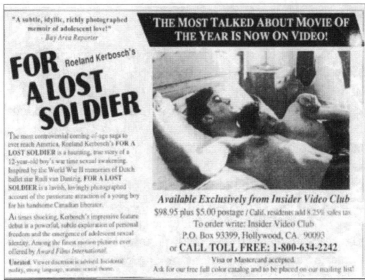

Pederast film, advertised in a homosexual magazine. The only barrier to pederasty in America today is age-of-consent laws. Elimination of age-of-consent laws was one of the planks of the 1972 "Gay Rights" Platform.

sexual acts? And if public health considerations no longer outweigh the "right" to sexual freedom under the law, what justifies continued limitations upon sado-masochism, incest, beastiality and even pedophilia? A society is left with no bases for regulating sexual conduct but its surviving moral standards and the legal concept of "mutual consent."

Can we have confidence that America's moral standards will present a lasting barrier to the continued escalation of sexual deviance? Certainly not with regard to consensual sex between adults. A quick perusal of the menu of available pornography on the Internet reveals that battle has been lost. But will the line hold against the legitimization of adult-child sex? The answer to that lies in the hands of the "gay" activists, whose dedication to their own sexual freedom has driven the sexual revolution.

Pederasty in the "Gay" Movement

The 1973 victory of "gay" politics over scientific objectivity in the American Psychiatric Association had far-reaching consequences. After the fall of the APA's medical standard against the normalization of homosexuality, "gay rights" activists made tremendous gains in public acceptance of, or at least tolerance for, open homosexuality. This fact is especially alarming when we consider that the APA has now taken action which some construe as "normalization" of pedophilia as well. The September, 1994 issue of "Regeneration News," the newsletter of a homosexual recovery group in Baltimore, features an article about this change. Regeneration Director, Alan Medinger compares the new set of criteria for diagnosing pedophilia with the prior standard:

Legitimization of homosexuality in schools prepares children for re-cruitment into the "gay" lifestyle.

In the earlier DSM-III-R [Diagnostic and Statistical Manual for Psychiatrists], pedophilia was diagnosed as a disorder if "[t]he person has acted out on these urges or is markedly distressed by them...*but the new standard defines pedophilia as a disorder only if the fantasies, sexual urges, or behaviors cause clinically significant distress or impairment in social, occupational, or other important areas of functioning"* (Medinger, reprinted in *Stop Promoting Homosexuality*

Hawaii Newsletter, November, 1994. Emphasis ours).

The APA has taken a step which can be interpreted to imply that adult sex with children is normal as long as the perpetrators are not unhappy with their sexual orientation. The APA has taken exception to this interpretation.

Although many contemporary homosexual activists, especially lesbians, attempt to distance themselves from their pederastic comrades, the fact remains that pederasts (as was true in Germany) have always been at the forefront of the movement, albeit often "in the closet." And the "right" of adults to have sex with children has always been a basic goal of the movement. In February of 1972, for example, a national coalition of homosexual groups met in Chicago to draw up a list of priorities for the movement. Prominent on the list was the demand for "a repeal of all laws governing the age of sexual consent" (Rueda:201ff). Already in Canada the age of consent has been lowered to age 14 (Mulshine:10).

The organizations dedicated specifically to "pedophile rights" or "pederast-rights" in the United States are made up of homosexual men (Rueda:173ff), and in major cities with an active homosexual community "gay" bookstores carry numerous titles which endorse man/boy sex (Grant, 1993:22). Tom Reeves, a self-admitted pederast who was part of the early "gay rights" movement, is one of a number of writers in an anthology called <u>Varieties</u>

Cover of a NAMBLA newsletter. The most vocal advocates of "children's rights" (i.e. pedophilia) are male homosexuals.

of Man/Boy Love. He explains the role of pederasts in homosexualist activism:

> Almost every one of the early openly homosexual writers was a pederast. Pederasty was a constant theme of early gay literature, art, and pornography. The Stonewall riots

Pederast Leland Stevenson (left) leads a NAMBLA contingent in the 1993 "Gay Pride" parade in Washington, D.C.

were precipitated by an incident involving an underage drag queen, yet that detail was not viewed as significant. Curtis Price, a fourteen-year-old, self-described "radical hustler," formed the first gay liberation organization in Baltimore. Many of the leaders of early gay liberation and the founders of the major gay groups in the U.S. were boy-lovers (Reeves in Pascal:47).

Another of the early leaders of the "gay rights" movement was David Thorstad, also a self-identified pederast. Thorstad was president of the Gay Activist Alliance (*Stop Promoting Homosexuality Hawaii Newsletter*, November, 1994:6), one of the largest of the groups which formed in New York in the wake of the Stonewall riot. The GAA invented "the strategy of 'zapping' politicians," writes Marotta, "that would later become [its] trademark...[they] had learned that homosexuals could infiltrate political gatherings and make themselves heard through sheer brashness" (Marotta:137). The GAA also developed the strategy of using these "carefully staged confrontations" to force politicians to enact "anti-discrimination" policies (ibid.:150). The GAA reorganized early in 1974 as the National Gay and Lesbian Task Force (Adam:88).

Thorstad, along with Reeves and others, later went on to form the North American Man/Boy Love Association in Boston in 1978 (*NAMBLA Bulletin*, September, 1992:2). NAMBLA, which is the largest "pederast rights" organization in the country, cloaks its agenda in rhetoric about concern for the rights of children to have "sexual freedom." (Pascal:49). In recent years NAMBLA has come under attack by some elements of the "gay rights" alliance, who have tried to exclude the group from some of the higher profile media events. But this has evoked a violent response from its defenders. When NAMBLA was denied a role in the 1986 Los Angeles "Gay Pride Parade," marcher Harry Hay donned a sweatshirt printed with the legend, "NAMBLA Walks With Me." Timmons writes that Hay, "could not contain his outrage" that NAMBLA was excluded (Timmons:296). More recently, as reported in the *NAMBLA Bulletin*, Hay was a featured speaker at NAMBLA's annual membership conference, June 24-25, 1994:

> [He] gave an inspiring talk about reclaiming for the 1990's the spirit of homoerotic sharing and love from various ancient Greek traditions of pederasty. A remarkably balanced and sensitive account of the conference appeared in the August 23 Advocate from a writer who was invited to attend (*NAMBLA* Bulletin, September, 1994:3).

Other homosexualist-run "children's-rights" organizations include the Rene Guyon Society, which was formed in 1962 "to make it possible for adults to provide sexual stimulation for virtually all children" (Rueda:177), and a group called Project Truth (*NAMBLA Bulletin*, September, 1994). (While we're discussing homosexual splinter groups we should mention the Eulenspiegel Society, formed in 1971 to promote "Sado-masochist rights" for homosexuals whose "special concern is freedom for sexual minorities and particularly those whose sexuality embraces S/M" — Rueda:175).

Membership of groups such as these in the International Lesbian and Gay Association (ILGA) caused it to be expelled from the United Nations Economic and Social Council in September of 1993. Attempting to forestall its expulsion, ILGA tried to separate itself from pederast groups but quickly learned that support for the "boy-lovers" was too deeply entrenched in the association. ILGA's ouster of ten-year member NAMBLA and a couple of other high-profile groups caused European pederast member-organizations to step forward in protest. Division within ILGA continues (*NAMBLA Bulletin*, September 1994:3).

Another apologist for pederasty is Larry Kramer, founder of ACT-UP. In <u>Report from the Holocaust: The Making of an AIDS Activist</u>, Kramer had this to say about adult/child sex: "In those instances where children do have sex with their homosexual elders, be they teachers or anyone else, I submit that often, very often, the child desires the activity, and perhaps even solicits it" (Kramer:234). According to Reeves, "Queer Nation and Act-Up" were home to "both boys and men" who wanted "additional cultural activity beyond...their illegal relationships" (Reeves in Pascal:73).

Pedophilia and its promotion is not limited to male homosexuals. Virginia Uribe, a lesbian teacher in Los Angeles, has been at the forefront of a movement to "affirm gay teenagers," through school-based pro-homosexual "counseling" (*Homosexuality, the Classroom and Your Children*, 1992) Her own program, called Project 10 (named for the oft-quoted "statistic" of 10% homosexuality in the U.S. population, a figure demonstrated in several re-

cent studies to be nearer 2%), included a book for young
people called <u>One Teenager in Ten</u>. This "resource" for
troubled teens features lurid pornographic stories, includ-

ing a graphic lesbian sex scene
between a twelve-year-old girl
and her twenty-three-year-old
dance teacher. The apparent
goal is to activate children's
sexuality at increasingly younger ages. At a conference promoting Project 10 to public
school teachers in Oregon,
University of Washington sociologist Pepper Schwartz admits targeting prepubescent
children for "affirmation," saying, "At this point, getting the
majority to say 'gay' is good' at nine or ten years old is going to be difficult, but just because it is difficult doesn't
mean it's not the right thing" (*Homosexuality, the Classroom and Your Children*, 1992).

The beneficiaries of "sexual freedom" for children and
teens are often predatory adult homosexuals. The National
Gay and Lesbian Task Force is on record that "gay teens
should be supported in coming out" (Mulshine: 10), but
writer Paul Mulshine notes that "the guidance, and the sex,
tends to come from adult gays who bring the teens out...A
study published in the *Journal of Pediatrics* showed that of
a sample of gay teenagers who had steady sexual partners,
the mean age of the partners was 25 years" (ibid.:10). He
cites a "1985 study of arrests in 12 U.S. jurisdictions [for
child sex abuse, which] showed...on average, about 40 percent of arrests for pederastic homosexuals" (ibid.:11).

Though some deny that the "right" of adults to have sex
with children remains a fundamental component of the
"gay rights" movement, the evidence suggests otherwise.

Alyson Publications, the leading publisher of "gay" titles, markets books aimed at pre-schoolers, such as Daddy's Roommate and Heather Has Two Mommies, right alongside Gay Sex: A Manual for Men Who Love Men. The latter contains detailed instructions for pedophiles and pederasts on how to successfully avoid discovery and arrest. "Avoid situations," advises author Jack Hart, "where a number of men have sex with the same boy, or group of boys, over a period of time" (Hart:123). No doubt these guidelines are gratefully received by pederasts in the community, a constituency that is larger than most people realize. For example, Reeves claimed in a 1979 speech that he personally had met "over 500 men" who "were struggling with their attraction to boys." "Almost to a man," said Reeves, "they are teachers and boy scout leaders and boys club leaders" (Rueda:97).

Scouts Under Siege

Fortunately, America's version of the *Wandervoegel*, the Boy Scouts of America, has largely been spared the problems associated with its German cousin. This can be attributed to its commitment to Judeo-Christian ideals as represented in its pledge to be "reverent toward God" (Hillcourt:10). Still, the number of homosexuals that have infiltrated the organization is alarming. From 1973 to 1993 over 1,416 scout leaders were expelled for sexually abusing boys (*The Washington Times*, June 15, 1993).

Beginning in 1991 and continuing to the present time, the Boy Scouts have been targeted by "gay rights" militants for their policy against allowing homosexuals to be scout leaders. An ostensibly "spontaneous" outcry against the Boy Scouts arose across the country, led by the once-venerable United Way agency, which pulled its funding from the Scouts in various cities. United Way's funding withdrawal was quickly followed by other homosexual-controlled or co-opted entities including Levi Strauss, Wells Fargo, Seafirst Bank and Bank of America (which later reversed itself) (*Oregonian*, July 11, 1992). Self-admitted lesbian, Roberta Achtenberg, then serving on the San Francisco Board of Supervisors, led a campaign to coerce the Bank of America into support for the homosexuals' demands. Shortly thereafter, Achtenberg was appointed Assistant Secretary for the Department of Housing and Urban Development (*Los Angeles Times*, January 29, 1993), one of more than two dozen homosexuals appointed to high-level posts in the Clinton Administration (Grant, 1993:107).

In the streets, the Boy Scouts was mocked by "Queer Scouts, a focus group of Queer Nation" (*Bay Area Reporter*, August 1, 1991), while homosexualists at the highest levels of government attempted to intimidate the organization into submission. Surgeon General Joycelyn Elders used her post to castigate Scout officials (*U.S.A. Today*, June 2, 1994) and Interior Secretary Bruce Babbitt signed an order prohibiting Boy Scouts from volunteering in national parks (*The Washington Times*, May 28, 1993). In San Francisco and San Diego the Boy Scouts were barred from operating day programs in the public schools (*San Francisco Chronicle*, September 14, 1991) and in San Diego, city officials launched an investigation of the Scouts under its legal powers to prevent "discrimination" against homosexuals (*San Francisco Chronicle*, October 18, 1992).

So far the Boy Scouts have withstood the onslaught, but late in 1992 the organization received a letter from NAMBLA predicting that it will eventually succumb to homosexual demands. The letter is addressed to Ben Love, Chief Scout Executive, Boy Scouts of America, and was published in the *NAMBLA Bulletin*, November, 1992:

Dear Mr. Love,

At its 16th membership conference, held in Chicago, August 7-9-1992, the North American Man/Boy Love Association unanimously adopted the following resolution:

"NAMBLA calls on the Boy Scouts of America to cease its discrimination against openly gay or lesbian persons in the appointment of its scout masters. This will permit scouts to be exposed to a variety of lifestyles and will permit more of those individuals who genuinely wish to serve boys to do so."

I feel especially honored to have been asked to alert you of this resolution...I have also been a scout and a scout leader and share with so many in NAMBLA affection for the movement.

We recognize, of course, that the action for which we call is inevitable. What a great added contribution your organization will make possible to all the boys and girls who participate in it when you take this step. May it be taken in the near future.

We share a common mission — to bring greater understanding and light and purpose to the young as they grow. We invite you to join with us in cherishing individual integrity, and in seeking the opportunity for every boy and girl in our country *to find their own truth*. We encourage you to help every person associated with your organization to be able to express those values from themselves which to them represent for themselves the Good, the True, and the Beautiful. As we work together toward these ends Light will guide our way.

We express these sentiments most respectfully,
Very Cordially,

Leland Stevenson
Co-Recording Secretary, NAMBLA (NAMBLA Bulletin, November 1992. Emphasis ours).

Stevenson's letter is reminiscent of the one Wilhelm Jansen sent to *Wandervoegel* parents in which he told them, "you will have to accustom yourselves to the presence of so-called homosexuals in your ranks" (Mills:167). As we see, however, Stevenson's ideological allies have far greater political power in the United States today than Jansen's had in Germany in 1912.

On June 28, 2000, the Boy Scouts prevailed in the landmark Supreme Court case of Dale v. Boy Scouts of America. Dale, an open homosexual, had sued the Scouts under a New Jersey anti-discrimination statute for denying him the opportunity to be a scout leader. The court ruled that forcing the Boy Scouts to accept practicing homosexuals would violate their constitutional right of "expressive association." Rather than accepting this ruling, however, the "gay" movement stepped up its campaign against the Scouts, targeting the donor base of the organization. To this date, the Boy Scouts has stood firm.

Unfortunately, the moral courage of the Boy Scouts of America is not shared by all youth organizations. The Girl Scouts allows lesbian leaders in its organization and has expelled at least one heterosexual leader who refused to keep this policy secret from parents. Brenda Mailand, a Girl Scout employee in Lansing Michigan was fired after she refused to sign the following pledge:

> As an employee of the Michigan Capitol Girl Scout Council, you may not proactively inform members, parents of members, prospective members or parents of prospective members, or members of the general public (including media) of the Council's and GSUSA's position on sexual orientation (Private letter, February 9, 1993).

The Big Brothers/Big Sisters organization actively promotes "gay rights" through its organization. In 1991 Big Brother/Big Sisters' Board of Directors lobbied the Boy Scouts to change its policy against homosexual leaders, saying "the use of 'non-traditional' volunteers in the service delivery to youth can serve the best interest of children" (Private letter, August 9, 1991). Homosexual "big brothers" and "big sisters" are actively recruited in some cities (*Just Out*, March 1, 1993).

Absent a reversal in American cultural trends, it seems likely that the barrier to adult-child sex will fall in the not-too-distant future. What then? Can any society hope to escape disaster whose citizens have, to such a profound degree, lost the capacity to restrain themselves and others regarding sexual perversion? We cannot necessarily predict the future from what happened in Germany, but the possibility of following a similar path is very real. That path leads from sexual license to violence, murder and sadistic cruelty.

Atrocities

> *"The wicked prowl on every side when vileness*
> *is exalted among the sons of men"* Psalms 12:10.

Has sexual perversion led to increasing violence in America? Fortunately, to this point America has not experienced the wide-scale atrocities perpetrated by the Nazis in Germany, but the actions of certain male homosexuals in recent history are reminiscent of the worst SS butchers. As noted in a January 21, 1984 editorial in *The New York Times*, "Many of the most violent multiple murders have been committed by homosexual males." The correlation is even closer that the *Times* observation would suggest. Robert Hazelwood, a well-respected former agent of the FBI's Behavioral Science unit, offered the following insights:

> With reference to your question about homosexual killings, I will provide you with what I have learned in more than 34 years of professional law enforcement experience, countless training and educational programs provided by the forensic communities (pathologists, mental health, legal) and law enforcement, as well as my own experience in having consulted on more than 4,000 homicide cases (cases involving from 1-30 victims) including over 300 homicides involving homosexual males.
>
> When a deceased male is found nude or partially clothed and the murder involves "overkill" (i.e., much more violence than necessary to kill) and/or multiple stab wounds to the heart or throat and/or mutilation of the genitals then the investigator begins with the supposition that the crime is a homosexual-related murder. From my own experience, I can assure you that this assumption is proven true in at least 95% of the cases (Private letter, July 12, 1999).

Dr. Brian Clowes cites some alarming statistics showing that eight of the top ten serial killers in the United States
were homosexuals and that homosexuals were responsible
for 68 percent of all mass murders (Clowes:97). The following is a list of nine leading homosexual serial killers,
eight of which were among the top ten most prolific killers
as of 1992. Clowes' sources are listed in the text and are reprinted from *Debating the "Gay Rights" Issue*:

Donald Garvey: 37 Murders...[a] nurse's aide [who] was
convicted of 37 murders in Kentucky and Ohio. Psychol-
ogists testified that "Harvey said he was a homosexual."
The New York Times, August 20, and August 17th, 1991.

John Wayne Gacy: 33 Murders...[a] professed homosexual ...who killed 33 young men and boys and buried them
in his basement. *The New York Times*, February 22, 1980.

Patrick Wayne Kearney: 32 Murders...The New York
Times described him as "an acknowledged homosexual"
and "...perpetrator of the 'homosexual trash bag murders.'" *The New York Times*, July 27, 1977.

Bruce Davis: 28 murders...killed 28 young men and boys
after having sex with them. *The New York Times*, January
21, 1984.

Corll, Henley and Brooks: 32 Murders. Dean Corll,
Elmer Wayne Henley, and David Owen Brooks were the
members of a Texas homosexual torture/murder ring that
captured and mutilated 27 young men. *The New York
Times*, July 27, 1974.

Juan Corona: 25 Murders...an admitted homosexual,
killed 25 male migrant workers. *The New York Times*,
October 4, 1972.

Jeffrey Dahmer: 17 Murders...a convicted child molester

and practicing and admitted homosexual, lured 17 young men and boys to his apartment, had sex with them, then killed them and dismembered them. He ate parts of his victims bodies...Dahmer was active in "gay rights" organizations and had participated in "gay pride" parades. Michael C. Buelow. "Police Believe Suspect Killed 17." *The Oregonian*, July 26, 1991, pages A1 and A24. Also: "Relative in Dahmer Case Sues." *USA Today*, August 6, 1991, page 3A. Also October 1991 Focus on the Family Letter.

Stephen Kraft: 16 Murders...killed at least 16 young men after drugging, sodomizing and torturing them. Robert L. Mauro. "The Nation's Leading Serial Killers." *The Wanderer*, October 31, 1991.

William Bonin: 14 Murders...tortured and killed 14 young men...had sex with his victims before and after they died. Robert L. Mauro. "The Nation's Leading Serial Killers." *The Wanderer*, October 31, 1991. (Clowes:96)

William Bonin was executed by lethal injection at California's San Quentin prison on February 23, 1996. As reported in the *Orange County Register*, February 22, 1996, Bonin, the so-called "Freeway Killer," killed at least 21 boys and young men and dumped their bodies along California freeways (our original source mentioned only 14). After having been jailed in the early 1970s for raping boys, Bonin had vowed that in the future "there will be no witnesses."

Although various stories reported that Bonin had raped men at gunpoint in the army and had been engaged in sex with a man at the time of his final arrest, the media failed to identify Bonin as "gay." Standard "gay" rhetoric denies that male-on-male child molestation qualifies as homosexual conduct. Here, the perpetrator clearly was homosexual in his adult sexual relations as well, but the "gay" label was scrupulously avoided.

Thomas Hamilton of Dunblane, Scotland, is Britain's

worst mass-murderer in modern history. Hamilton killed 16 children at an elementary school on March 13, 1996. According to *The New York Times*, Hamilton was obsessed with boys. Ousted from the Boy Scouts in 1974 for "complaints about unstable and possibly improper behavior following a Scout camp," Hamilton later formed his own boys' club. Once again, children complained that "he was overly familiar, made them take their shirts off and was obsessed with photographing them." Upset that he had been branded a "pervert," Hamilton apparently took his revenge against the town of Dunblane by killing their children.

In a spree of "gay-on-gay" violence not seen since Nazi Germany, one homosexual man, Gaetan Dugas, was directly responsible for killing over a thousand homosexual men by deliberately infecting them with the AIDS virus. Indirectly he may be responsible for tens of thousands, eventually perhaps hundreds of thousands of AIDS deaths. One of the first known AIDS carriers, Dugas was known as "Patient Zero" because he caused so many of the earliest infections (Clowes:97).

Even after his diagnosis Dugas "justified his continued sodomy with the excuse that he was free to do what he wanted with his own body. Even when he was in the final stages of AIDS he would have anonymous sex with men in homosexual bathhouses, and then show his sexual partners his purple Kaposi's Sarcoma blotches, saying, 'Gay cancer. Maybe you'll get it'" ("The Columbus of AIDS." *National Review,* November 6, 1987:19).

As reported in the *Marin Independent Journal*, February 5, 1996, the first known murder connected to the Internet resulted from a homosexual encounter between two men in East Windsor, New Jersey. After meeting "through an online chat room, an electronic gathering place for gay men," they decided to get together. "But their offline meeting Jan. 4 turned deadly, police say, when George Hemenway shot Jesse Unger in the head, as a

15-year-old boy looked on." According to the story, the last homicide in this Trenton suburb of 22,000 was 10 years ago and also "stemmed from a homosexual 'street encounter,' police say."

Other major news stories have had a homosexual element that assumes greater significance when viewed in the context of the homo-fascist connection. For example, just days after du Pont fortune heir John E. du Pont attracted national attention for his role in a shooting and a dramatic police standoff at his Pennsylvania mansion, details of his bizarre private life began to emerge. A single man who lived with his mother until her recent death, du Pont used his personal fortune to support his hobbies, which centered on traditionally ultra-masculine themes: collecting guns and military artifacts (such as an armored personnel carrier he drove around his estate) and collegiate-style Greco-Roman wrestling.

A Gannett News Service report published in the January 30 edition of the *Marin Independent Journal* contains allegations that du Pont was a homosexual who used his wealth to recruit others into the homosexual lifestyle. "'You really don't want to hear the whole truth. It would blow you away,' said Andre Metzger, a wrestling coach who sued du Pont for sexual harassment. Metzger said du Pont used the Foxcatcher training facility to gain access 'to kids and adults' for homosexual relationships."

Around the turn of the millennium, America was stunned by a string of mass murders in public high schools. The most horrific of these was the attack by teenagers Dylan Klebold and Eric Harris on their classmates at Columbine High in Littleton, Colorado. Fifteen died that day, including Klebold and Harris, who committed suicide. There are two important facts which are relevant to our study. The first is that according to fellow students, the killers were homosexual. The *Gay Today* news website reported, in an article titled "The Waking Dream: Homoerotic violence at Columbine High," that "according to some accounts, Klebold and Harris were allegedly 'bisexuals,' which is a teenage code word for the "G" (gay) word, which teens, especially high school teens in Colorado, cannot use." NAMBLA Bulletin editor, Bill Andrietti wrote that

> A gay angle surfaced almost as soon as the shootings hit the news, with rumors circulating that the boys with the bombs and guns were -- variously -- certainly gay, absolutely heterosexual, or self-avowed bisexuals...Many gay public relations experts thought it best to downplay Eric Harris and Dylan Klebold's possible homosexuality....[while a press release from the homosexual Metropolitan Community Church reported that] Campus jocks remember calling Eric and Dylan "faggot," "homo," and "queer" because "they showered together" or "were seen holding hands."
> But asking whether Klebold and Harris were "really" gay misses the point. Like a wick soaked in gasoline, their relationship was soaked with homoeroticism. The theme of braving death together in battle runs through the literature of queer love....In his diary, one of the two spun out a fantasy of living on an island alone with the other....Whether they had girlfriends or not, Harris and Klebold shared a pact unto death that, if twisted horribly, also was romantic (Andrietti, Bill. "Homosexuality and the Massacre, *The Guide*, June 1999).

The second relevant fact is that the killers deliberately selected April 20th to launch their killing spree because it was Adolf Hitler's birthday. This choice was attributed, by surviving students, to the fact that "they believed in...what Adolf Hitler did"...."They're white supremacists" (Meek, James Gordon. "Littleton's Casualties of War," *Gridlock Magazine*, undated, quoting from *The Washington Times* and *The Washington Post*).

Not all of the school mass killers were alleged to be ho-

mosexuals, although a possible homosexual connection was raised in several of the incidents with the highest number of victims. Michael Carneal killed three and wounded five students as the victims prayed together at Heath High School in Paducah, Kentucky. Carneal denied being a homosexual, but had been accused of being "gay" by fellow students (Martinac, Paula. "Lesbian Notions" Called Out LGBT Religious News Service, May 24, 1999).

Mitchell Johnson (13), the older of the two boys who killed five and wounded ten at Westside Middle School in

Jonesboro, Arkansas had been repeatedly sexually abused by a relative of his day care provider when he was six or seven years old. It is assumed that the abuser was male. (*Arkansas Democrat Gazette*, April 7, 1998).

Luke Woodham attributed his murder of his mother and two students (nine others were wounded) to rage over a failed romance with a girl, but he had also been angered over being called "gay" at school (*Time.com*, July 6, 1998). By itself, this is rather unpersuasive evidence that Woodham struggled with homosexuality. However, we find it most interesting that in a pre-rampage explanatory note to a male friend, Woodham referred those who would be looking for clues about his motives to a section from The Gay Science by Friederich Nietzsche (*The Cincinnati Post* website, 11-09-98). The section contains Nietzsche's famous commentary on the theme that "God is dead." The Gay Science is not about homosexuality, but we wonder if reference to it might be intended to convey a cryptic message about Woodham's struggles. (Nietzsche's homosexuality is an acknowledged fact in "gay" circles these days -- see Charles Stone, "Of Whom Nietzsche dreamed," *Harvard Gay and Lesbian Review*, Winter 1999.) Interestingly, Woodham identified this and two other books as his favorites: Necronomicon, a book of magic, and Mein Kampf (ibid.).

More significant than the possible homosexual inclinations of the killers is the fact that school shootings have arisen in the context of rampant moral degeneracy among students. The degree to which America's children have been corrupted was documented in a 1999 PBS *Frontline* special "The Lost Children of Rockdale County." Following a 1996 outbreak of syphilis among teenagers in the middle-class community of Rockdale, Georgia, officials were shocked to learn that large numbers of local schoolchildren, from twelve years old and up, were routinely engaging in group sex together. Girls of fourteen were admitting to having had from 30-100 sex partners. Not only were the children not ashamed of their actions, according to one health care worker, students were "laughing and high-fiving" each other as they tested positive for syphilis.

Three years later, on the one-month anniversary of the Columbine massacre, Rockdale County became the site of its own school shooting. Fifteen-year-old Thomas Solomon shot and wounded six of his fellow students at Heritage High School in the city of Conyers (Grigg, William Norman. "Another Lost Generation?," *The New American*, October 23, 2000). Grigg writes

> To [the] grim indices of cultural decline must be added the recently coined category of "school shooters" -- murderous teenage sociopaths....One of the most potent indictments of our degenerate culture is found in the...FBI report "The School Shooter: A Threat Assessment Perspective"...listing the warning signs intended to help school officials recognize and evaluate potential shooters within their student populations. Relatively few social commentators have been willing to explore the unspoken assumption behind that report -- namely, that our present culture...can be expected to generate teenage mass murderers on a regular basis (ibid.).

As we can see, our nation is already reaping the destructive consequences of having embraced the "gay" ethic of sexual license. Once a nation of high moral values and strong families, we are now a fractured and morally confused society. It is not certain that we shall go the way of Germany, but absent a reversal of the current trend, it is very likely that we shall face some form of cultural disaster before the homosexualization of America is complete.

Chapter Ten

CLOSING THOUGHTS

The Danger of "Gay Rights"

Scott Lively

I am writing this conclusion to the third edition on the same day that President Bill Clinton has called for "hate crimes" legislation based on "sexual orientation" (code words for homosexuality). A few days ago, in an act unprecedented in the history of the presidency, Mr. Clinton aligned himself with the homosexual cause at a fund-raiser for the Human Rights Campaign Fund, the "gay" movement's largest political action committee. Knowing what it cost this president in 1993 to endorse "gays in the military," I am wondering what "gay" leaders might have promised the president in exchange for this new endorsement. Or can it be that public perception of the "gay" movement has changed so much that the Clinton administration (notorious for its reliance on polls and "focus groups") has decided that it is now safe for the president to identify himself and his office with the "gay" political agenda.

This question has personal significance for me, since I was one of the few people to publicly challenge then-candidate Clinton on his support for "gay" issues during his first run for presidential office. In response to my questions during a live *Town Hall* television program (simulcast from Seattle, Washington and Portland, Oregon), Mr. Clinton said he was against promoting homosexuality as a valid, alternative lifestyle to young people. At that time he also affirmed the right of the Boy Scouts to exclude "gay" scout leaders.

I raise this issue to contrast the benign public image of "gays" with the face of the "gay" movement that we have seen in these pages. Those whose perceptions of the "gay" movement have been shaped primarily by the popular media may find President Clinton's pro-"gay" political actions appropriate, even laudable. Such people have been persuaded that "gays" are society's victims in need of protection. But the "gay" movement I have seen and investigated is neither benign, nor are its members "victims." It is vicious, deceptive and enormously powerful. Its philosophy is Machiavellian and its tactics are (literally) Hitlerian.

What explains the dichotomy of perspectives on the "gay" movement? If any of the facts in this book are true, then the image of the "gay" movement Bill Clinton and other pro-"gay" opinion makers would like you to accept cannot be true. Are typical heterosexual supporters of "gay rights" simply unconcerned about the association of homosexuality with personal and societal dysfunction and violence? Or have these presumably well-intentioned people been denied complete information?

I have always been cautious of the word conspiracy, yet this is the word which best describes how the "gatekeepers" of American popular culture have helped to shape public opinion on this issue. The truth about homosexuality and the Nazi Party (indeed most information that might reflect negatively on the "gay" movement) appears to have been deliberately suppressed. We know that so-called "gay rights" has become a virtual *cause celebre* among the self-styled cultural elites in government, academia and the news and entertainment media. Over fifty years ago Samuel Igra also observed that homosexualism "had become a veritable cult among the ruling classes" in Germany prior to the rise of Hitler. I have come to believe that America's cultural elitists, perceiving themselves to be the moral arbiters of our society and the protectors of "gays," have used their power and their positions to protect and shield the "gay" movement from all unfavorable publicity. More than this, they have colluded to promote an image of "gays" as sterling citizens.

When I initially learned the truths set forth in this book, I was first astonished and then angered. Why had this information never surfaced during the many months in which the Oregon campaign to stop the "gay" agenda was continually being compared (in the local and national media) to the Nazi regime? The information is certainly not hidden. Anyone with the most basic research skills could easily find many of the two hundred-odd sources we have cited in this book. Are we to believe that the hundreds of trained journalists, college professors and politicians who helped guide the debate on that campaign (and many similar events) failed to discover any of these sources? We must assume that at least some of these professionals knew of these facts but decided not to inform the public. At best this represents an appalling level of arrogance (allowing that they might have disregarded these facts as not credible — denying "common" people the right to make up their own minds). The more plausible (and more frightening) conclusion is that the facts were withheld because of their likely negative impact on the "gay" movement.

"Gay" political power derives in large part from the public perception that homosexuals are victims. As Kirk and Pill so baldly admitted in *The Overhauling of Straight America,* "gays must be cast as victims in need of protection so that straights will be inclined by reflex to assume the role of protector." What would happen to the protective instinct of Americans if they knew that many of the worst villains of the Third Reich were "gay"? How closely would America scrutinize the "gay" agenda if "homoeroticism" were revealed as the very foundation of Nazism? (And I believe the movement would not survive such scrutiny). The evidence points to a conspiracy of silence — a nearly universal self-censorship by the same opinion-makers who mock conspiracy theories and decry any form of censorship.

If the facts in this book are true, and if it is also true that the "gatekeepers" of our public information are deliberately keeping these facts from us, can we hope to educate our fellow citizens before the "gay agenda" plunges this nation into social chaos? The outcome is uncertain. Surely, however, there have been times in the past when the inevitable repetitions of history were derailed by a few warning voices. It is our hope that the facts we have presented here will penetrate the fog of media-sponsored misinformation and "political correctness."

Have we exaggerated the urgency of our task? I think not. The future of America, indeed of civilization itself, depends upon the preservation of the natural family -- God's model for effective human society and the training ground for healthy human relationships. Yet the goal of the "gay" movement is the devaluation of the Judeo-Christian sexual ethic (monogamous heterosexual family-centered marriage) and its replacement with a "gay" affirming pagan alternative.

The "gay" movement in America (as contrasted with the German version) is different in style but not in substance. It remains characteristically selfish and hedonistic, but more importantly it continues to be defined by what it is *against:* Judeo-Christian family-based society. This "gay" vision for America is best defined in a widely circulated satirical essay written by a homosexualist under the pseud-

onym "Michael Swift" (probably to remind us of the
political satire of Jonathan Swift. Although the writer in-
tends to discredit this view of the homosexual agenda, its
very eloquence (in the context of our study) belies this attempt. Echoing from the ancient Spartan culture, from the
Teutons, from the Knights Templar, from the SA under
Ernst Roehm, and now from the American "gay rights"
movement comes this, our final glimpse into the fascist
heart of homosexualism:

> This essay is outre, madness, a tragic, cruel fantasy, an
> eruption of inner rage, on how the oppressed dream of be-
> ing the oppressor.
>
> We shall sodomize your sons, emblems of your feeble
> masculinity, of your shallow dreams and vulgar lies. We
> shall seduce them in your schools [Project 10], in your
> dormitories [forced homosexual roommates], in your
> gymnasiums, in your locker rooms, in your sports arenas,
> in your seminaries, in your youth groups [*Wandervoegel*,
> Boy Scouts], in your movie theater bathrooms, in your
> army bunkhouses ["gays in the military"], in your truck
> stops, in your all-male clubs, in your houses of Congress,
> wherever men are with men together. Your sons will be-
> come our minions and do our bidding. They will be recast
> in our image. They will come to crave and adore us.
>
> Women, you cry for your freedom. You say you are no
> longer satisfied with men; they make you unhappy [radi-
> cal feminism, lesbian separatist movement]. We, con-
> noisseurs of the masculine face, the masculine physique,
> shall take your men from you then. We will amuse them;
> we will embrace them when they weep. Women, you say
> you wish to live with each other instead of men. Then go
> ahead and be with each other. We shall give your men
> pleasures they have never known because we are fore-
> most men too and only one man knows how to truly
> please another man; only one man can understand with
> depth and feeling the mind and body of another man.
>
> All laws banning homosexual activity will be revoked

[anti-discrimination ordinances, minority status based on homosexuality]. Instead, legislation shall be passed which engenders love between men [graphic "pro-gay" sex and AIDS education, mandatory "sensitivity training,"].

All homosexuals must stand together as brothers; we must be united artistically, philosophically, socially, politically and financially [the multi-faceted and powerful "gay rights" movement]. We will triumph only when we present a common face to the vicious heterosexual enemy [suppression of internecine conflicts and other negative information about homosexuals by the homosexualist dominated media].

If you dare to cry faggot, fairy, queer, at us, we will stab you in your cowardly hearts and defile your dead puny bodies ["hate crimes," speech codes, fines].

We shall write poems of the love between men; we shall stage plays in which man openly caresses man [the play *Bent* and a multitude of others; the lesbian counterpart in the television show, *Ellen*]; we will make films about the love between heroic men which will replace the cheap, superficial, sentimental, insipid, juvenile, heterosexual infatuations presently dominating your cinema screens [Hollywood promotion of homosexual "love-making" and of the "gay rights" agenda in movies and television]. We shall sculpt statues of beautiful young men, of bold athletes which will be placed in your parks, your squares, your plazas [public funding of homosexual pornography by the National Endowment for the Arts, National Public Broadcasting Service]. The museums of the world will be filled only with the paintings of graceful, naked lads.

Our writers will make love between men fashionable and *de rigeur,* and we will succeed because we are adept at setting styles [invention of "gay-speak" — "gay," "homophobia," "diversity," "sexual orientation"]. We will eliminate heterosexual liaisons through usage of the devices of wit and ridicule which we are skilled in employing.

We will unmask the powerful homosexuals who masquerade as heterosexuals [outing]. You will be shocked and frightened when you learn that your presidents and

their sons, your industrialists, your senators, your may-
ors, your generals, your athletes, your film stars, your
television personalities, your civic leaders, your priests
are not the safe, familiar bourgeois, heterosexual figures
you assumed them to be. We are everywhere [a commonly used bumper-sticker]; we have infiltrated your
ranks [strategic "surprise" announcements by "conservative" homosexuals, e.g. Mel White, former ghostwriter
for Christian leaders]. Be careful when you speak of homosexuals because we are always among you; we may be
sitting across the desk from you; we may be sleeping in
the same bed with you.

There will be no compromises. We are not middle class
weaklings. Highly intelligent, we are the natural aristocrats of the human race, and steely-minded aristocrats
never settle for less [Brand/Friedlander, *Fuehrer* princi-
ple]. Those who oppose us will be exiled [the "Fems"].

We shall raise vast, private armies, as Mishima did, to
defeat you [Rossbach and Roehm, Frederick the Great].
We shall conquer the world because warriors inspired by
and banded together by homosexual love and honor are
invincible as were the ancient Greek soldiers [Plato's
Banquet].

The family unit — spawning ground of lies, betrayals,
mediocrity, hypocrisy and violence — will be abolished
[homosexual "marriage" and adoption]. The family unit,
which only dampens imagination and curbs free will,
must be eliminated [Plato's Republic]. Perfect boys will
be conceived and grown in the genetic laboratory. They
will be bonded together in communal setting, under the
control and instruction of homosexual savants [Sparta].

All churches who condemn us will be closed [attacks on
the McIlhennys, St. Patrick's Cathedral]. Our only gods
are handsome young men. We adhere to a cult of beauty,
moral and esthetic. All that is ugly and vulgar and banal
will be annihilated [*Kummerlings*]. Since we are alienated from middle-class heterosexual conventions, we are
free to live our lives according to the dictates of the pure
imagination [Nietzsche, Hitler]. For us too much is not

enough.

The exquisite society to emerge will be governed by an elite comprised of gay poets [Adolf Brand, Stefan George, Plato's "philosopher-kings"]. One of the major requirements for a position of power in the new society will be indulgence in the Greek passion [pederasty]. Any man contaminated with heterosexual lust will be automatically barred from a position of influence [SA leadership]. All males who insist on remaining stupidly heterosexual will be tried in homosexual courts of justice and will become invisible men.

We shall rewrite history [Holocaust revisionism, extravagant claims that historical figures (like Lincoln) were homosexual], history filled and debased with your heterosexual lies and distortions. We shall portray the homosexuality of great leaders and thinkers who have shaped the world. We will demonstrate that homosexuality and intelligence and imagination are inextricably linked, and that homosexuality is a requirement for true nobility, true beauty in a man [Hans Blueher].

We shall be victorious because we are filled with the ferocious bitterness of the oppressed who have been forced to play seemingly bit parts in your dumb, heterosexual shows throughout the ages [victim-plunder strategy]. We too are capable of firing guns and manning the barricades of the ultimate revolution [ACT-UP, Queer Nation, blood terrorism].

Tremble, hetero swine, when we appear before you without our masks.

(By Michael Swift, "Gay Revolutionary." Reprinted from *The Congressional Record* . First printed in *Gay Community News, February 15-21, 1987).*

B" H

The Final Word

Kevin E. Abrams

"The foundation of any 'human' civilization is a moral and healthy
sexual constitution, everything else is window-dressing."
The Jerusalem Post, May 21, 1996

After we learn of the role "gays" played in the National
Socialist movement, the Nazi attitude towards homosexuality may still seem contradictory and confusing, a riddle
only partially solved. We may still wonder, if so many of
the leading Nazis were "gay," why they would target homosexuals for incarceration or extermination as today's "gay"
activists claim. How can today's "gays," who express so
little regard for Biblical ethics, now portray themselves as
joint victims with the very Jews who suffered persecution
and virtual extermination at the hands of the largely "gay"
Nazis? How do the official Nazi invectives against homosexuality reconcile with the fact that "gays" held key positions in the Nazi government throughout its despotic reign,
inclusive of the Holocaust. Were the Nazis then victims of
their own persecution?

And why are we so compellingly urged by the Left to
sanction "gay rights," when, as the wide spectrum of "gay"
and non-"gay" sources listed in this book's bibliography in-
controvertibly show, Germany's militant "gays" were
largely responsible for propelling Hitler into the Chancellor's office? And now, knowing the extent to which German "gays" contributed to the success of the Nazi
movement, how should we interpret a looming "gay" swastika over America?

Spiritual Truth

Jewish scholar Rabbi Samson Raphael Hirsch who lived in the last century, is remembered for his most profound and extensive treatise on Torah philosophy. HOREB, meaning Sinai (the mountain where the original Torah was given by God and received by Moses), was written and published as a refutation to the Jewish pretensions of the German Reform Religion, which, today, is at the forefront of the movement to promote "gay rights" in America's Jewish community and within Israel. In opposition to both natural and Divine law, Reform has ordained lesbians as "rabbis" and sanctioned "gay" unions. "Gay" Jews have also imposed themselves on the Holocaust, cynically and pragmatically exploiting the deaths of six million Jewish men, women and children as a dramatic metaphor to portray themselves as victims, as if Hitler had targeted Jewish homosexuals primarily because they were "gay." But what of the truth in history?

From an ethical monotheistic perspective, Rabbi Hirsch points out in the following excerpt from HOREB, how it is the primary concern and duty of each of us to guard the dignity of our fellow man:

> God, who created man to be just, that is to say, to leave and give to all entities in all their relations that which is their due, has also endowed his mind with the faculty of mirroring the reality of things in their various relations so that man may be able to perceive the entities and their relations, and, on the strength of this knowledge, give to them what the teachings of justice lay down as their right.
>
> This reproduction of reality in the mind is truth. Truth therefore, is a precondition of justice; for only according to the image of the things and their relations which appears in man's mind can man behave towards them; if this image be false, his behavior will be different from what is due to them: he becomes unjust. And thus, if nothing else,

justice itself - which is our Divine calling - will guarantee that, as far as that calling of ours demands, we shall be able to perceive the reality of external things from their reflection within ourselves.

God has knitted together the community of man with the vital thread of love, and has ordained that man should rely on his brother for the spiritual good - namely, truth. But he who, instead of truthfully expressing in words what he has experienced to be real, communicates a false image of it to his brother, who accepts it and bases his behavior on it - either being unjust to his fellow-creatures or, having a wrong conception of their intentions towards him, being destroyed by them - that man turns into a curse that supreme blessing of the Creator; for he who denies truth to his brother, thus violating the highest duty towards him which God has imposed, calls down a curse - he who lies calls down a curse. And as material property is valuable only as a means for a life devoted to justice, and the liar steals the first condition of that justice - namely, truth, and gives falsehood in exchange, thus giving birth to injustice, the liar is even more dangerous than the thief.

The thief takes only the means of life as such, while the liar takes those of a just life, producing, in turn, injustice - and misery. For just as God links the supreme good, justice, to truth, so does He do the same with regard to the minor good, happiness. For to appreciate the nature of things you rely on your knowledge of them; and if somebody deceives you about their true nature, he robs you of a support or causes you to lean on a support that is insecure. And by stealing from another directly something precious - truth - and so indirectly the most precious thing - justice - the liar also kills himself spiritually; for he extinguishes in himself that Divine spark which alone makes of a him a human being created for the benefit of his fellow-men (Hirsch:248ff). [And what of "gay rights?" Never have so few taken so much from so many.]

Who were the Nazis?

We must recognize who the Nazis were. Ideologically, the Nazis were pragmatic, technocratic, tribal pagan utilitarians. They viewed human life with a detached and cynical pragmatism. They exploited whomever and whatever they could to achieve their political and military goals. Typically, the Nazis approached such issues as euthanasia, homosexuality and abortion with a ruthless expedience. Sterilization and abortion were preferred for anyone classified inferior or defective (but never for healthy Aryans).

To the technocratic Nazi mind truth was dictated by the necessity of the moment (dealing thus in lies they brought a curse upon themselves and all they touched). "Defectives" were euthanized and inferiors sterilized, while it was a crime for Aryan maidens to have abortions. While privately tolerating and even promoting homosexuality, the Nazis denounced it frequently in public using trumped-up charges of homosexuality to arrest and remove those who disagreed with Hitler's military and political goals. Former neo-Nazi Ingo Hassellbach, in his revealing 1996 book, <u>Fuhrer-Ex</u>, confirms how the utilitarian Nazi double standard was applied in other areas: "Opposition to abortion had been one of the consistent planks in the Nazi platform since the Movement's beginnings in the 1920s, and for a simple reason: abortion was race murder. While permissible, even desirable, among the colored women and Jews of the world, among Aryans it was the ultimate sin" (Hasselbach:111).

The Nazi version of racial eugenics evolved into the key political and military platform of the Nazi Party, which enabled the Nazis to portray the Jewish people as a defective and inferior class, along with the physically deformed and other non-productive members of German society. In effect, however, the Nazis simply projected their own depravities upon the Jewish people, demonized and dehumanized them, and then used them as scapegoats as they themselves proceeded to plunder the world. Nazi racial theories served as a pretext to justify the elimination of a people whose deeper "offense" was its commitment to an unyielding moral standard.

As Professor Giora Shoham explains in his book, <u>Valhalla, Calvary &</u> <u>Auschwitz</u>, the Nazis, like today's "gays," "longed to shed the normative constraints of Judaeo-Christian law and morals and to return to the amoral irresponsibility of their paganism. They resented the Jews, who symbolized to them the imposition of restraints on their hedonistic paganism....When this sense of law and justice is rejected, the tribal chieftain, [and homoerotic warrior] reigns supreme. Thus, the separant power of Odin knew no limits; consequently, the omnipotence of Adolf Hitler, der Fuehrer, recognized no boundaries of law, morality or mercy" (Shoham:27).

Increasingly, as they emerge from the closet, today's "gays" do bear a striking resemblance to yesterday's Nazis.

Left-Right Polarities

To understand the pagan mind in this context we must recognize the truth about left-right polarities in the political sphere. With minor discrepancies, all left-wing ideology can be identified as "regressive," and right-wing ideology as "progressive." Left-wing regressives incite mutual plunder, encourage dependency and pragmatically aspire to the lowest common denominator. Genuine right-wing progressive conservatives encourage creativity, inspire mutual affirmation, trust and human productivity. By nature, all socialism falls on the regressive side, in that "socialism," is simply a political ideology which often lacks a true sense of social justice. Evil disguises itself as virtue (e.g., the goal of racial purity) because it has no life of its own (which is why sad bondage wishes to be known as "gay liberation.")

Generally, adherents of the Left fail to do what is necessary to guard the dignity of their fellow man. A left-leaning historian, for instance, would fatalistically argue that "history" repeats itself, while a conservative like Voltaire could observe correctly how it is instead "man who always repeats himself." No wonder left-regressives cannot learn from history. If history just "happens" then little can be learned from it or done to prevent it from happening again. Basing one's decisions on a revised, corrupted or inverted version of history, however, is another matter. Some of man's worst follies are committed because of erroneous or falsified information.

In trying to understand the Nazi phenomenon we often ask ourselves how a gang of murdering thugs could have seized power in such a *civilized* nation? The truth is that Germany during the Weimar period was one of the most *uncivilized* nations in the world. Hitler himself referred to Berlin as the whore of Babylon. We consistently err in judging the advancement of human civilizations on the basis of art and technology. The Nazis loved classical music, and they were astute in the use of science and technology. The question we must ask about every society is, to what end is human culture is employed?   For left-wing regressives, culture serves destruction and death.   For right-wing progressives, culture focuses upon life.

A positive and utilitarian attitude toward homosexuality, euthanasia and abortion would therefore (then as now) be a left-wing regressive orientation, and a typical Nazi profile (with very specific contradictions and qualifications). It bears repeating that the Nazis were first and foremost technocratic, utilitarian pragmatists who believed in the survival of the fittest and the societal goals of physical beauty and racial perfection, Aryans being the "fittest" and most perfected, and Jews the least "fit" and least perfect. In truth, racial characteristics are irrelevant. Only the morality of a individuals and nations can determine whether they are civilized or barbarians -- builders or plunderers.

How do homosexuals fit into this picture? Although Nazi rhetoric listed homosexuals among the unfit, the Nazis never targeted homosexuals for destruction. To the contrary, unless the homosexual in question was Jewish, or a political enemy, the Nazi organization was often protective of homosexuals. Originally, the SS was founded for precisely the purpose of protecting Viennese homosexuals. The Nazis actually attempted to cure homosexuals at the Goering Institute, albeit in many ways which proved futile. (forcing a gender-weak frightened male to sleep with a female prostitute proved ineffective). "Gay" rights activists often take Nazi propaganda against homosexuals and regurgitate it as historical truth. Nazi and "gay" historical revisionism, with their inversion of history and civilized values, are one. In today's "gay" victim strategy, the perpetrator is posing as the victim.

Fifth Columns

In their quest for power, Nazi homosexuals were no different from today's "gays." Then, as now, the strategy was one of deception, infiltration and subversion. Our study of "gay" history reveals how Nazi "gays," both historically and today, act as subversive fifth columns in their host communities, preparing the way for "gay" Nazi power while overtly and covertly spreading anti-"gay" propaganda in an attempt to veil their own goals. The Pink Swastika documents how top French and British Nazis were "gays" and that American Nazi Frank Collin, who led the 1977 march on Skokie Illinois, was a "gay" pederast. So what of so-called 'liberty?'"

The idea of liberty held by modern liberals is quite new. According to them, liberty connotes a radical individualism that rejects all social norms and institutions which the individual has not agreed to. Subscribers to this idea defend the right of Nazis (who themselves despise the idea of rights) to

march through Skokie, Illinois, but not the right of
Skokians and their elected leaders to maintain order and defend the dignity of the principles and customs they hold
most dear. Likewise, they support the right of homosexuals
and atheists to invade and destroy the Boy Scouts.

In Nazi history, failed fifth column sedition activities in
target nations are recorded in the October 12, 1937 *The New
York Times* in bold headlines reading, "Czech Nazi Official
Is Seized by Police." The Prague dispatch quoted in the
Times reports "a major political sensation caused by the ar-
rest, under the criminal code 'dealing with homosexuality,'
of Hans Rutha, a high official in the country's camouflaged
Nazi Party." And from October 17, 1937, further headlines
read, "14 members of Czech Nazi Party Held for Morals
Offences," identifying Rutha, as the "'right hand man' of
the Nazi Party Chief," i.e., as "gay" Ernst Roehm was to
Hitler. On December 3, headlines report, "Members of
Youth Organization Face Homosexual Charges." And on
December 10, 1937, a *Times* story from Prague announces
that "fourteen Czechs, all the accused, had received 'sus-
pended sentences' after trial on homosexual charges" (J.
Katz:553f).

Despite such random clues, the world of that day was
duped. Left-regressive, self-identified lesbian, Gertrude
Stein, felt that Hitler should have received the Nobel Peace
prize in 1937. Apparently, Britain's Prime Minister,
Neville Chamberlain, also thought Hitler could be bribed to
honor peace with the September 30, 1938 Munich agree-
ment. His payment was Czechoslovakia, but "peace in our
time" only cleared the way for Hitler's invasion of Poland
on September 1, 1939. History shows that militant "gay"
efforts often produce a result that is anything but peaceful.
Further, while individual "gays" may "come out of the
closet" for various reasons, their agenda and the truth about
the depth of their infiltration of powerful institutions,
remans hidden. We can also learn from the Nazis' victims

that bribery never satisfies extortionists. They always come back for more, which is why (in our day) demands for "rights" have no end. Each capitulation of American society to "gay" demands draws increasing demands, which will continue until they destroy the institutions which support society, including the homosexuals themselves.

The age of AIDS has launched "gay" activism into full gear. As the liberal dogma would have it, no one is responsible for AIDS; it just happens. Taking its cue from no-fault divorce and no-fault insurance, the Left has also created the concept of no-fault utilitarian sex. British occultist and Satanist, Aleister Crowley sums it up: "do what thou wilt, shall be the whole of the law."But "do what thou wilt" is no law at all! Crowley's maxim is in reality a negation of all natural and spiritual law; it only promotes chaos and a left-wing regressive descent into oblivion and non-existence. His maxim reflects a complete lack of concern and respect for the dignity of his fellow man and a contempt for life.

"Gay" Sedition

"Gay" strategists choose to employ the biological model of homosexuality for the dual purpose of denying choice and escaping responsibility. In calling for research into a so-called "gay" gene, their purpose was never to cure or rectify, but to justify homoerotic conduct and the homosexual identity. "Gays" correctly reason that if sexual behavior is a choice, it carries with it both responsibility and accountability. Their insistence that homosexuality is "not a choice" functions to bring ever more recruits into the "gay" fold and keep them there by discouraging them from seeking change. For many of today's young men, their ability to choose has been hijacked by a sophisticated program of psychosexual sedition and manipulation, largely sustained by the social weaknesses of our time.

To limit the animating source for human behavior to the brain and animal instinct (as many of today's behavioral scientists do) is both reductionist and left-wing regressive. Human motives and actions are, to a significant extent, determined by the vastly greater non-physical aspects of human existence. Inclinations are non-physical, and behavior causes physical change. (Planting the seed of human life in the passage designed for the expulsion of waste not only causes disease, but also exerts a destructive force upon the individual soul and on the value of all human life).

"Gays" have forgotten that responsibility for personal conduct goes hand-in-hand with our personal dignity and authority. Realistically, we can never dignify something which is profoundly undignified, no matter how hard we strive to.   This brings us to another seditious element of "gay" culture, pornography. Dr. Judith Reisman, co-author of <u>Kinsey Sex & Fraud</u> and Founder of the Washington based Institute for Media Education, is an expert on the impact of pornography on society. During a lengthy private conversation, Dr. Reisman asserted that "all pornography promotes homosexuality." I have pondered her comment many times since then, and have come to see its correctness. In her 1994 analysis, *Kinsey, Hefner & Hay, The Indoctrination of Heterophobia in American Men & Women*, Dr. Reisman explains;

Pragmatically, *Playboy* (*that is*, all pornography) manifests a blatant homosexual ethos. Its heterophobia is sustained by an utilitarian analysis of *Playboy* images and philosophy. It is not too much to say, that just as the imagery of stained glass windows and holy cards once initiated, instructed and indoctrinated potential adherents in a religious faith, the didactic images in "soft" and "hard" pornography similarly initiate, instruct and indoctrinate potential believers in the tenants of its religion, its homosexual morality. Hugh Hefner took great pains to write his own bible; he called it the "*Playboy* Philosophy." And on this note, it is well accepted that "Alfred Kinsey...gave Hefner the research base for the "*Playboy* Philosophy."...In fact Kinsey can properly be identified along with his supporters and co-workers, as the one most responsible for justifying the kind of behavior which led to AIDS, and more than Harry Hay, the real father of American's homoerotic revolution (Reisman, 1994:7f). [In reality, pornography expresses a vicious hatred and contempt for the dignity of all men in that it treats men as nothing more than an appendage to be manipulated by the twisting and exploitation of female sexuality.]

Sons of Oedipus

Clinical research concludes that the target of human sexual affections is not predetermined at birth, but conditioned by a combination of environmental and sociological factors. It would be helpful to turn back to the "Oedipus complex," to present a psychosexual model for the roots of homoerotic attraction. [Oedipus was the legendary figure who killed his father and married his mother.]

Although "gay" research mocks and rejects the validity of this Freudian construct, the idea offers helpful insight into the complex structure and development of the homosexualities. The classic Oedipus complex may be defined as a lust-hate demeanor towards the mother and an irreconcilable combination of longing and contempt for the father. In the words of Dr. Joseph Nicolosi,

Homosexuality is a developmental problem that is almost always the result of problems in family relations, particularly between father and son. As a result of failure with father, the boy does not fully internalize male gender-identity, and develops homosexuality. This is the most commonly seen clinical model (Nicolosi, 1991:25).

Analyst Peter Loewenberg in <u>The Nazi Revolution,</u> <u>Hitler's Dictatorship and the German Nation</u>, writes, "Boys who become homosexuals are often those who were left alone with their mothers and formed an intense attachment to them that was unmediated by the father's presence and protection."

The regressive promotion of an androgynous culture advances an equality in which gender distinctions, roles and identity are blurred and inverted. This leads to a loss of healthy self-identity. Paradoxically, the freedom of choice being offered by liberal left-regressive social theorists to today's youth destroys a child's ability to choose. In a similar vein, radical feminism actually destroys femininity while emasculating males, and socialism destroys social justice. By robbing our children of their ability to conduct themselves morally, today's left-wing regressives are grooming a new generation of potential Nazis.

Today, while chronic homoerotic behavior is limited to a small percentage of the population, its roots (either deficiencies in psychic gender patterning, or deviance initiated by adult-child sexual abuse) may be more widespread. Clinical studies reveal that the sexualization of a search for masculinity is the genesis of homoerotic attraction. It follows that the current generation of fatherless youth may be prime candidates for homosexual recruitment. And the same amoral thinking which allows them to consider homosexuality as a "normal" option may also make them dangerously susceptible to the next Hitler. It is no accident that Hitler and his cronies came to power on the backs of emasculated German male youth.

Akhtar's Metaphor -- A New Beginning

A primary goal of any people striving to maintain a civilized human society must be to prepare our children to become reliable and loyal husbands and wives and competent fathers and mothers. There is nothing in the world a young man wishes to do more than to be able to love, admire and respect his father. This vision can only be fully realized in the context of a healthy natural family.

There are two primary obligations which the parent has toward his children: to instill in them a moral and healthy sexual constitution and to ensure they are equipped with an honest and productive way of providing for themselves and their families. These two personal assets enable any person to live life as a dignified human being. The parents' obligation, therefore, is to guard the dignity of their children. Conversely, the Biblical injunction contained within the principle of the family is for the children to guard the dignity of their parents. If we kept this in mind, many families could be reunited and divisions resolved. Our challenge is to repair America's soul before the body perishes.

Dr. Salman Akhtar's book, Broken Structures, offers a metaphor for healing the broken person which is also applicable to the mending of a nation. Teaching a course on character pathology to a class of clinical psychology interns, Dr. Akhtar was asked if a severely disturbed client could ever be so completely healed by psychotherapy that he would be indistinguishable from a person who had always been well-adjusted. From the book Broken Structures in which Dr. Akhtar tells "The Parable of Two Flower Vases," I will conclude with his words:

> I thought for a moment. Then, prompted by an inner voice, I spontaneously came up with the following answer. Well, let us suppose that there are two flower vases made of fine china. Both are intricately carved and of comparable value, elegance, and beauty. Then a wind blows and one of them falls from its stand, and is broken into pieces. An expert from a distant land is called. Painstakingly, step by step, the expert glues the pieces back together. Soon the broken vase is intact again, can hold water without leaking, is unblemished to all who see it.

Yet this vase is now different from the other one. The lines along which it had broken, a subtle reminder of yesterday, will always remain discernible to an experienced eye. However, it will have a certain wisdom since it knows something that the vase that has never been broken does not: it knows what it is to break and what it is to come together .

Kevin E. Abrams
November 14, 1997

BIBLIOGRAPHY

A

*** Adam, Harry D. The Rise of a Gay and Lesbian Movement. Boston, Twane Publishers, 1987. *** Agonito, Rosemary. History of Ideas on Women: A Source Book, New York, G.P.Putnam & Sons, 1977. *** Alyson Almanac. Boston, Alyson Publications Inc., 1990. *** American Family Association Journal. January, 1988. *** Anderson, Shelly. "Youth." The Advocate. January 26, 1993. *** Andriette, Bill, "Is Gaie France Fascist?" NAMBLA Bulletin, September, 1992. *** Andrietti, Bill. "Homosexuality and the Massacre, The Guide, June 1999 *** Arkansas Democrat Herald. In Life Advocate, February, 1994.

B

*** Bay Area Reporter. August 1, 1991. *** Beard, Mary. The Sex Life of the Unmarried Adult. Garden City Publishing, New York, 1934. *** Berenbaum, Michael. The World Must Know. Boston, Little, Brown and Company, 1993. *** Bergler, Edmund, M.D. Homosexuality: Disease or Way of Life?. New York, The Macmillan Company,1956. *** Bergsson, Snorri G. Muftism and Nazism, at www.notendur.centrum.is/˄snorrigb, *** Berry, Jason. Lead Us Not Into Temptation: Catholic Priests and the Sexual Abuse of Children. New York, Doubleday, 1992. *** Bessel, Richard. Political Violence and the Rise of Nazism. New Haven, Yale Press, 1984. *** Bianco, David, "What Was The Scientific Humanitarian Committee?, Washington Blade, August, 1997. *** Blachford, Gregg. "Male Dominance and the Gay World," in Kenneth Plummer, ed. The Making of the Modern Homosexual, 1981. *** Bleuel, Hans Peter. Sex and Society in Nazi Germany. New York, J.B. Lippincott Company, 1973. *** Blueher, Hans. *Die deutsche Wandervogelbewegung als erotisches Phanomen*, Templehof-Berlin, 1914. *** Bonetti, David. "Muscling in on the Mainstream." *San Francisco Examiner*, June 26, 1992. *** Buchmayr, Friedrich. *Biographisch-Bibliographisches Kirchenlexicon*, Vol. XVI, 1999. *** Burleigh, Michael, and Wipperman, Wolfgang. The Racial State: Germany 1933-1945. New York, Cambridge University Press, 1993. *** Butler, Ewan and Young, Gordon. The Life and Death of Hermann Goering.

C

*** Calic, Edouard. Reinhard Heydrich: The Chilling Story of the Man Who Masterminded the Nazi Death Camps. Military Heritage Press, William Morrow and Company, 1982. *** Cantarella, Eva. Bisexuality in the Ancient World. New Haven, Yale University Press, 1992. *** Cavendish, Richard, Man, Myth & Magic: An Illustrated Encyclopedia of the Supernatural. New York, Marshall Cavendish Corporation, 1970. *** Clowes, Brian. Debating the "Gay Rights" Issue. Brooks, Oregon, Oregon Citizens Alliance, 1993. *** Cory, Donald Webster, and LeRoy, John P. The Homosexual and His Society: A View from Within. New York, Citadel Press, 1963. *** Costello, John. Mask of Treachery: Spies, Lies, Buggery and Betrayal. New York, William Morrow and Company, 1988. *** Costello, John and Tsarev, Oleg. Deadly Illusions. Crown Publishers, New York, 1993. *** Cowan, Thomas. Gay Men and Women Who Enriched the World. Boston, Alyson Publications, 1988. *** Crompton, Louis. "Gay

Genocide: from Leviticus to Hitler." The Gay Academic.   Palm
Springs, California, ETC Publications, 1978.

D

*** *Daily Telegraph*, "How sex became a weapon of war," July 23,
1998. *** Davidson, Michael. The World, the Flesh, and Myself. London, Arthur Baker Ltd., 1962. *** *Dateline World Jewry*. New York,
Institute of the World Jewish Congress, August, 1994. *** Donohue,
William A. "Culture Wars Against the Boy Scouts". *Society Magazine*,
May/June 1994. *** Dunne, Bruce. "Power and Sexuality in the Middle East," *Middle East Report*, Spring, 1998. *** Dynes, Wayne. The
Encyclopedia of Homosexuality.   New York, Garland Publishing,
1990.

E

*** Ebert, Michael. "Pedophilia Steps into the Daylight." *Focus on the
Family Citizen*. November 16, 1992. *** Eder, Dr. Asher. "How to
Disarm the Terrible Jihad Psychosis Against Jews and Israel that Af-
flicts the Muslim World Today," www.rb.org, February 24, 2000. ***
Evans, Arthur. Witchcraft and the Gay Counterculture. Fag Rag Books,
Boston 1978.

F

*** Facts on File Yearbook, 1941, Volume 1, New York, Persons In-
dex, Facts on File Inc. *** Fee, Elizabeth. "Science and Homosexuality." The Universities and the Gay Experience. New York, Gay
Academic Union, 1974. *** Fest, Joachim C. The Face of the Third

Reich: Portraits of the Nazi Leadership. New York, Pantheon Books, 1970. *** Fest, Joachim C. Hitler. New York, Vintage Books, 1975. *** Flaceliere, Robert, Love in Ancient Greece, Crown Publishers, New York, 1962. *** Flemming, Gerald. Hitler and the Final Solution. Berkeley, University of California Press, 1982. *** Flood, Charles Bracelen. Hitler, The Path to Power. Boston, Houghton Mifflin Company, 1989. *** Friedlander, Benedict. "Memoirs for the Friends and Contributors of the Scientific Humanitarian Committee in the Name of the Succession of the Scientific Humanitarian Committee." Journal of Homosexuality, January-February, 1991. *** Friedlander, Henry, and Milton, Sybil (Eds.). Simon Wiesenthal Center Annual, Volume 7. New York, Allied Books, 1990. *** Friedrich, Otto. Before the Deluge. (Harper and Row, New York, 1986. *** Fuchs, Thomas. The Hitler Fact Book. New York, Fountain Books, 1990.

G

*** Gallo, Max. The Night of the Long Knives. New York, Warner Books, 1973. *** Garde, Noel I. Jonathan to Gide: The Homosexual in History. New York, Vantage Press, 1969. ***The Gay Agenda (video). Lancaster, California, The Report, 1992. *** Gay, Peter. Weimar Culture: The Outsider as Insider. New York, Harper and Row, 1968. *** Genese, Cecil. The Holocaust: Who Are The Guilty. Sussex, England, The Book Guild Ltd., 1988. *** Germino, Dante. "Fascism." Collier's Enclyclopedia. Volume 9. New York, Macmillan, 1991. *** Glaser,Herman. The Cultural Roots of National Socialism. University of Texas Press, Austin, 1964. *** Glazov, Jamie. "Sexual Rage Behind Islamic Terror," FrontPage magazine, October 4, 2001. *** Goodrick-Clarke, Nicholas. The Occult Roots of Nazism: Secret

Aryan Cults and their Influence on Nazi Ideology. New York, New York University Press, 1992. *** Graber, G.S. The History of the SS: A Chilling Look at the Most Terrifying Arm of the Nazi War Machine. New York, Charter Books, 1978. *** Grahn, Judy. Another Mother Tongue. Boston, Beacon Press, 1984. *** Grant, George. Grand Illusions: The Legacy of Planned Parenthood. Brentwood, Tennessee, Wolgemuth and Hyatt, Publishers Inc., 1988. *** Grant, George, and Horne, Mark. Legislating Immorality. Chicago, Moody Press, 1993. *** Grau, Gunter. Hidden Holocaust? London, Cassells, 1993. *** Greenberg, David F. The Construction of Homosexuality. Chicago, University of Chicago Press, 1988. *** Greif, Martin. The Gay Book of Days. The Main Street Press, 1982. *** Grigg, William Norman. "Another Lost Generation?," The New American, November 12, 2001. *** Grunberger, Richard. The 12-Year Reich: A Social History of Nazi Germany 1933-1945. New York, Ballantine Books, 1971. ***Guthrie, W.K.C. "The Republic." Grolier Electronic Publishing, 1992.

H

*** Hasselbach, Ingo. Fuhrer EX. Random House, 1996. *** Haeberle, Irwin J. "Swastika, Pink Triangle, and Yellow Star: The Elite Rights Committee, 1992. *** Harvard Gay and Lesbian Review Summer, 1995. *** Healy, Murray, Gay Skins: Class, Masculinity and Queer Appropriation,Cassell, 1996. *** Heiden, Konrad, History of National Socialism, New York, A.A. Knopf, 1935; Der Fuehrer, 1944. *** Herdt, Gilbert. The Sambia , CBS College Publishing, New York, 1987. *** Herzer, Manfred. "Communists, Social Democrats, and the Homosexual Movement in the Weimar Republic." In Heckma, et al

(Eds.). Gay Men and the Sexual History of the Political Left. New York, Haworth Press, 1995. *** Hirsch, Rabbi Samson Raphael. HOREB: A Philosophy of Jewish Laws and Observances. Jerusalem, Soncino Press, 1962. *** Howard, Michael. The Occult Conspiracy. Rochester, Vermont, Destiny Books, 1989. *** Howe, Ellic. Astrology: A Recent History Including the Untold Story of its Role in World War II. New York, Walker and Company, 1967. *** Hutton, Dietrich, *Defilement of Race*, Duesseldorf, "Duetsche Revolution."

I

*** *IGLA Euroletter* 52, "Gay Holocaust Survivors to get Swiss Money," August, 1977. *** Igra, Samuel, Germany's National Vice . London: Quality Press Ltd., 1945, Igra, Samuel, The "Doctor's Plot" in Moscow and the Protocols of the Wise Men of Zion, 1960.

J

*** Jackson, Robert H., The Nurnberg Case, New York, Cooper Square Publishers, Inc. 1971. *** Jay, K., and Young, A. The Gay Report. Summit, 1979. *** Johansson, Warren, "Pink Triangles." In Dynes, Wayne (ed.). Encyclopedia of Homosexuality. New York, Garland Publishing, 1990. *** Johansson, Warren, and Percy, William A. "Homosexuals in Nazi Germany." In Henry Friedlander (ed.), Simon Wiesenthal Center Annual: Volume 7. New York, Allied Books, Ltd., 1990. *** Johansson, Warren, and Percy, William A. Outing: Shattering the Conspiracy of Silence. New York, Harrington Park Press, 1994. *** Jones, H. Kimball. Toward a Christian Understanding of the Homosexual. New York, Association Press, 1966. *** Jones, J. Sydney. Hitler in Vienna 1907-1913. New York, Stein and

Day, 1983. *** Jones, Nigel H.. Hitler's Heralds: The Story of the Freikorps 1918-1923. London, John Murray, 1987. *** *Just Out.* March 1, 1993.

K

*** Karlen, Arno. Sexuality and Homosexuality. New York, W.W. Norton, 1971. *** Katz, Jonathan. Gay American History. New York, Thomas Y. Crowell Company, 1976. *** Katz, Jonathan Gay and Lesbian Almanac. *** Katz, Steven T. "Quantity and Interpretation — Issues in the Comparative Historical Analysis of the Holocaust." In Holocaust and Genocide Studies: Volume 1. Oxford University Press, New York, 1994; Volume 4, Number 2, 1989. New York, Pergamon Press, 1989. *** Kennedy, Hubert. "Man/Boy Love in the Writings of Karl Heinrich Ulrichs" in Pascal, Mark (ed.). Varieties of Man/Boy Love. New York, Wallace Hamilton Press, 1992. *** Kennedy, Hubert. Ulrichs: The life and works of Karl Heinrich Ulrichs, Pioneer of the Modern Gay Movement, Boston, Alyson Publications, 1988). *** Kirk, Marshall, and Pill, Erastes. "The Overhauling of Straight America." *Guide Magazine*, November, 1987. *** Knickerbocker, H.R. Is Tomorrow Hitler's ? New York, Reynal and Hitchcock, 1941. *** Koch, H.W. The Hitler Youth: Origins and Development 1922-1945. New York, Stein and Day, 1976. *** Koehl, Robert Lewis. The Black Corps: The Structure and Power Struggles of the Nazi SS. Madison Wisconsin, University of Wisconsin Press, 1983. *** Kogon, Eugen. The Theory and Practice of Hell. New York, Berkley Publishing Company, 1950.

370

L

*** Langer, Walte_r. The Mind of Adolf Hitler: The Secret Wartime Report. Signet, 1972. *** Lauritsen, John, and Thorstad, David. The Early Homosexual Rights Movement:1864-1935. New York, Times Change Press, 1974. *** League of Nations International Health Year-book. Geneva, League of Nations Health Organization, 1924. *** Lee, Martin. The Beast Reawakens. New York, Little, Brown and Co., 1997. *** Leo, John. "When Activism Becomes Gangsterism." U.S. News and World Report. February 5, 1990. *** Levi, Primo. Survival in Auschwitz. New York, Macmillan Publishing Company, 1961. *** The Limbaugh Letter. May, 1995. *** Linsert, Richard. Kabale und Liebe: Uber Politik und Geschlechtsleben. Berlin, Man, 1931. *** Lombardi, Michael A.. "Research on Homosexuality in Nineteenth Century Germany" (Parts I and II). Los Angeles, Urania Manuscripts, 1977. *** Los Angeles Times. January 29, 1993.

M

*** Mac Mathuna, Sean. "Postwar Arab links to the ODESSA network," Flame Magazine, 1999, www.flamemag.dircon.co.uk. *** MacDonald, Callum. The Killing of SS ObergruppenFuehrer Reinhard Heydrich. New York, The Free Press, 1989. *** Macintyre, Ben. Forgotten Fatherland: The Search for Elisabeth Nietzsche. New York, Farrar Straus Giroux, 1992. *** The Mail on Sunday (UK), "The Gay Acolytes haunting Haider," April 30, 2000 *** Manchester, William. The Arms of Krupp. Little, Brown and Co., Boston, 1968. *** Manchester, William. The Last Lion: Winston Spencer Churchill. London, Little, Brown and Company. *** Marotta, Toby. The Politics of Homosexuality. Boston, Houghton Mifflin Company, 1981. *** The

Massachusetts News, "Holocaust Survivor: Molested by Guards," April 5, 2000 *** Martinac, Paula. "Lesbian Notions" Called Out LGBT Religious News Service, May 24, 1999. *** Mauro, Robert L. "The Nation's Leading Serial Killers." *The Wanderer*. October 31, 1991. *** McIllhenny, Chuck & Donna, and York, Frank. When the Wicked Seize a City. Lafayette, Louisiana, Huntington House, 1993. *** Meade, Marion, Madame Blavatsky: The Woman Behind the Myth. New York, G.P. Putnam & Sons, 1980. *** Miles, David H. "George, Stefan." Grolier Electronic Publishing, Inc., 1992. *** Miller, Neil. Out of the Past: Gay and Lesbian History from 1869 to the Present. New York, Vintage Books, 1995. *** Mills, Richard. "The German Youth Movement." In Leyland, Winston (Ed.). Gay Roots: Twenty Years of Gay Sunshine: An Anthology of Gay History, Sex, Politics, and Culture. San Francisco, Gay Sunshine Press, 1989. *** Mosse, George L. Nationalism and Sexuality: Respectability and Abnormal Sexuality in Modern Europe. New York, Howard Fertig, 1985. *** Mulshine, Paul. "Man/Boy Love." *Heterodoxy*, September, 1994. *** Munk, Rabbi Elie. Call of the Torah. Feldheim Publishing, 1980.

N

*** *NAMBLA Bulletin*. November 1992; September, 1992. *** *NARTH Bulletin*. March, 1994. *** *National Review*. November 6, 1987; June 24, 1991. *** Nethercot, Arthur H.. The First Five Lives of Annie Besant. Chicago, University of Chicago Press, 1960. *** *The New York Times*. October 4, 1972; July 27, 1974; July 27, 1977; February 22, 1980; January 21, 1984; August 17 and August 20, 1991. *** Newman, Leslea. Heather Has Two Mommies. Boston, Alyson Publications, 1989. *** Newton, Michael. Raising Hell: An Encyclopedia

372

of Devil Worship and Satanic Crime. New York, Avon, 1993. ***
Newton, Michael, and Newton, Judy Ann. The Ku Klux Klan: An En-
cyclopedia. New York, Garland Publishing, 1991. *** Nicolosi, Dr.
Joseph. Reparative Therapy of Male Homosexuality: A New Clinical
Approach. Jason Aaronson Inc., 1991. ***Nicolosi, Dr. Joseph.
Healing Homosexuality: Case Stories of Reparative Therapy. Jason
Aaronson Inc., London, 1993. *** Noebel, David, The Homosexual
Revolution: A look at the Preachers and Politicians Behind it, Manitou
Springs, Colorado, Summit Press, 1984.

O

*** Oosterhuis, Harry. The "Jews" of the Antifascist Left: Homosexuality and Socialist Resistance to Nazism." In Heckma, et al (Eds.). Gay
Men and the Sexual History of the Political Left. Haworth Press, 1995.
*** Oosterhuis, Harry, and Kennedy, Hubert (eds.). Homosexuality
and Male Bonding in Pre-Nazi Germany: the youth movement, the gay
movement and male bonding before Hitler's rise: original transcripts
from Der Eigene, the first gay journal in the world. New York, Harrington Park Press, 1991. *** Oregonian. July 26, 1991; July, 11 1992;
August 26, 1992; December 10, 1992. Oosterhuis, Harry and Steakley,
James. "Leftist Sexual Politics and Homosexuality: A Historical Over-
view. In Heckma, et al (Eds.). Gay Men and the Sexual History of the
Political Left. Haworth Press, 1995.

P

*** Pacifici, Sergio. "D'Annunzio, Gabriele." Grolier Electronic Publishing, Inc., 1992. *** Parshall, Gerald. "Hitler's Horrors." U.S.
News & World Report. April 3, 1995. *** Pawelczynska, Anna.

Values and Violence in Auschwitz. Berkley, California, University of California Press, 1979. *** Perrault, Gilles, and Azema, Pierre. Paris Under the Occupation. New York, Vendome Press, 1987. *** Peters, H. F., Zarathustra's Sister: The case of Elisabeth and Frederich Nietzsche. Crown Publishers, New York, 1977. *** Peukert, Detlev J.K. The Weimar Republic: The Crisis of Classical Modernity. New York, Hill and Wang, 1987. *** Plant, Richard. The Pink Triangle: The Nazi War Against Homosexuals. New York, Henry Holt and Company, 1986. *** Poliakov, Leon. Harvest of Hate: The Nazi Program for the Destruction of the Jews of Europe. New York, Walden Press, 1979. *** Pollard, Walter. Medical Block Buchenwald. New York, Ballentine Books, 1960. *** Pronger, Brian. The Arena of Masculinity: Sports, Homosexuality and the Meaning of Sex, New York, St. Martins Press, 1990.

Q

*** Quigley, Carroll. Tragedy and Hope. Macmillan Company, New York, 1966.

R

*** Rauschning, Hermann. Men of Chaos. New World Books, 1942.*** Read, Anthony, and Fisher, David. Kristallnacht: The Nazi Night of Terror. New York, Times Books,1989. *** Rector, Frank. The Nazi Extermination of Homosexuals. New York, Stein and Day, 1981. *** Reeves, Tom. "Reviving and Redefining Pederasty." In Pascal, Mark (Ed.). Varieties of Man/Boy Love. New York, Wallace Hamilton Press, 1992. *** Reich, Wilhelm. The Mass Psychology of Fascism. Farrar, Straus & Giroux, New York, 1970. *** Reisman, Dr.

374

Judith A. "A Content Analysis of Two Decades of *The Advocate*, the Gay and Lesbian National News Magazine." Work in progress. *** Reisman, Dr. Judith A. *Kinsey, Hefner and Hay, The Indoctrination of Heterophobia in American Men and Women*. Arlington, VA. Institute for Media Education, 1994. *** Reisman, Dr. Judith A., and Eichel, Edward W. Kinsey, Sex and Fraud: The Indoctrination of a People. Lafayette, Louisiana, Huntington House, 1990. *** Reiter, Joseph A. "Death in Venice." Grolier Electronic Publishing, Inc., 1992. *** Rempel, Gerhard. Hitler's Children: The Hitler Youth and the SS. Chapel Hill, North Carolina, The University of North Carolina Press, 1989. *** Reuth, Ralf George. Goebbels. Harcourt Brace, New York, 1993. *** Riley, Patrick G. D. "Homosexuality and the Maccabean Revolt." *New Oxford Review*, September 1997. *** Rhodes, James M. The Hitler Movement: A Modern Millenarian Revolution. Stanford, California, Hoover Institution Press, 1980. *** Robinson, Jacob. "The History of the Holocaust." Holocaust. Jerusalem, Keter Publishing House, 1974. *** Rosan, Laurence J. "Philosophies of Homophobia and Homophilia." The Gay Academic. Palm Springs, California, ETC Publishing, 1978. *** Rose, Rick. "Museum of Pain." *The Advocate*, October 19, 1993. *** Rosenthal, A. M., and Gelb, Arthur. One More Victim: The Life and Death of a Jewish Nazi. New York, The New American Library Inc., 1967. *** Rossman, Parker. Sexual Experience Between Men and Boys. New York, Association Press, 1976. *** Rowse, A.L. Homosexuals in History: Ambivalence in Society, Literature and the Arts. New York, Macmillan Publishing Company, 1977. *** Rueda, Enrique T. The Homosexual Network: Public Lives and Private Policy. Old Greenwich, Connecticut, The Devon Adair Company, 1982. *** Runes, Dagobert D. Pictorial History of Philosophy.

New York, Philosophical Library, 1959. *** Rutledge, Leigh W. The
Gay Book of Lists. Boston, Alyson Publications Inc., 1987.

S

*** *San Francisco Chronicle.* September 14, 1991; October 18, 1992.
*** Sanger, Margaret. The Pivot of Civilization. New York,
Bentano's, Inc., 1922. *** Schaeffer, Francis A. The Great Evangeli-
cal Disaster. Westchester, Illinois, Crossway Books, 1984.   ***
Schmidt, Dr. Matthais. Albert Speer:The End of a Myth. St. Martins
Press, New York. *** Schwarzwaller, Wulf. The Unknown Hitler: His
Private Life and Fortune. National Press, Inc., and Star Agency, 1989.
*** *Searchlight* magazine. "Gay nazi -- A contradiction in terms?"
September, 1999. Also "A very English extremist." August, 2000. ***
Sereny, Gitta. Albert Speer: His Battle With Truth. Alfred A. Knopf.
New York, 1995. *** Seward, Desmond. Napoleon and Hitler. New
York, Simon and Schuster. *** Shaul, Elisheva. "Homosexuality in
the Third Reich." In Gutman, Israel (Ed.). Encyclopedia of the Holo-
caust. Tel Aviv, Sifriat Poalim Publishing House, 198?. *** Shirer,
William. The Rise and Fall of the Third Reich. New York, Fawcett
Crest, 1960. *** Shoham, S. Giora. Valhalla, Calvary and Auschwitz.
Bowman and Cody Academic Publishing, 1995. *** Simonelli, Freder-
ick J., American Fuehrer: George Lincoln Rockwell and the American
Nazi Party, University of Illinois Press, 1999. *** Sklar, Dusty. The
Nazis and the Occult. New York, Dorset Press, 1989. *** Skousen, W.
Cleon. The Naked Communist. Salt Lake City, Utah, Ensign Pub-
lishing Co., 1958. *** Snyder, Dr. Louis L. Encyclopedia of the Third
Reich. New York, Paragon House, 1989. *** Southern Poverty Law
Center Intelligence Report, "Fringe of the Fringe" Issue number 100,

Fall, 2000. *** Spence, Lewis. The History of Origins of Druidism. Great Britain, EP Publishing Ltd., 1976. *** Star, Susan Leigh. "Swastikas: The Street and the University." In Linden, Robin Ruth, Pagano, Darlene R, Russell, Diana E.H., and Star, Susan Leigh (eds). Against Sadomasochism: A Radical Feminist Analysis. East Palo Alto, California, Frog in the Well, 1982. *** Steakley, James D., The Homosexual Emancipation Movement in Germany. New York, Arno Press, 1975. *** Steiner, Jean-Francois. Treblinka. New York, Simon and Schuster, 1979. *** Stevenson, William A Man Called Intrepid: The Secret War Harcourt Brace Jovanovich, 1976. *** Stone, Charles. "Of Whom Nietzsche dreamed," *Harvard Gay and Lesbian Review*, Winter 1999. *** *Stop Promoting Homosexuality Hawaii Newsletter*. April, 1994; November, 1994. *** Strasser, Otto. Hitler and I. Boston, Houghton Mifflin Company, 1940. *** Strasser, Otto, and Stern, Michael. Flight From Terror. New York, Robert M. McBride & Company, 1943.

T

*** Taylor, Fred. The Goebbels Diaries: 1939-1941. New York, G.P. Putmans' Sons, 1983. *** Theweleit, Klaus. Male Fantasies. Volumes 1 and 2. Minneapolis, Minnesota, University of Minnesota Press, 1987. *** Timmons, Stuart. The Trouble With Harry Hay: Founder of the Modern Gay Movement. Boston, Alyson Publications Inc., 1990. *** Toland, John. Adolf Hitler. Anchor Books, New York, 1976. *** Tripp, C. A. The Homosexual Matrix. Signet, 1975. ***Tompkins, Peter. The Magic of Obelisks. Harper and Row, 1981.

U, V

*** Ulrichs, Karl Heinrich. *Forschugen uner das Ratsel der Mannmanlichen Liebe*. Leipzig, Max Spohr Verlag, 1989. *** *U.S.A. Today*. August 6, 1991; June 2, 1994. *** *U.S. News and World Report*. October, 1994.

W

*** Wagner, Nike. The Wagners: The dramas of a musical dynasty. Princeton University Press, 1998. *** Waite, Robert G.L. Vanguard of Nazism: The Free Corps Movement in Postwar Germany 1918-1923. New York, W.W. Norton and Company, 1969. *** Waite, Robert G.L. The Psychopathic God Adolf Hitler. New York, Signet Books, 1977. *** *Washington Blade*, January, 1992. *** *The Washington Times*. May 28, 1993; June 15, 1993. *** Webb, James. The Occult Underground. LaSalle, Illinois, Open Court Publishing Co., 1974. *** Weber, Eugen. Varieties of Fascism: Doctrines of Revolution in the Twentieth Century. Princeton, New Jersey, D. Van Nostrand Company Inc., 1964. *** Westwood, Gordon. A Minority: A Report on the Life of the Male Homosexual in Great Britain. London, Longman's Green and Co. Ltd., 1960. *** Wiesel, Elie. Night. New York, Avon Books, 1969. *** Willhoite, Michael. Daddy's Roommate. Boston, Alyson Publications, 1990. *** Wilrich, Michael. "Uncivil Disobedience." *Mother Jones*. December, 1990. *** Wistrich, Robert. Who's Who in Nazi Germany. New York, Bonanza Books, 1984. *** Wockner, Rex. Wockner Wire, www.PlanetOut.com, November 9, 2001. *** Wolff, Charlotte M.D. Magnus Hirschfeld. Quartet Books, New York, 1986. *** Wren, Thomas E. "Nietzsche, Friedrich Wilhelm." Grolier Elec-

378

tronic Publishing, 1992. *** Wright, Michael Phillip. <u>War on Hetero-</u>
<u>sexuality: The Gay Patriarchy Advances</u>. 1998.

X, Y, Z

***Young, Ian. "Gay Resistance: Homosexuals in the Anti-Nazi Un-
derground." In Leyland, Winston (Ed.). <u>Gay Roots: Twenty Years of</u>
<u>Gay Sunshine: An Anthology of Gay History, Sex, Politics, and Cul-</u>
<u>ture</u>. San Francisco, Gay Sunshine Press, 1989. *** Zentner, Christian
and Bedurftig, Friedmann, <u>The Encyclopedia of the Third Reich</u>, New
York, De Capo Press, 1997. *** Ziegler, Herbert F. <u>Nazi Germany's</u>
<u>New Aristocracy: The SS Leadership, 1925-1939</u>. Princeton, New Jer-
sey, University Press, 1989.

INDEX

A

ACT-UP: 325

ACT-UP: 290, 292, 296, 303, 325, 348

ADVOCATE: 279 - 280, 283, 287, 324

AIDS: 283, 291, 295, 318, 325, 335, 346, 357, 359

AMERICAN NAZI MOVEMENT: 279

ANTHROPOSOPHICAL SOCIETY: 124

ANTI-SEMITISM: 33, 61

ARIOSOPHY: 111, 116

ARMANEN ORDER: 35, 108, 110

ARYAN: 17, 35, 106, 108 - 110, 116 - 119

ARYAN BROTHERHOOD: 286

AUSCHWITZ: 15, 232 - 233, 236 - 237, 239 - 240, 242

B

BAAL: 59, 98

BABYLON: 97, 354

BATHHOUSE: 315, 317 - 318

BAVARIA: 120, 124, 144, 163, 221

BELZEC: 232

BERLIN: 39, 47, 49 - 51, 155, 172, 179, 182, 185, 188, 193, 205, 207 - 208, 246, 283, 307, 315, 354

BESANT: 106, 108

BIBLE: 15, 59, 98, 102, 260 - 261

BLACK BERTHA: 154

BLACKMAIL: 183, 208, 219 - 220, 242

BLAVATSKY, HELENA PETROVNA: 35, 104, 106, 108, 120, 128

BLOMBERG: 199, 201, 219

BLONDE BEAST: 219

BLUEBEARD: 240

BLUEHER: 11, 32, 49 - 50, 70 - 71, 73, 75, 81, 348

BOY SCOUTS: 32, 75, 328, 331, 342, 345, 356

BOY-LOVERS: 51, 57, 323, 325

BRAND, ADOLF: 38, 42, 60 - 61, 63 - 64, 66 - 67, 70, 89, 92, 110, 114, 169 - 170, 347 - 348

BRATWURSTGLOECKL: 32, 41, 91, 145

BRESLAU: 87, 174, 188

BROWN FAIRIES: 166

BROWNSHIRTS: 35 - 36, 41, 75, 198, 207, 246, 277, 293

BRUCKNER: 146

BUCH: 165, 203

BUCHENWALD: 232, 235, 237, 243

BURGESS: 80, 139

BUTCHER OF HANOVER: 226

BUTCHES: 39, 42, 67 - 68, 70, 213, 313

C

CABARET: 288

CALICLES: 130

380

CANAAN: 104

CANARIS: 207, 220 - 221

CATAMITE: 55

CATHOLIC: 39, 58, 108, 192, 199, 263, 265, 290

CHELMNO: 232

CHICAGO: 275

CHRISTIAN: 15, 19, 42, 57 - 58, 60 - 61, 63 - 64, 84, 95 - 97, 99 - 100, 103, 106, 259

CHRISTIANITY: 257

CLINTON: 328, 341 - 342

COLLIN: 280 - 281, 355

COMMODUS: 98

COMMUNISTS: 171

COMMUNITY OF THE ELITE: 38, 60 - 61, 64 - 67, 71, 76, 92, 118, 133, 135, 213, 258

CONCENTRATION CAMP: 5, 33, 38, 43, 177, 179, 193, 222, 229, 231 - 233, 235, 237, 241, 243, 246

COOLEY: 293

COPROPHILE: 151

CROWLEY: 33, 120, 122, 302, 357

D

DACHAU: 199, 231 - 233, 237 - 238

DAHMER: 334

DALUEGE: 228

DANZIG FREE STATE: 207

DEGRELLE: 139

DER EIGENE: 61

DER EIGENE: 38, 51, 60, 65, 109, 114, 118, 169

DER STUERMER: 147

DIELS: 151

DOLLFUSS: 208 - 209

DOLLMAN: 151

DOLLY BOYS: 236

DORIOT: 81, 139

DREXLER: 124

DUGAS: 335

E

EBERMAYER: 151

EBERSTEIN: 220 - 221

ECKART: 35, 121 - 122, 143

ELEGABALUS: 99

ENGELS: 47

EUGENICS: 352

F

FASCISM: 57, 129, 133, 135, 139 - 141, 172, 275, 277, 283, 289, 291, 295, 303

FASCIST: 17, 43, 57, 75, 80, 85, 130, 140 - 141, 168, 269, 275, 277, 282 - 283, 285, 287 - 288, 291 - 292, 302, 336

FASCIST: 130

FATHERLAND: 288

FEMMES: 39, 41, 43, 50, 64 - 65, 67, 69 - 70, 192 - 193, 213, 313, 347

FINAL SOLUTION: 255 - 256

FISCHER: 32, 70 - 71

FLOSSENBERG: 222

FOERSTER: 153, 207

FRANK: 146, 165, 206

FRAULEIN ANNA: 154

FREDERICK THE GREAT: 114, 130, 141, 151, 347

FREIKORPS: 35, 82 - 83, 85, 87, 141, 219, 228, 239

FRIEDLANDER: 43, 61, 64 - 66, 70, 73, 81, 89, 92, 110, 118, 213, 258

FROMM: 140

FUEHRER: 32, 71, 75 - 76, 84, 92, 118, 124, 134, 148, 166 - 167, 172, 184, 207, 222, 224, 233, 257, 267, 353

FUNK: 146, 206

FURSTENFELDER HOF: 143

G

GANYMEDE: 55

GAULEITER: 147, 267

GAY AGENDA: 344

GAY HOLOCAUST: 177, 179

GAY LIBERATION FRONT: 312

GAY RIGHTS: 37, 44, 51, 67, 70, 121, 141, 166, 178 - 179, 185, 190, 216, 275, 288, 303, 310, 312, 318, 320 - 321, 323, 327, 331, 334, 342, 345 - 346, 349 - 351

GAY RIGHTS: 295, 333

GEORGE: 69, 135 - 136, 348

GERBER: 275, 277

GERMAN FAITH MOVEMENT: 263

GERMAN WORKER: 32, 35, 68, 121, 124, 143 - 144

GERMAN WORKER'S PARTY: 32

GERMANY'S NATIONAL VICE: 78

GESTAPO: 192 - 193, 226, 242, 263

"GAY" MOVEMENT: 344

GINSBERG: 5

GIRL SCOUTS: 330

GNOSTICISM: 95

GOEBBELS: 148 - 149, 172, 224, 267

GOERING: 87, 146, 162, 172, 192, 199, 201, 206, 222, 257, 269, 355

GOERING INSTITUTE: 355

GORKY: 140

GRAF: 165

GRANNINGER: 93

GRAVELLE: 108, 118

GRUNDGENS: 192

GRYNSZPAN: 222 - 223, 225 - 226

GUIDO VON LIST SOCIETY: 33

H

HADRIAN: 98

HAECKEL: 116

HAMILTON: 334

HANFSTAENGL: 151

HASSELLBACH: 352

HAUSHOFER: 122 - 123, 156

HAY: 301, 303, 305, 316, 324, 358

HEFNER: 358

HEINES: 36, 83, 85, 87, 91, 172, 174, 200, 239

HELLDORF: 172, 207

HELLDORF, WOLF VON: 91, 149

HELLENIC: 56

HELLENISM: 58

HEROIC MALES: 73

HESS: 90, 121, 143, 146, 154, 206 - 207, 267

HEYDRICH: 94, 199, 204, 219 - 222, 227, 269

HILDEBRANDT: 66

HILLER: 43, 193

HIMMLER: 74, 79, 91, 110, 114, 118, 127, 173, 179, 182, 192 - 193, 195, 199, 206, 210, 212, 214, 217, 219 - 220, 230, 245, 256 - 257, 267

HINDENBERG: 199, 201, 204

HINDU TANTRISM: 33, 109

HIRSCHFELD: 36 - 38, 42 - 43, 48 - 51, 60 - 61, 63 - 65, 67 - 68, 70, 73, 155, 185, 187, 193, 277

HITLER YOUTH: 32, 43, 77, 79, 84, 135, 146, 168, 175, 193 - 195, 197, 266

HOESS: 239

HOFFMAN: 71, 184

HOFMANN: 152

HOLOCAUST: 96, 99 - 100, 177, 179, 229 - 230, 233, 245 - 246, 256 - 257, 269, 280, 348 - 350

HOMOEROTIC: 57, 73 - 74, 136, 324, 344

I

IRGUN: 5

ISLAMISTS: 269, 271

J

JANSEN: 61, 70 - 71, 330

JENNINGS: 302

JUDAISM: 58

K

KAHNERT: 121, 275

KAISER WILHELM: 31

KALTENBRUNNER: 221

KAPOS: 237

KAPOS: 236

KARL ERNST: 91, 172, 200

KINSEY: 304 - 305, 316, 358

KINSEY INSTITUTE: 307

KNIGHTS TEMPLARS: 112

KRAMER: 290, 325

KRISTALLNACHT: 36, 222, 226, 269

KUBIZEK: 151

KUHNEN: 283

L

LANDSBERG: 154, 163

LANZ: 33, 35, 108, 111, 114, 116 - 117, 119, 122, 128, 133, 216 - 217, 256 - 257, 269

LASSALLE: 132

LEADBEATER: 35, 106 - 107

LEBENSBORN: 217, 256

LEFT-RIGHT POLARITIES: 353

LENZ: 36

LESBIAN: 35

LESBIANS: 44, 242, 315, 321, 350

LIDICE: 228

LIEBENFELS: 33

LIST: 33

LUDECKE: 151

LUSTKNABEN: 173

M

MACCABEAN: 58

MADAGASCAR: 256

MAENNERBUND: 42, 127

MAIDENEK: 232

MALE BONDING: 73

MALE PROSTITUTE: 98

MANICHAEISM: 96

MANN, THOMAS: 135 - 136

MARCUSE: 312

MARRIAGE: 59

MARX: 47

MARXIST: 129

MATTACHINE SOCIETY: 301 - 303, 313

MAURICE: 90, 146, 203

MEIN KAMPF: 35, 90, 116, 135, 200

MENGELE: 137

MENNINGER: 276

MILITARY: 54

MOLESTATION: 44

MOTHERING SUNDAY: 264

MUNICH: 41, 47, 89, 91 - 93, 117, 124, 143, 155 - 156, 172, 199, 203, 209 - 210, 221, 356

MUSSOLINI: 137, 155, 200, 208 - 209

N

N.S. MOBILIZER: 279

NAMBLA: 324, 328 - 329

NATIONAL GAY AND LESBIAN TASK FORCE: 313

NATIONAL SOCIALIST LEAGUE: 279

NATIONAL SOCIALIST MOVEMENT: 89

NATIONAL SOCIALIST WHITE PEOPLE'S PARTY: 279

NAZI TEACHERS ASSOCIATION: 264

NAZISM: 32

NEO-NAZI: 283, 352

NERO: 99

NEW YORK CITY: 316

NIETZSCHE: 133 - 137, 141, 259, 347

NIETZSCHEANISM: 136

NIGHT OF THE LONG KNIVES: 195

NOAH: 103

NOBEL PEACE PRIZE: 289

NOTRE DAME DE PARIS: 225

NUEVA GERMANIA: 137

NUREMBERG: 266

O

OCCULTIC: 101

OCCULTISM: 95

OCCULTISM: 95

OEDIPUS: 359

OLCOTT: 104

ORDENSBURGEN: 74, 265

ORDO NOVI TEMPLI: 33, 111

OSTARA: 114, 116 - 117, 121

P

PAGAN: 97

PARAGRAPH 175: 37 - 39, 46, 48, 65, 189, 191 - 192, 195, 221

PEDERASTY: 37

PFEIFFER: 80, 139

PHOENIX: 275

PINK TRIANGLE: 38 - 39, 43, 75, 180, 239, 241 - 242, 311

PLANETTA: 209

PLATO: 30, 45, 53 - 54, 57, 130 - 131, 141, 347

PORNOGRAPHY: 190, 322, 346, 358

PROJECT 10: 325

PROSTITUTE: 97 - 98, 156, 165 - 166, 173, 183, 317, 355

PROSTITUTION: 243

PROTESTANT: 263

Q

QUEER NATION: 292 - 293, 325, 328, 348

QUEER SCOUTS: 328

QUISLING: 140

R

RACIAL PURITY: 116

RADICAL FAERIES: 302

RASPUTIN OF HIMMLER: 127

RATH: 223

RAUSCHNING: 153

REICHSTAG: 36, 68, 132, 171 - 172, 204

ROEHM: 31, 36, 38, 42, 68 - 70, 81, 83, 85, 87 - 89

ROEHM PURGE: 66, 149, 207

ROEHM PURGE: 81, 172, 182, 195, 199, 203, 206, 212, 276

ROEHM'S AVENGERS: 245

ROMANS: 74

ROME: 99

ROSENBERG: 57, 124

ROSSBACH: 35, 77, 82 - 85, 87, 119 - 120, 149, 228, 239

ROSSBACHBUND: 35

RUNE: 109

RUNE OF LIFE: 264

S

SA: 66

SADISM: 90

SAN FRANCISCO: 288

SCHACHT: 146

SCHILLJUGEND: 36, 84, 87

SCHIRACH: 78, 84, 94, 146

SCHWEITZER: 132

SCIENTIFIC-HUMANITARIAN COMMITTEE: 37, 49, 51, 60, 63, 65, 67

SERIAL KILLERS: 333 - 334

SEX RESEARCH INSTITUTE: 36 - 39, 50, 155, 182, 185, 187, 307

SEXUAL ORIENTATION: 197, 313, 321, 330, 341, 346

SEYSS-INQUART: 139, 209

SHAMANISM: 97

SHC: 37 - 38, 43, 49, 64, 68 - 69, 188

SHR: 66, 275

SKOKIE: 281

SOBIDOR: 232

SOCIAL DEMOCRATS: 168

SOCIALISM: 129

SOCIETY FOR HUMAN RIGHTS: 38, 66 - 67, 92, 121, 226, 275

SOCRATES: 53 - 54, 130

SODOMY: 43

SPARTA: 54, 130 - 131, 345

SPARTAN: 131

SPEER: 149 - 150

SPRETI: 174

SS: 43

STEIN: 289

STEINER: 138

STENNES: 167

STONEWALL BAR: 311

STORM TROOPERS: 35, 83 - 84, 87, 91, 177, 197, 245 - 246, 288

STREICHER: 147, 206

SUMMER SOLSTICE: 264

SWASTIKA: 32

TIBET: 127

TIENE: 240

TORAH: 350

TRANSVESTITE: 49, 269, 315 - 316

TREBLINKA: 232, 234

TRESCKOW, HANS VON: 48

U

ULRICHS: 38, 42, 44 - 46, 48, 50 - 51, 64, 67, 70, 165, 225, 303

URANIANS: 45

V

VAN DER LUBBE: 171 - 172

VERSAILLES: 31, 163

VHEME: 119 - 120

VIENNA: 156

VOLTAIRE: 131

VOM RATH: 223 - 224

VON LIST: 33, 108 - 110, 116 - 118, 216, 256 - 257

T

TEN COMMANDMENTS: 268

TERRORISM: 120

TEUTONIC: 127

TEUTONIC KNIGHTS: 112, 131, 217

TEUTONS: 97, 114, 170, 345

THEBES: 55

THEOSOPHICAL SOCIETY: 35, 104

THULE SOCIETY: 35, 119 - 121, 124, 143, 275

W

WAGNER: 134

WANDERVOEGEL: 32, 49, 70 - 71, 74 - 76, 81, 83 - 84, 121, 327, 330, 345

WEININGER: 122, 265

WIESEL: 233

WILIGUT: 127

WINTER SOLSTICE: 264

WOTAN: 36, 108, 114, 261

Y

YAD VASHEM HOLOCAUST
MEMORIAL: 229

Z

ZAPPING: 323

ZBONSZYN: 223

ZEUS: 55, 59

For further study on this topic, read
<u>The Poisoned Stream:</u>
<u>"Gay" Influence in Human History</u>,
Volume One, Germany 1890-1945.
Scott Lively, 1997, second printing 2001.
Available through Veritas Aeterna Press
PO Box 3691, Sacramento, California.
Ordering inquiries call 1-800-834-1508
or visit www.abidingtruth.com